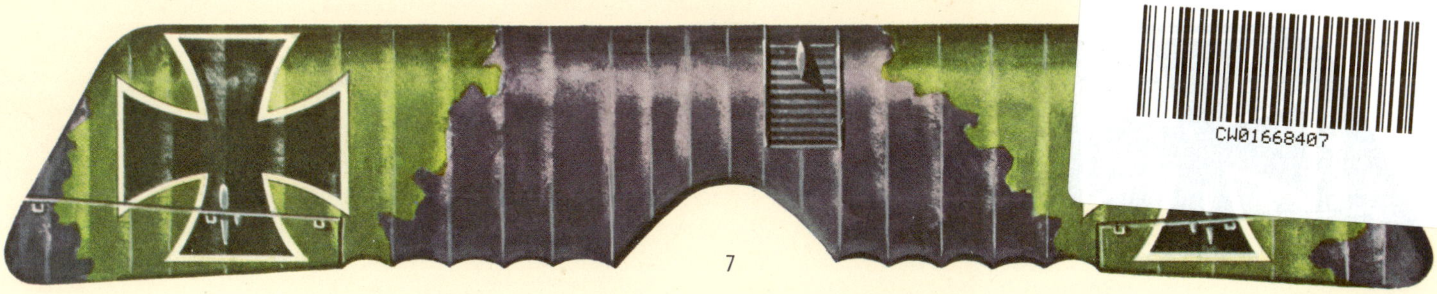

7

8

9

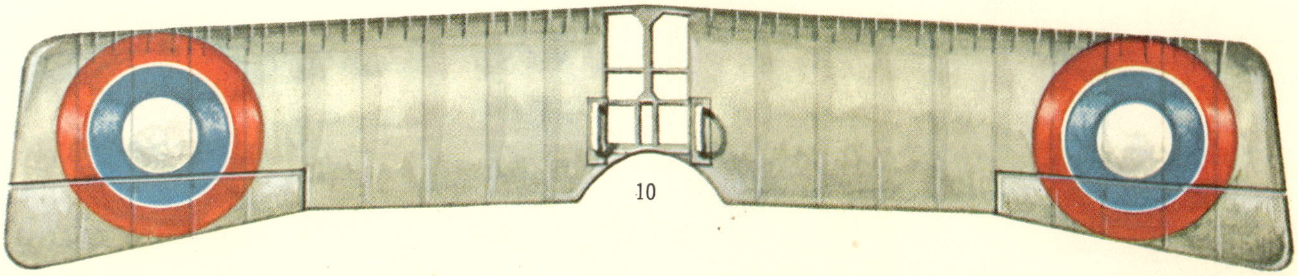

10

11

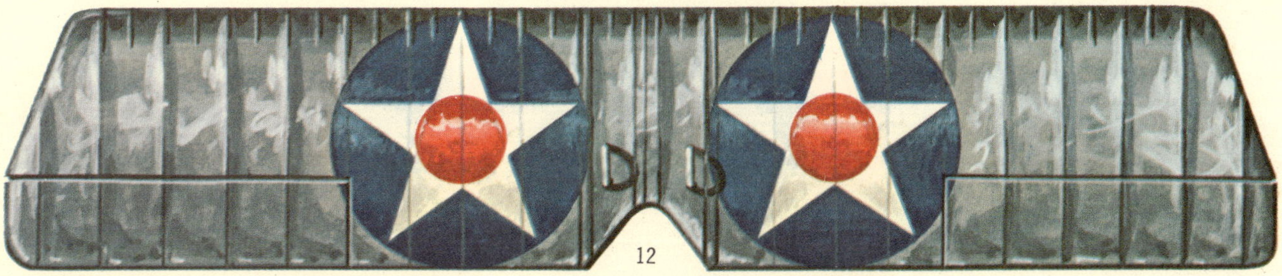

12

7/ Albatros D V. Germany. 1917-1918 8/ Ansaldo S.V.A.5. Italy. 1917-1918 9/ Sopwith F.1 Camel. Great Britain. 1917 (night fighter)
10/ Nieuport 17. France. 1916 (in Russian colors) 11/* Fokker D VII. Germany 1918 12/ Thomas-Morse S 4C. United States. 1918 (U.S. naval colors)

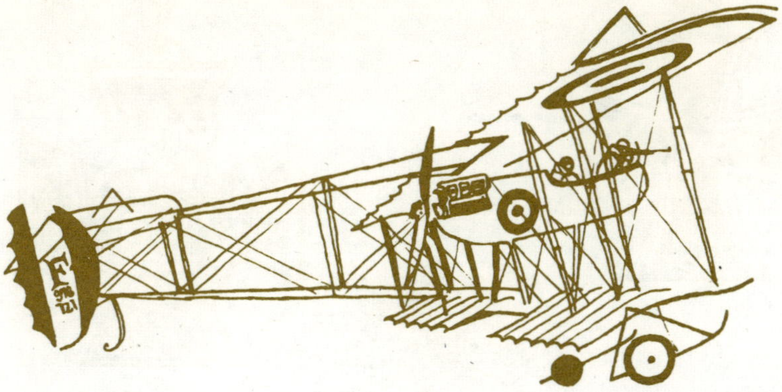

Aircraft and Flyers
of the First World War

MILITARY ORDERS & DECORATIONS

1/ Distinguished Service Order, Great Britain 2/ Order of Leopold, Belgium 3/ Medjidie, Turkey 4/ Iron Cross, Germany 5/ Victoria Cross, Great Britain 6/ St. George, Russia 7/ Legion of Honor, France 8/ Chrysanthemum, Japan 9/ Distinguished Service Cross, United States 10/ Congressional Medal of Honor, United States 11/ Pour le Mérite, Germany 12/ Croix de Guerre with star, France 13/ Military Medal, France 14/ St. Stephen, Hungary 15/ Order of the Red Eagle, Germany 16/ The Distinguished Service Cross, Great Britain 17/ Distinguished Flying Cross, Great Britain 18/ Military Cross, Great Britain

Aircraft and Flyers of the First World War

Originally titled Heroes & Aeroplanes of the Great War 1914-1918

by Joseph A. Phelan

PSL Patrick Stephens, Cambridge

First published in Great Britain in 1974 under the title
Aircraft and Flyers of the First World War

Originally published under the title
Heroes & Aeroplanes of the Great War 1914-1918

ISBN 0 85059 187 2

Printed in the United States of America

The Foreword is from *The Book of Flight* and is reprinted with the kind permission of American Heritage and the Oral History Collection of Columbia University.

To Marc, my son

For their friendly help, advice, and encouragement, the author wishes to thank his fellow-members of the New York Metropolitan Chapter of the Cross & Cockade Society of World War I Aero Historians. In particular he wishes to acknowledge the generous contributions made by Peter M. Grosz, Ola A. Sater, Thomas E. Andrews, and Thomas R. Funderburk.

1/ 1903. U. S. Wright Flyer. (Man's first powered flight, distance: 120 feet; time: 12 seconds; place: Kitty Hawk, North Carolina)

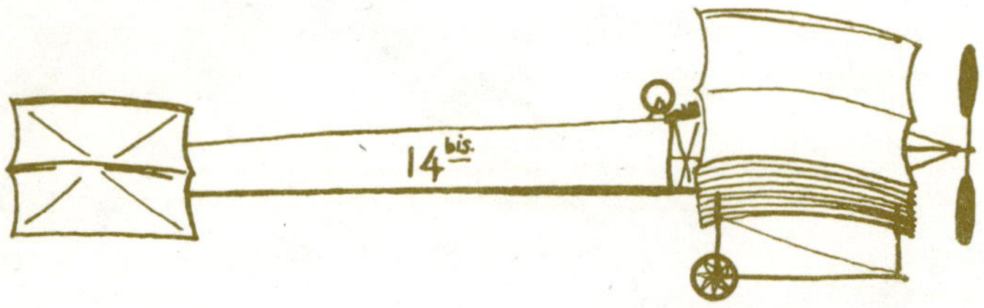

2/ 1906. France. Santos-Dumont 14bis

3/ 1907. France. Voisin-Farman biplane

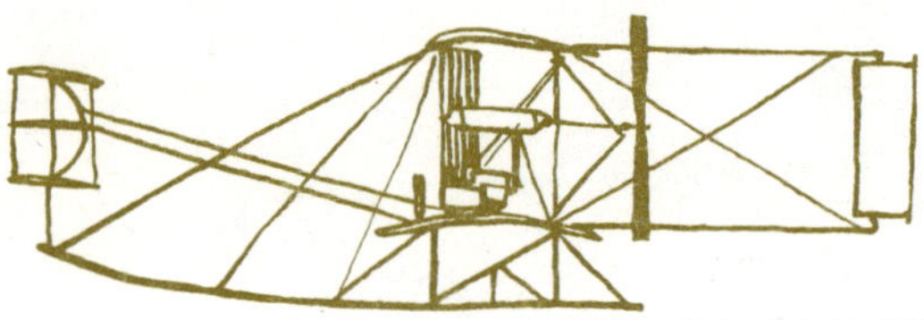

6/ 1909. U. S. Wright "A" flyer

7/ 1909. France. Blériot No. XI

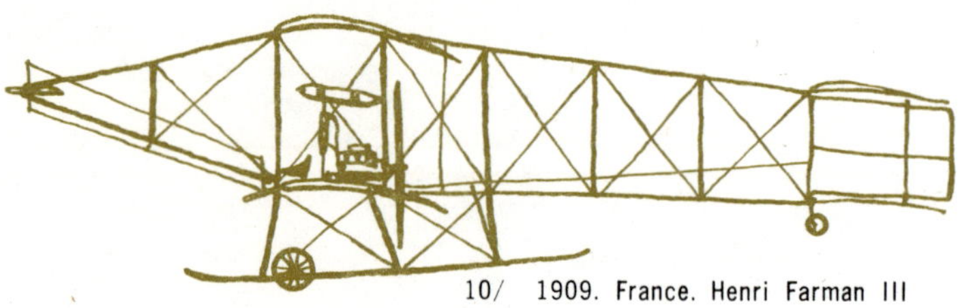

10/ 1909. France. Henri Farman III

11/ 1910. U. S. Curtiss pusher

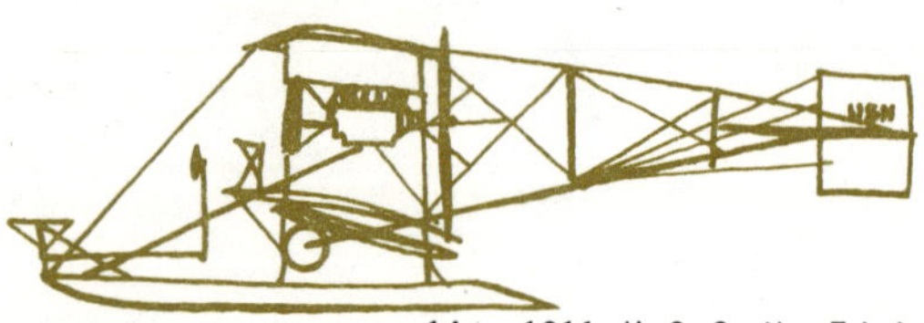

14/ 1911. U. S. Curtiss Triad

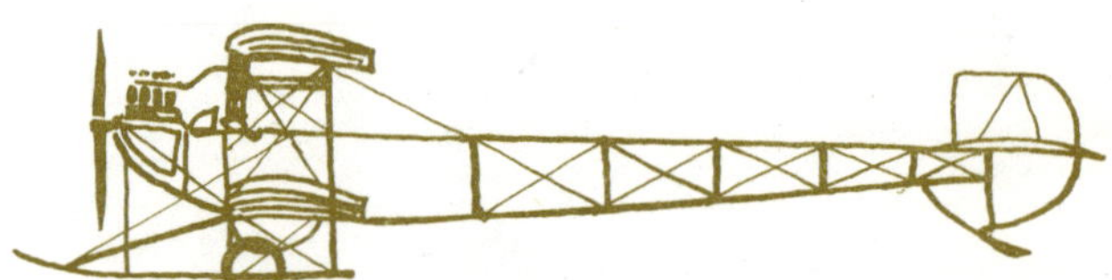

15/ 1911. Britain. Avro biplane

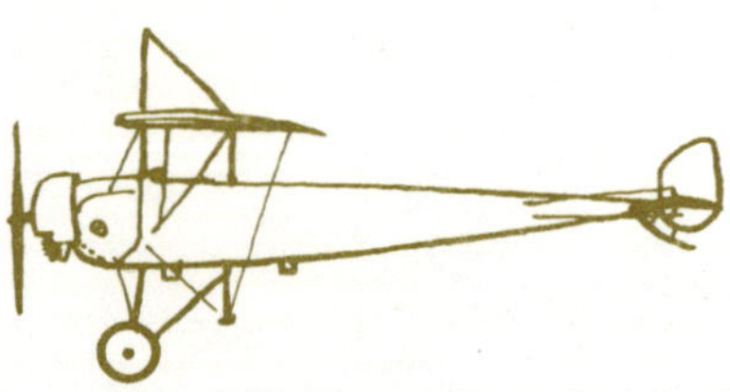

18/ 1913. France. Morane-Saulnier Type L

19/ 1913. France. Deperdussin monoplane

20/ 1913. Britain. Sopwith Tabloid

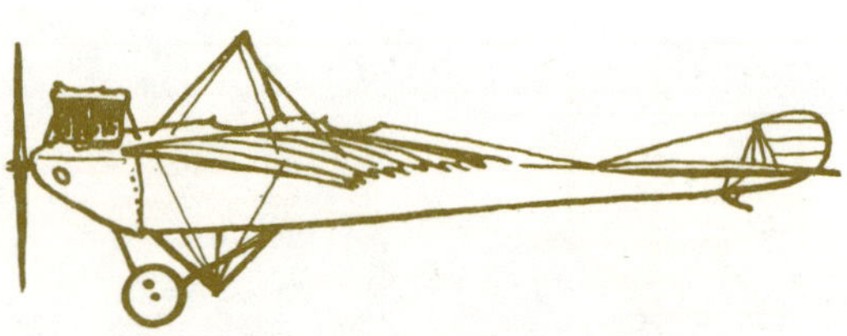

22/ 1913. Germany. Rumpler Taube

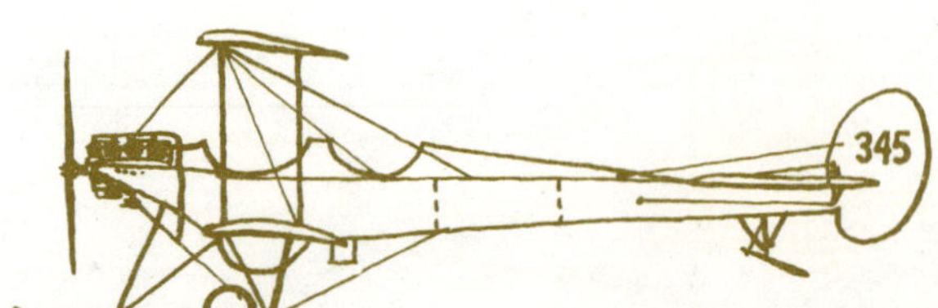

23/ 1913. Britain. Royal Aircraft Factory B.E.2

THE ANTIQUE AEROPLANES shown here represent a capsule history of the development of aviation from 1903 to 1913. In the ten short years that followed the first success of the Wright brothers, aeroplanes grew from powered gliders to four-engined transports capable of carrying a dozen people, and were at home on land, in the air and on the sea.

4/ 1908. U. S. Curtiss "June Bug"

5/ 1908. Britain. A. V. Roe "Avroplane"

8/ 1909. France. Santos-Dumont Demoiselle

9/ 1909. France. Lavavasseur Antoinette

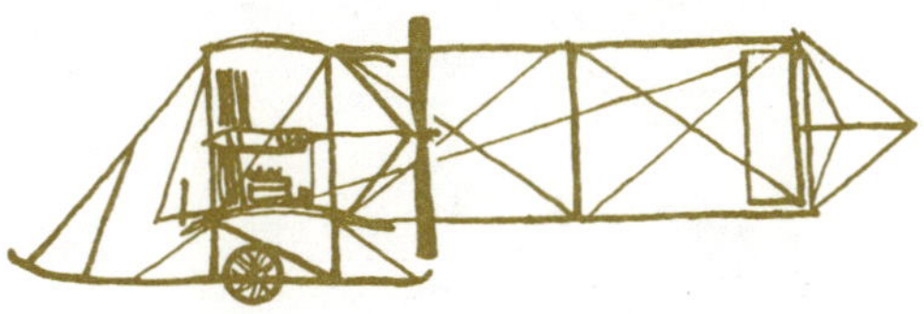

12/ 1910. U.S. Wright "B" Flyer

13/ 1910. France. Nieuport Type 6

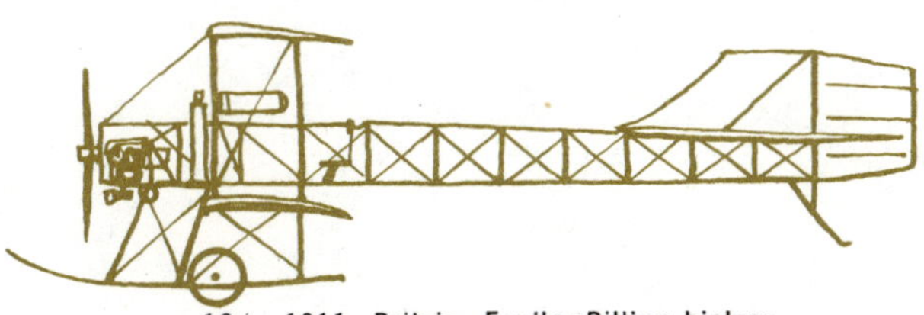

16/ 1911. Britain. Eardley-Billing biplane

17/ 1913. Britain. Vickers E.F.B.2

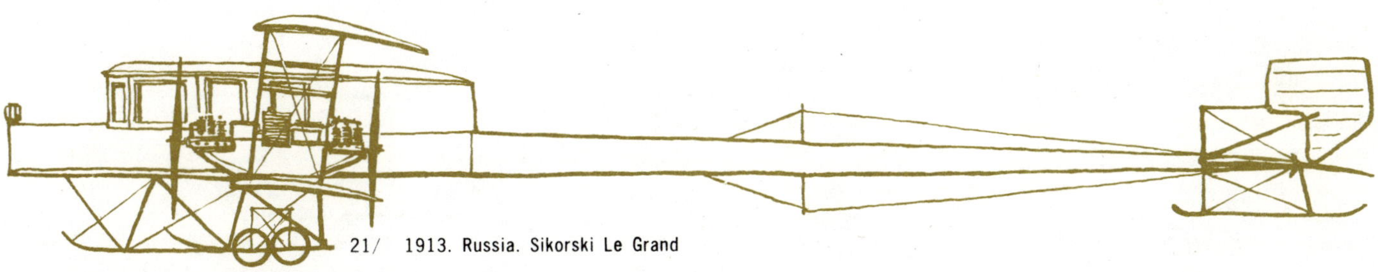

21/ 1913. Russia. Sikorski Le Grand

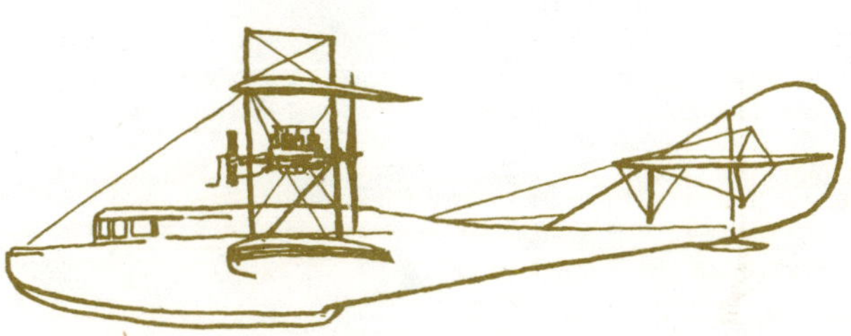

24/ 1913. U. S. Curtiss "America"

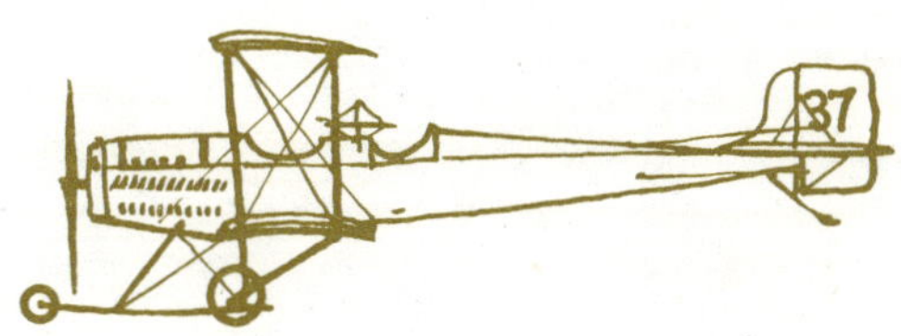

25/ 1913. U. S. Martin "TT"

Contents

Illustration Index

THE ALLIES

AERO INSIGNIA

AEROPLANES

GREAT BRITAIN

FRANCE

Sopwith Snipe 1918. 230 h.p. Bentley.

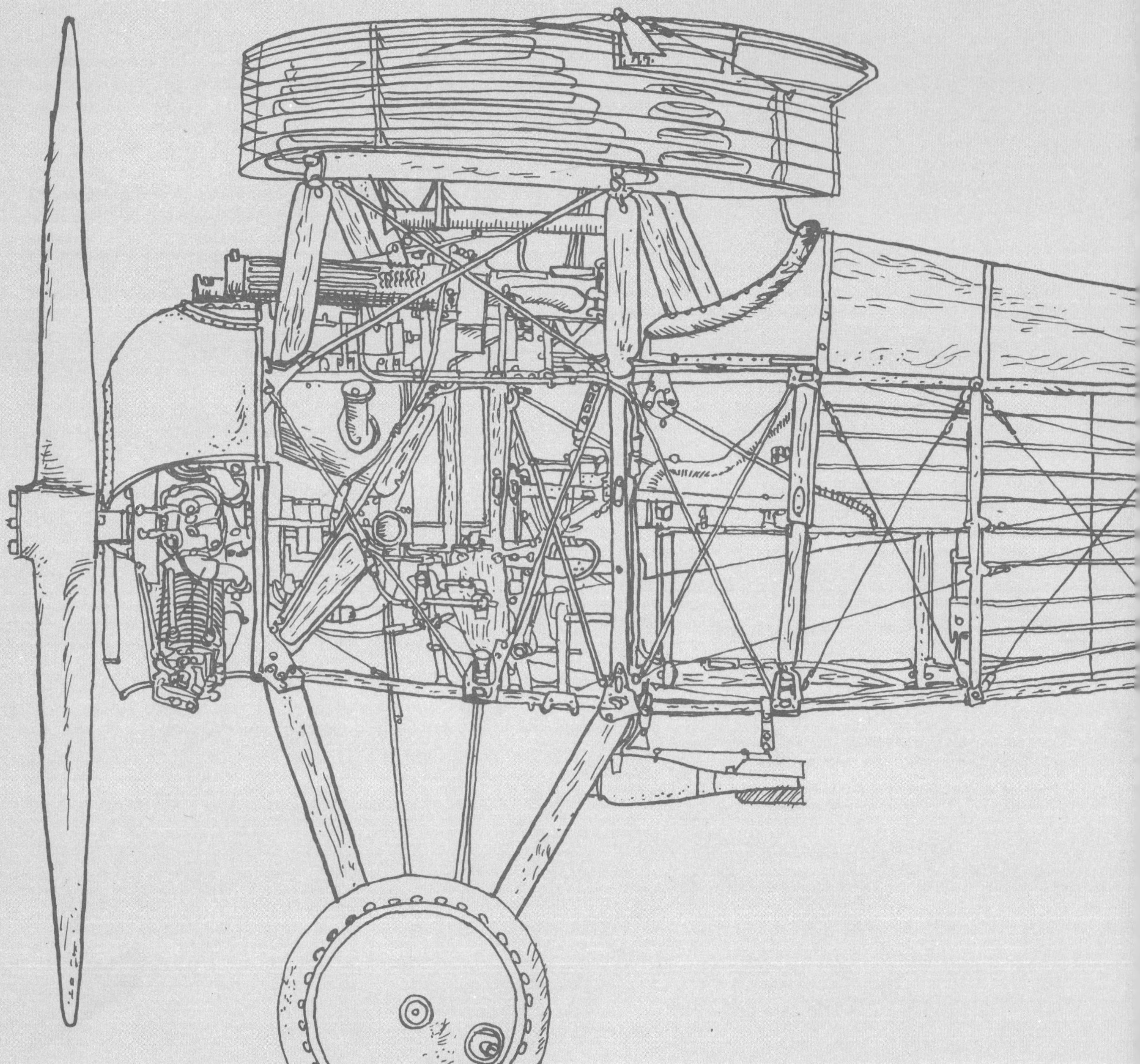

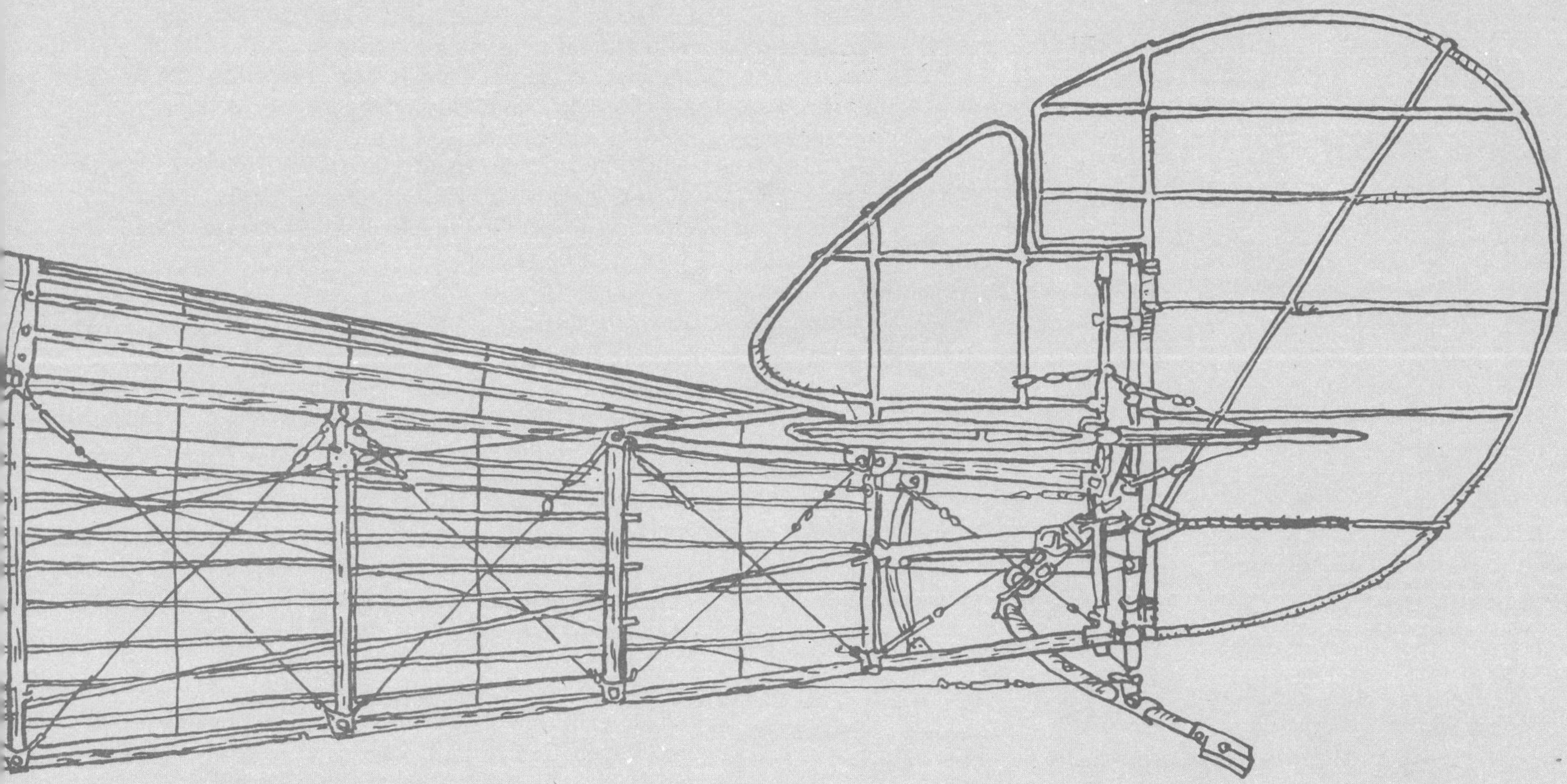

When we started the First World War, there were no fighters. The small, rather high-performance—for their day—aircraft that were building were really built as scouts. From scouts they developed into fighters, literally—from going up with rifles and revolvers to the day when we learned to fire through the propeller.

Development was so fast! We literally thought of and designed and flew the airplanes in a space of about six or eight weeks. Now it takes approximately the same number of years.

From sketches the designs went to chalk on the wall. Until about the middle of the war there was no stressing at all. Everything was built entirely by eye. That's why there were so many structural failures. We didn't start to stress airplanes at all seriously until the Camel, in 1917.

Flying in those days was empirical. We really weren't structural engineers at all. It was a constant gamble, in a way. We just flew by the light of nature. Some of us were lucky and some of us weren't.

Sir Thomas Octave Murdoch Sopwith, C.B.E., of the Sopwith Aviation Co., Ltd.

MILITARY AVIATION BEGINS

with the balloon, the first device of man's ingenuity which permitted him to fly. The first military use of the balloon occurred during the French Revolutionary Wars. In 1794 at the seige of Manberg the French sent up a balloon to try to get a look at the dispositions of the Austrians and the Dutch. The observations made were not necessary, for the besiegers, supposing incorrectly that their moves were being perfectly observed, quitted the field in dismay.

The first successful flying with wings was done in a long series of gliding experiments performed by a German engineer named Otto Lilienthal (1848–1896), who based his wing shapes on those of birds. He made over 2,000 safe glides between 1891 and 1896 and was finally killed when a gust of wind caused him to lose his equilibrium and he tumbled fifty feet to the ground. His last words were, "Sacrifices must be made."

In the United States, two brothers named Wilbur (1867–1912) and Orville (1871–1948) Wright, bicycle manufacturers of Dayton, Ohio, were much impressed with the work of Lilienthal and other pioneers of flight. They studied the writings of such men and profited by their experiences, evolving in addition their own ideas through experimentation. They were patient and methodical and were motivated by scientific curiosity rather than by any burning desire to fly. Neither brother was ever much interested in flying for its own sake. In 1903 they built and flew the first aeroplane, a motorized version of one of their early gliders. The Wright brothers shunned publicity and so little was heard about their success at the time that other experimenters in Europe and America proceeded on their own intuition, without benefit of the Wright brothers' knowledge.

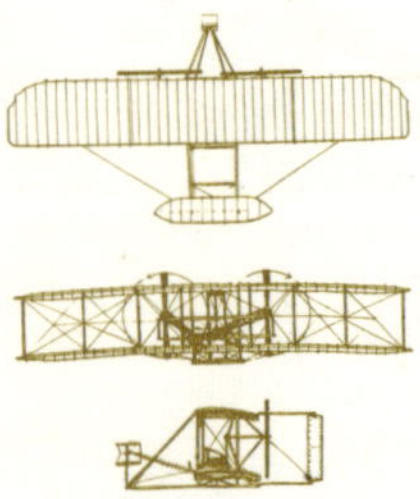

The Wright Flyer. 1903

Wright Type A Biplane. 1908

Alberto Santos-Dumont (1873–1932), a Brazilian living in Paris, built and flew fourteen motor-driven airships between 1898 and 1906. An airship is a dirigible—a floating aircraft equipped with some form of propulsion by means of which it can be driven forward and so steered instead of being compelled to drift with the wind. In 1906 Santos-Dumont used airship *No. 14* to launch a machine called 14*bis,* the first aeroplane to fly in Europe. The 14*bis* was a box kite with a fuselage projecting out forward of the wings instead of aft of them, the tail assembly at the forward end of the fuselage, and the motor at the rear. To modern eyes, it had the appearance of an aeroplane going backwards. The

14*bis,* for its first flight, was carried into the air slung underneath airship *No. 14* and released. Santos-Dumont flew the machine to a safe landing. Thereafter he took off from the ground in it and made many successful, though short, flights.

The first British aeroplane to fly was the invention of A.V. Roe (later Sir Alliot Verdon Roe), who also used a launching method for his first flight in 1908—at the Brooklands motor course his machine was towed by an automobile to develop flying speed. The first all-British aeroplane was Roe's triplane, called an "Avroplane," built in 1909 and powered by a J.A. Prestwich motorcycle engine.

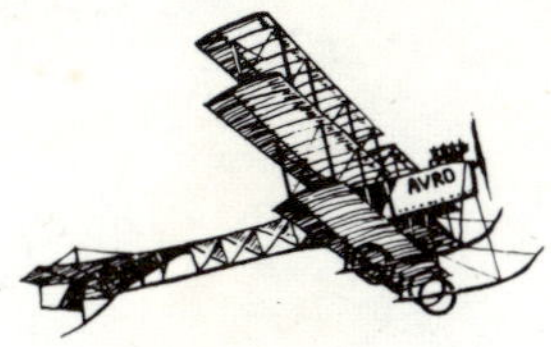

One of the most successful of the early aeroplanes was designed by the Frenchman, Louis Blériot. His model No. XI was a monoplane powered by a 25 h.p. Anzani engine. On 25 July 1909, Blériot flew No. XI across the English Channel from Calais to Dover, the flight lasting about half an hour and winning for Blériot the £1,000 prize put up by the London newspaper, *Daily Mail.* Both before and during the 1914–1918 war, the Type XI was manufactured in large numbers as a reconnaissance and training machine for the military of France and Britain.

Count Ferdinand von Zeppelin (1838–1917) was born in southern Germany and received an army commission in 1858. He made his first ascent in a balloon in America in 1863 while he was serving as a volunteer with the Union army. In 1891 he retired from the army with the rank of general and devoted thenceforth all his time, effort and substantial fortune to developing an airship. On 2 July 1900, the first Zeppelin airship, the *Luftschiff-Zeppelin 1* or LZ.1, took off from a floating hangar on Lake Constance. The LZ.1 was built of aluminum girders and covered with cotton cloth. It was supported by nearly 390,000 cubic feet of hydrogen contained in several individual cells of rubberized cloth. The LZ.1 was 420 feet long, and because of its great length was obliged to take off into the wind to avoid lateral stresses. The floating hangar was moored at one end only and swung free with the wind, keeping the Zeppelin's nose into the wind like a weathervane.

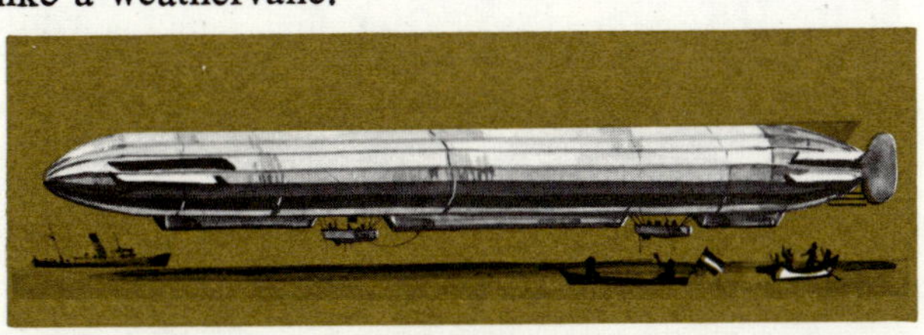

The first time an aeroplane ever took off from a ship was on 14 November 1910. The American aviator Eugene B. Ely took off in a Curtiss pusher from a ramp over the quarterdeck of the U.S.S. *Birmingham* moored in Chesapeake Bay. Ely, a well-known stunt pilot, was killed in a flying accident

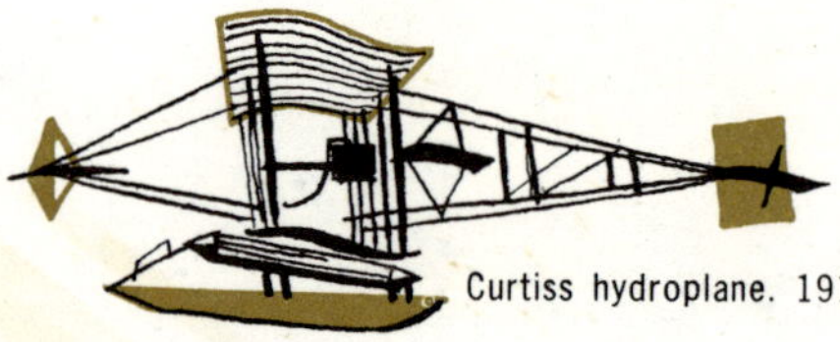

Curtiss hydroplane. 1911

shortly afterward. The Curtiss pusher was the invention of Glenn Hammond Curtiss (1878–1930) of Hammondsport, New York. A designer and builder of motorcycles and motorcycle engines, Curtiss became interested in flying when he went to Dayton to work on the engines of an airship flown by Captain Thomas S. Baldwin and there met the Wright brothers. In 1911 Ely, a graduate of Curtiss' flying school, made the first landing on a ship—the U.S.S. *Pennsylvania* moored in San Francisco Bay—in a Curtiss aeroplane. In the same year the first American seaplane, another Curtiss machine, made its first successful take-off from water. The first seaplane of all time was the invention of the brilliant young Frenchman, Henri Fabre, who built and flew his machine in 1910 near Marseilles without ever having taken a flying lesson. At the time of writing, Monsieur Fabre, although he has not flown for fifty years, is still active and is to be seen on fair days sailing alone in a small boat on the waters of the port of Marseilles where he once made his contribution to the history of aviation.

The first use of the aeroplane in war dates from 1912 when Italy seized Tripoli from the Ottoman Empire and made it into the Italian colony of Libya. The Italian machines were for the most part Farman pushers and their job was infantry reconnaissance. The first offensive use of the aeroplane occurred in the Balkan wars of 1912–1913 between the Ottoman Empire and Greece, Bulgaria, Serbia and Montenegro. The four last-named states wrested Macedonia and Thrace from the Turks in 1912, then fought among themselves in 1913 over the division of the spoils.

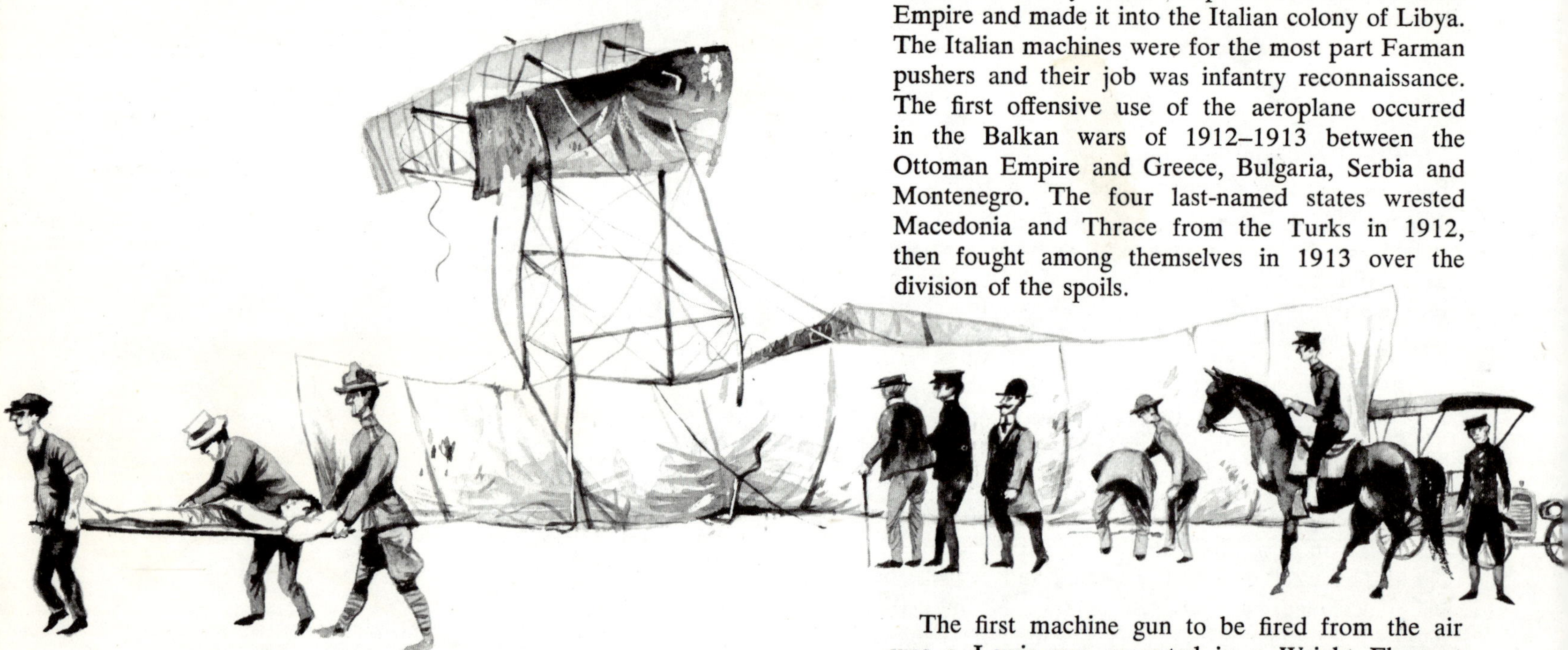

The first machine gun to be fired from the air was a Lewis gun mounted in a Wright Flyer at Fort Myer, Virginia, and it was there, on 17 September 1908, that Lieutenant Thomas E. Selfridge of the U.S. Army became the first American military man to be killed in an aeroplane crash. His pilot, Orville Wright, was seriously injured.

Igor Sikorsky, the Russian inventor and aviation pioneer, was born in Kiev in 1889, the son of a professor of medicine whose scientific interests were endless. Sikorsky was fascinated by the idea of flying from his boyhood and built his first aeroplane in 1910. By 1913 he had designed and built several, had won considerable recognition for his achievements, and was named head of the aeronautical division established in the Russian Baltic Railroad Car Factory at Petrograd. His first four-engined aeroplane, the *Le Grand,* was the first in the world. It flew in the spring of 1913 and completed over fifty trouble-free flights. In the summer of 1913 it was damaged beyond repair when the motor of another aeroplane fell on it.

Sikorsky's next four-engined aeroplane, named *Ilya Murometz* after the legendary Russian hero, first flew in January 1914. It could carry up to sixteen persons and minor engine repairs and servicing could be performed in flight. The *Ilya Murometz* was ordered in quantity by the Russian army, and by the time of the Revolution in 1917 about seventy-five had been delivered. The first four-engined bombers, they carried bombs weighing up to 1,000 pounds. They made some 400 bombing flights during the war, and were the first bombers to have a tail gunner's position. Only one *Ilya Murometz* was ever shot down by enemy fighters.

Leutnant R. von Thiedemann

When the war began, the German air service had developed to a fair degree the techniques of artillery observation with balloons and infantry co-operation with aeroplanes. *Leutnant* Richard von Thiedemann of the Hussars, who soloed at Döberitz, Berlin on 23 July 1910, was the first active-duty German officer to receive a pilot's license. *Leutnant* Ferdinand von Hiddessen, who soloed on 17 January 1911 at Darmstadt, flew over Paris on the afternoon of 30 August 1914, and dropped the first bombs ever dropped on a city. Three bombs fell on the Quai de Valmy, killing two persons and injuring several others. That night, the blackout was introduced. For some weeks after that, one or more German aeroplanes returned every evening at 6:00 p.m. to drop bombs in the hope of intimidating the populace. The Parisians referred to these aeroplanes collectively as the "Six O'Clock *Taube*" although the type was not a *Taube*. As the *Taube* (Dove) machines were the best known, all German aeroplanes were called *Taube* by the general public.

On 4 August, German cavalry crossed the Belgian frontier

1914 -1918

The eleventh hour, the eleventh day, the eleventh month

28 June at Sarajevo

1914

Not for the first time, nor for the last, the single irresponsible act of one misguided fanatic brought disaster to western civilization. The interlocked politics of the Balkans were convulsed by the assassination of the heir to the Austro-Hungarian throne, Archduke Franz Ferdinand. His assassin, a teen-aged Serb nationalist named Gavrilo Princip, was seized and imprisoned. He died of tuberculosis in prison in 1918.

B771

THE ACTUAL OUTBREAK of the 1914–1918 war was more like the spreading of a great fire than a single violent explosion. The nations of Europe, tangled in a web of alliances, reinsurance treaties and pledges of mutual support, fell one by one into the flames, each dragging his neighbor with him.

Some of the statesmen tried to avoid war; many of the army leaders openly planned for it. The statesmen were caught in their own traps, the army leaders caught in theirs, but it was the plain soldiers of all the armies who paid for the blunders of both. How the army men had fallen behind the times is illustrated in the scene below, which depicts Prussian officers with Napoleonic training about to send off a reconnaissance mission early in the war. The pilot of the aeroplane is merely a chauffer for the observer who is dressed exactly as if he were going on his mission on horseback rather than in an aeroplane—complete with sabre, spurs and *pickelhaube* helmet.

The traditional thinking of army leaders yielded slowly to the pressure of such new ideas as the exploitation of the air. Even after the war, which had been fought for four years along a deadlocked, stagnant, entrenched battleline that meandered from Switzerland to the Straits of Dover, Field Marshal Haig lectured the British Staff College on the uses of cavalry in modern war. Yet, even before the war, it had been demonstrated on maneuvers that a squadron of aeroplanes could penetrate far deeper behind the enemy lines than the cavalry, and its value for reconnaissance and observation was correspondingly greater. From this it was only a step to the notion that these same aeroplanes could drop bombs behind the enemy lines, disrupting supply and severing communications. Some army men never realized that the air age had dawned ten years before the war, and advocates of air power had an uphill struggle against official indifference throughout the course of the war—and for years afterward. About the only role that had been allotted the tiny air services when the war began was reconnaissance, and that grudgingly. Crusty army men hated aeroplanes because the racket they made frightened their horses.

The air services grew, however, in spite of indifference, obstruction and prejudice. By the time of the armistice in November 1918 the British Royal Air Force was operating in France and Belgium a total of ninety-nine squadrons with a strength of 30,000 officers and 22,000 aeroplanes. Germany was operating a comparable force (though a small one compared with the combined Allied services) of 21,386 aeroplanes and sixteen airships.

Germany was slow to abandon the airship (*Luftschiff* in German, but Zeppelin in English, after the man who perfected them). The air hopes of Germany were

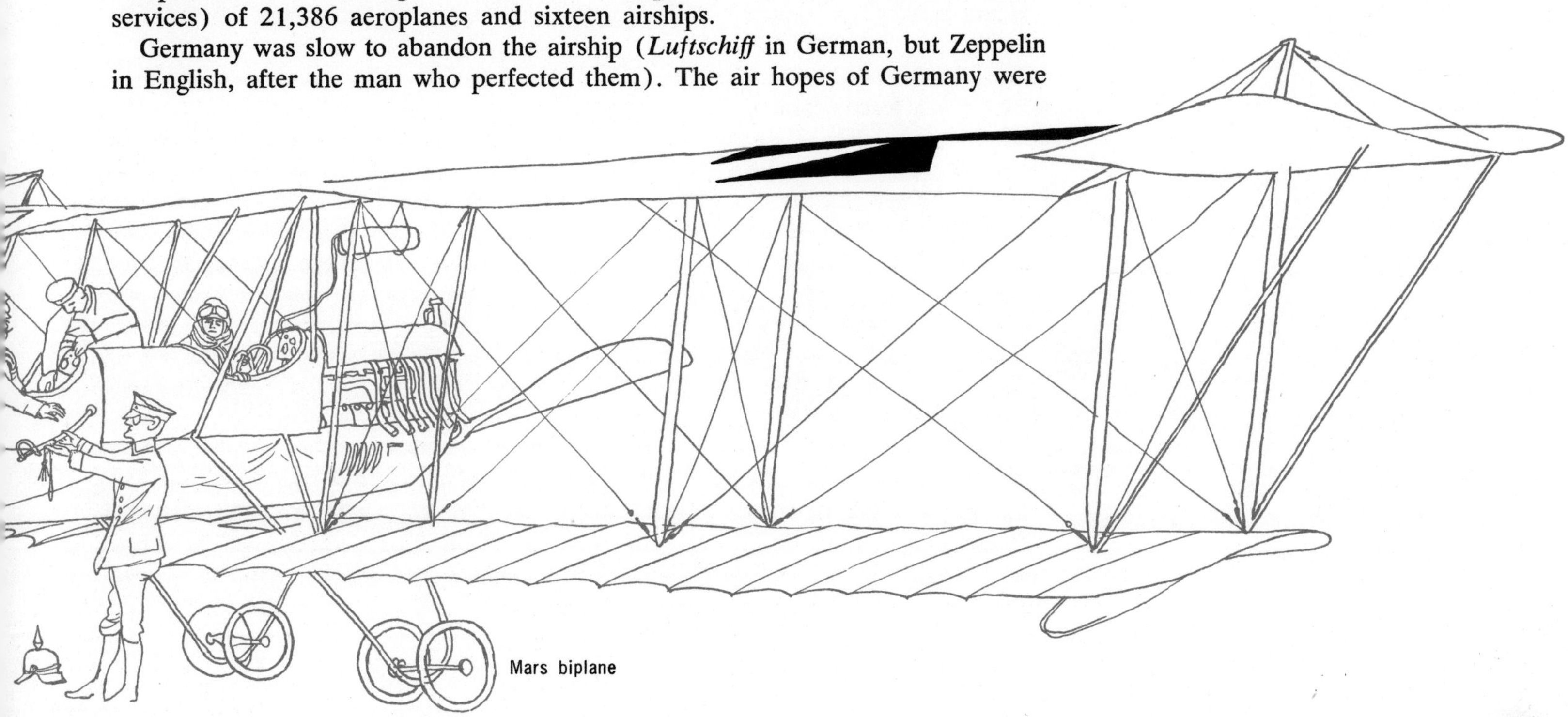

Mars biplane

based on the one quality the airships had that was unquestionably superior to that of aeroplanes—endurance. As early as 1908 airships in Germany had proved their ability to remain aloft for periods of up to twenty-four hours. It was with this endurance, giving them an operational range far greater than that of aeroplanes, that the Germans planned to terrorize the populations of London and Paris by bombing raids and so exact early peace offers. While the Germans expected to win the war in a few weeks and on the ground, the morale value of the airship thus had a place in the large scheme. It was a manifestation of this same technique of terror that prompted them to send the "Six O'Clock *Taube*" over Paris every evening in the first weeks of the war. The bugbear of the Zeppelins produced an unreasoning fear among the Allies who continued to regard them as a grave threat as bombers long after it had become apparent to the Germans that any attempt to bomb with them was doomed to fail because of weather, fighter defense or inevitable accidents. They were too vulnerable to storm and shell to be of much use, but an indication of the importance the Allies gave them was that the first British air raids of the war were launched against Zeppelin sheds.

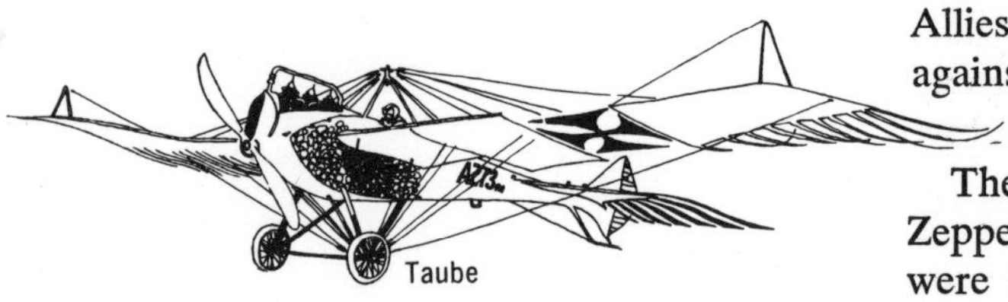
Taube

The backbone of the German air service, notwithstanding the celebrity of the Zeppelins, was the two-seater. Almost all the aeroplanes in the air services were two-seaters, of course, but the Germans developed more two-seater types than the French and the British put together. At the start of the war the German air service was composed of thirty-three *Feldfliegerabteilungen* (Field Flying Sections) of six aeroplanes each. These units, later called simply *Fliegerabteilungen* (Flying Sections, abbreviated *Fl. Abt.*), were assigned one to each German Army Headquarters for long-range strategic reconnaissance, and one to each corps headquarters (except for some reserve corps) for tactical reconnaissance.

There were seven and one-half *Festungsfliegerabteilungen* (Fortress Flying Sections) of four aeroplanes each assigned to the fortress garrisons of Metz, Strasbourg and Cologne in the Rhineland, and Posen, Lotzen, Grudziadz (Graudenz) and Königsberg clustered in northern Poland. The fortresses themselves, as the French forts of Belfort and Verdun and the Belgian fortress of Liège, were another holdover from Napoleonic times. The idea of assigning aircraft of any kind to a fortress garrison sounds today as anachronistic as the idea of issuing sails to a battleship.

The French air service, like those of Germany and Great Britain, was considered chiefly in the terms of an adjunct to the cavalry, which had always performed the duties of observation and reconnaissance on horseback. It had, however, the advantage of pre-war operational experience in Algeria and Morocco during the disturbances of 1912 through 1914. French air units had performed reconnaissance, observation and bombing missions, and the names of the first French airmen killed in action had been written on the Roll of Honor—*Capitaine* Hervé and his observer Roëland, slain by Arabs in Morocco early in 1914 following a forced landing in the desert.

French squadrons—*escadrilles*—were numbered in sequence according to the order of their establishment. There were twenty-one *escadrilles* of six two-seaters each for army co-operation when the war began, plus four units composed of three Blériot single-seaters each for the cavalry. Besides their basic numerical designation, the *escadrilles* were further identified by equipment, this being accomplished by prefixing a code letter representing aeroplane manufacturers and types. Thus, *V.B. 24* was Voisin bombing squadron number 24. The letters changed when the equipment did. Thus, one of the Stork squadrons changed its name three times—M-S 26, N. 26, Spa 26—as it progressed from Morane-Saulnier to Nieuport to Spad.

This system derived from the most significant characteristic of the French air service, one that was to stand the French in good stead at a later date, the fact that it was organized into homogeneous units. When, early in 1916, General Pétain ordered that the French must seize and hold aerial supremacy, the essential homogeneity of the *escadrilles* made it possible quickly to concentrate pure fighter units with which to accomplish the task.

Blériot XI

Reconnaissance

C 27 SAL 58 SAL 17 BR 14 SAL 33 SAL 264 ESC 204 SPA 59

Bombardement

BR 137 BR 107 VB 109 C 115 BR 205 BR 113 BR 201

Chasse

C 46 VB 137 SPA 571 SPA 68 SPA 89 SPA 153

SPA 48 SPA 168 SPA 95 SPA 62 SPA 88 SPA 160 SPA 32

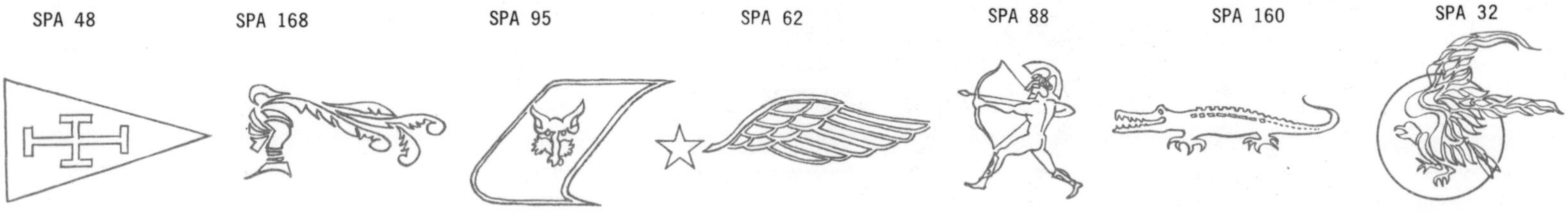

SPA 77 SPA 15 SPA 84 SPA 86 SPA 31 SPA 152 SPA 166

THE END OF POLITICAL ISOLATION

was dramatically symbolized by Louis Blériot's flight from Calais to Dover in the summer of 1909. His short flight from one country to another, scornful of the geographic barrier of the English Channel, showed with what ease peoples could be linked by the air—or how easily could be breached the "walls" of their national frontiers. It may truly be said that England was no longer an island once Blériot had come there on the unobstacled ways of the sky.

On 13 August 1914, the drama was replayed under the circumstances of war, for on that day Nos. 2 and 3 Squadrons of the British Royal Flying Corps, plus "A" and "B" Flights of No. 4 Squadron, flew across the Channel from Dover to Amiens to join the B.E.F. in France. Lieutenant H.D. Harvey-Kelly, formerly of the Royal Irish Regiment, flying B.E.2a number 347 in No. 2 Squadron, was the first to take off and the first to land (below). There had been a crash the day before, but on the occasion of the fly-over, all machines arrived safely. It was the first war-time mass flight across national boundaries in history.

Yet many of these pioneer aviators themselves were unable to grasp the significance of such flights. Group Captain R.J.F. Barton, who was later to serve as G.S.O. 1 to Major General H.M. Trenchard, was a youthful R.F.C. pilot in August of 1914. Concerning the fly-over he wrote: "I really do not think that the pilots of the Expeditionary Force had any feeling that the fly-over *en masse* was a historic event. It may have been the case with Squadron Commanders and Staff who were of riper years. It was just one big excitement to us younger ones."

347

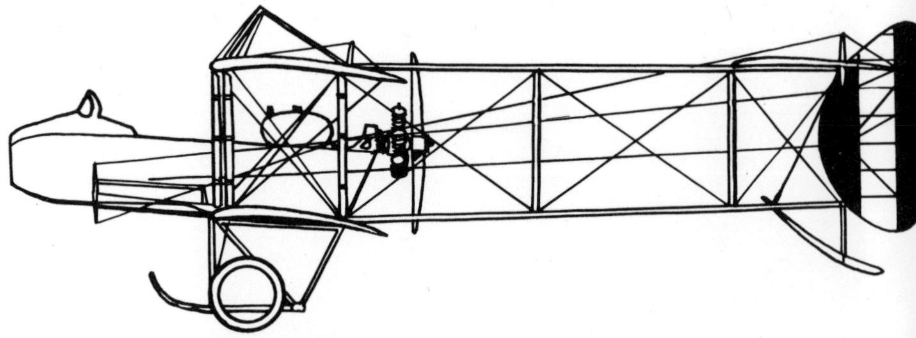

THE CRASH that had taken the lives of the first two men of the R.F.C. to be killed after the commencement of hostilities was the kind of meaningless tragedy that seems all the more bitter because it should not have happened. The squadrons that were to fly over the Channel assembled at Dover on 12 August, coming from Farnborough and Netheravon. No. 3 Squadron was at Netheravon under the command of Major John M. Salmond who in 1918 was a Major General and the Commanding Officer of the Royal Air Force in France. All the machines except one got off safely on that morning on the hop to Dover, the first leg of the trip to Amiens. The last machine, a Blériot two-seater of "C" Flight, had engine trouble and landed soon after take-off for some adjustment, taking off again with a mechanic named Keith Barlow as passenger and Second Lieutenant R.R. Skene as pilot. Taking off for the second time, Skene had just got his machine over the trees at the end of the field when the recalcitrant engine conked out altogether. The machine crashed into the trees, killing both men.

The first death in the German air service was that of *Oberleutnant* Reinhold Jahnow, who was born in Breslau on 27 March 1885. Jahnow had received pilot's license No. 80 in Germany, soloing on 10 April 1911, in a Harlan monoplane at Johannisthal, Berlin. He served in the Balkans in 1912, flying on several army co-operation missions for the Turks. He crashed fatally at Malmédy, Belgium, on 12 August 1914.

A tradition of stoicism developed early in the military aviation, an inheritance from the old regular armies who supplied the first officers of the new service. Before the war, Major Charles J. Burke of the Royal Irish Regiment, a veteran of the South African war appointed to the command of No. 2 Squadron, R.F.C., in 1912, wrote that waiting around on the aerodrome "has spoilt more pilots than everything else put together." To see a crash was an unnerving experience, even if there were many crashes in the early days, and unless a man had around him others who could calmly carry on in the face of tragedy, he was likely to become depressed by what he had seen. "*N'y pensez pas trop*," the French say: Don't think about it too much. It was an officer's job to keep the men busy so they would not have time to brood about death, and it was especially necessary to get them back in the air quickly if they had seen or survived a crash. To let them stand around and talk about it was to kill them—sooner or later.

At the front, the airmen who lived in reasonably comfortable quarters while the infantry lived in mud, were never envied or resented by the infantry. "You can have it," was what most of the infantry thought about flying. "It's a long way down and you only fall once."

The airmen paid for their dry beds and regular meals—they died. And they ignored the empty seats at the table, the empty cots in the huts. Somebody else was always available to sit in at an unfinished card game, and no place went vacant long. Each man coming into the squadron, whether he was an artist, a story-teller, a con man, a wire-puller, a clown or a killer, was one human being like all others who brought something of himself to the squadron. Something that became a part of it until he too failed to return.

Then his name would disappear from everyone's lips. The men would gather in the mess as usual, one, two or five missing would make no difference, and some would talk, some would drink, some would gamble, some would do all three, and some would do nothing. The party might end quietly or it might end in a shambles of broken crockery and smashed furniture.

And they would sing:

We meet 'neath the sounding rafters,
The walls around us are bare;
They echo the peals of laughter—
It seems that the dead are there.
So, stand by your glasses steady,
This world is a world of lies.
Here's a toast to the dead already;
Hurrah for the next man who dies.

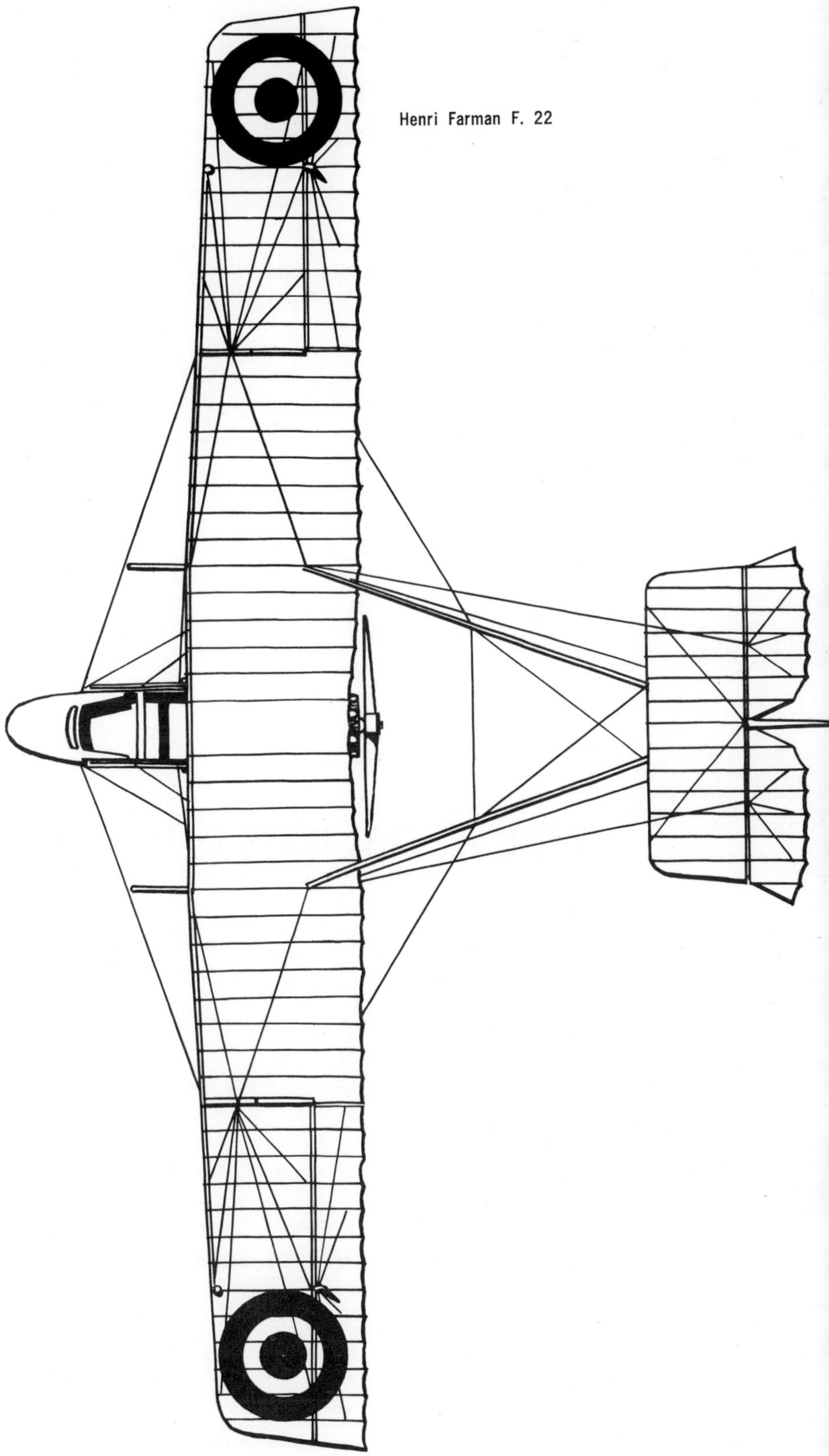

Henri Farman F. 22

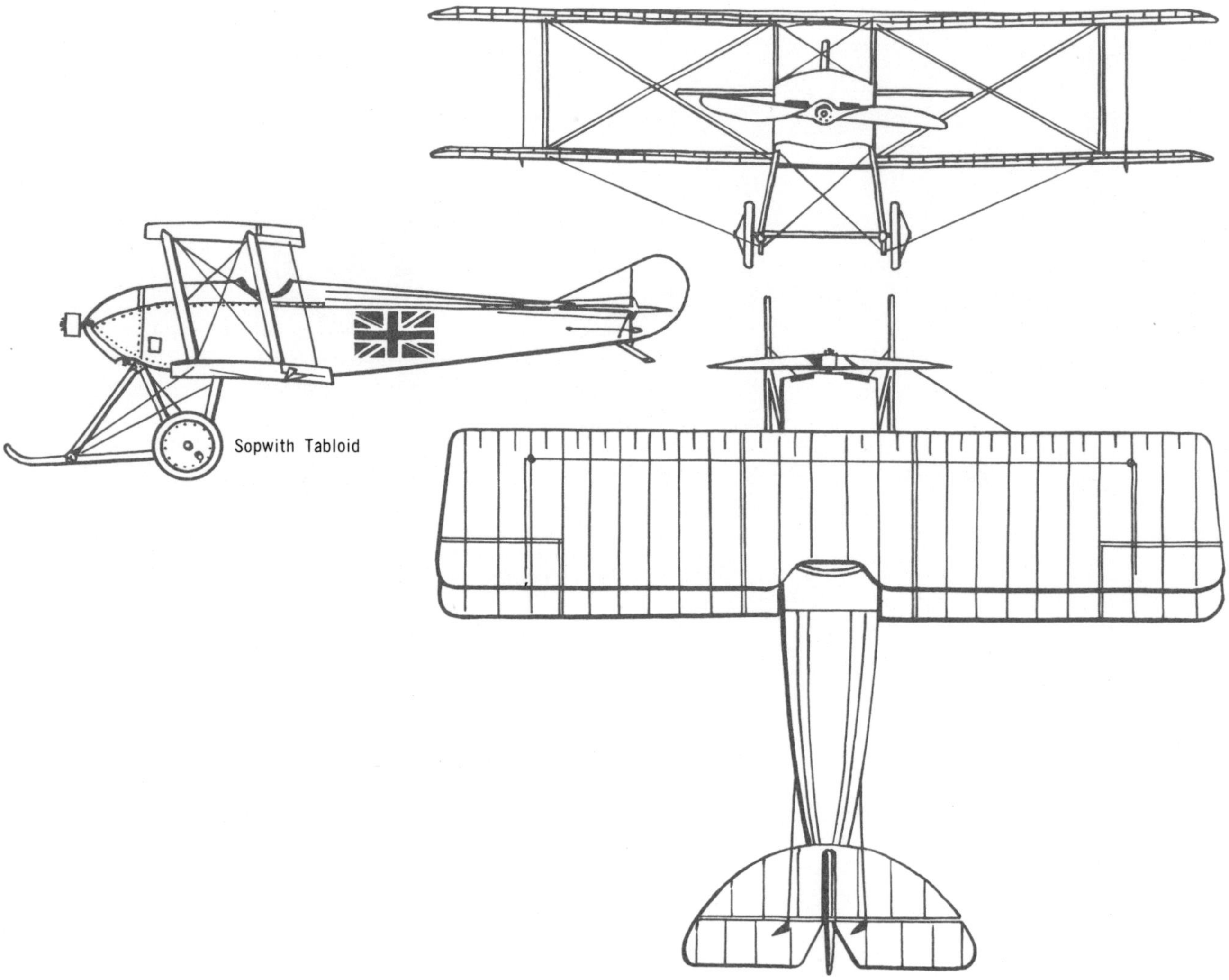

Sopwith Tabloid

DURING THE FIRST MONTH OF THE WAR,

from the beginning of August to the beginning of September 1914, the German army rammed its way almost to the gates of Paris. When it was stopped on the Marne it rapidly gathered its strength for a drive in another direction—to the Channel Ports. The British were not only concerned for the ports when they sent a naval division to Antwerp on 5 October, they hoped to force the Germans in France to retreat by aiming a blow at their flank. As it happened, the naval division was too small a force and was on the defensive from the start. On 8 October 1914, during the evacuation of Antwerp, and while the German artillery was bombarding the city, the small Royal Naval Air Service squadron was sticking determinedly to its aerodrome. The machines were wheeled out into the open and dispersed about the field to minimize damage from enemy shells. The weather was misty in the morning and there was concern that the flying conditions would be so poor that the R.N.A.S. would be deprived of the opportunity of getting in one good lick. They had one cherished goal: to bomb the Zeppelin sheds at Düsseldorf and Cologne. Time, however, was fast running out and the Germans were in the suburbs of the city.

At 1:20 p.m. Squadron Commander Spenser Grey took off in a Tabloid in poor visibility. He flew to Cologne in a thick mist and was unable to locate the sheds. He flew over the town for a short time and finally dropped his bombs on the main railway station. He got back to Antwerp at 4:45 p.m.

Flight Lieutenant R.L.G. Marix started off in his Tabloid at 1:30 p.m. and flew to Düsseldorf. The weather was somewhat better there than at Cologne and he was able to find the airship sheds. He dived on them and released his four 20-pound bombs from a height of about 600 feet. There was a colossal roar of flame that rose hundreds of feet into the air, and the destruction of the new Zeppelin Z.IX was complete. Marix weathered heavy gunfire from the ground and only just succeeded in running the gauntlet. His Tabloid was badly shot up and he nursed it along to within twenty miles of Antwerp where it finally gave up and he was forced to land. He managed, with the aid of a bicycle borrowed from a peasant, to return to the base just before the general evacuation was ordered at 6:00 p.m. The R.N.A.S. officers reached Ostend at noon the following day.

Flight Lieutenant R. L. G. Marix, R.N.A.S.

KAISER WILHELM II

Because of his family connections with the British royal house, the Kaiser was at first reluctant to give permission for the bombing of England. Grand Admiral Alfred von Tirpitz, the Prussian State Secretary of the Navy, however, was firm in his belief that the bombing of London was necessary for the psychological effect. In January of 1915 the Kaiser agreed to permit the bombing of targets in England provided that they were expressly military establishments. On 19 January the three navy Zeppelins L.3, L.4 and L.6, took off from Hamburg and Nordholz, headed across the Channel. The L.6 was forced to turn back because of engine trouble, but the L.3 and L.4 continued on, crossed the North Sea safely and arrived off Norfolk about 8:00 p.m. The L.3 dropped several bombs on Yarmouth and the L.4 dropped its load in the area of Norfolk. Several persons were killed and scores were injured in the first air raid against England. Bad weather intervened for a period of weeks. When it seemed fair enough to try again, on 17 February 1915, the L.3 and L.4 set out, but they ran into a storm over the North Sea, and were both wrecked on the coast of Jutland and their crews interned.

Before the war, the German Airship Travel Company (*Deutsch Luftschiffahrt A.G.—Delag*) operated by Hugo Eckener, Graf von Zeppelin's partner, flew airship routes carrying passengers and freight all over Germany. The airships were pressed into military service when the war began. One of them, the *Sachsen,*

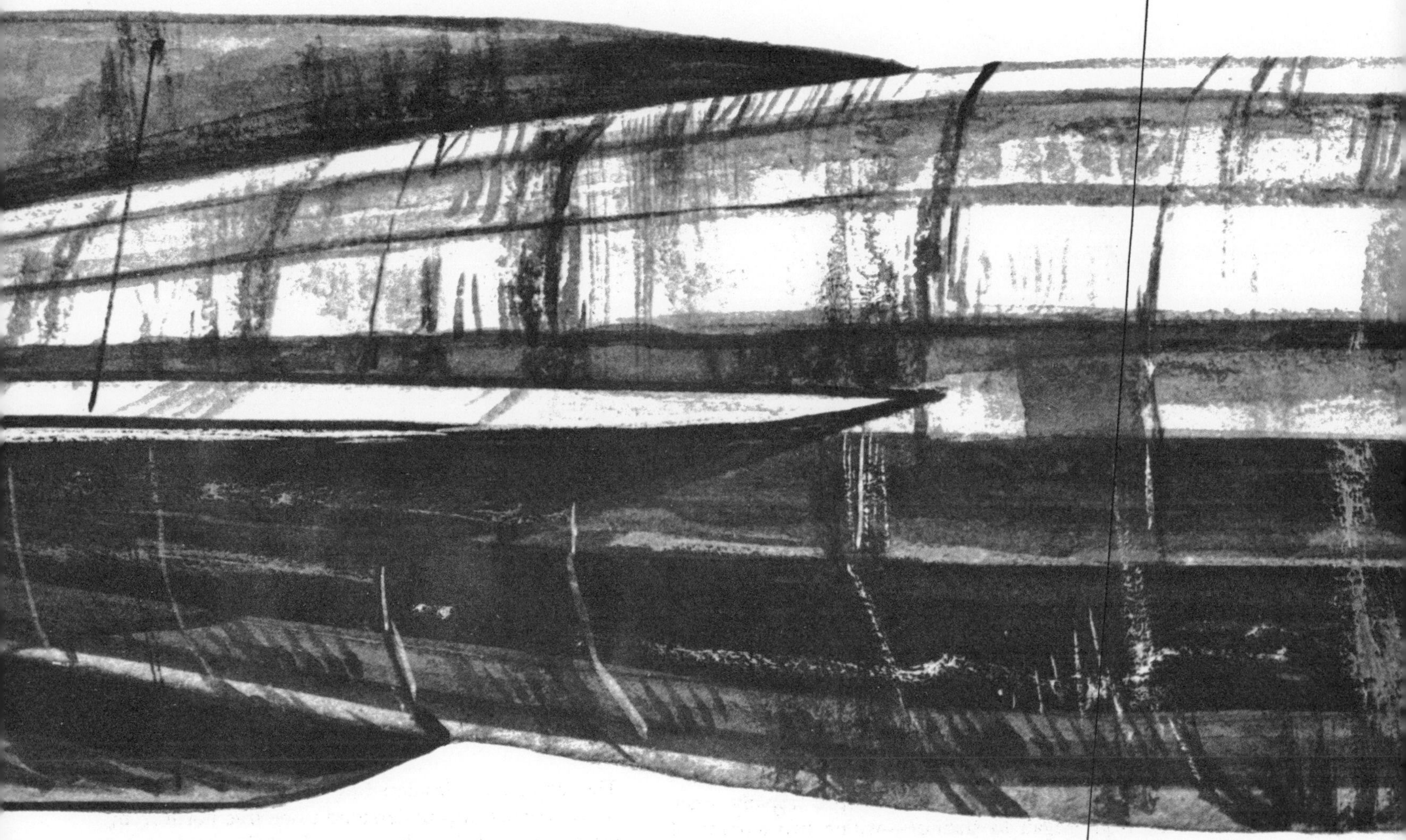

now bearing the army designation Z.12, was commanded by a naval officer, engineer and inventor named Ernst Lehmann. On 17 March 1915, Lehmann took the Z.12 on the first army airship mission to England. This was also the first occasion when the famous "cloud car" was used. The mission to England was frustrated by fog, but Lehmann was unwilling to give up so he cruised about trying to find the mouth of the Thames. It was no use so he turned back to France and soon raised Calais, whose lights were easily seen in the clear air on the other side of the Channel. Lehmann gave orders to throttle back the engines and lower the car. The car was an invention of Lehmann's, and consisted of a small plywood-covered tub with a cockpit, stabilizing fins and a telephone, the wires of which ran up to the cabin of the airship through the core of the steel cable by means of which the car was winched up and down. It was past midnight when the Z.12 ghosted over Calais, invisible from the ground and even from the cloud car. The observer later said that he felt lonely down there all by himself. By telephone he requested the dropping of small bombs, watched the strikes and made rough corrections to allow for forward speed, drift and altitude, and then requested larger bombs. On the ground, the engines of the Z.12 could barely be heard, and the fact that the Zeppelin was invisible caused more concern than the bomb damage. When all the bombs were dropped, the car was hauled up and in and the Z.12 went home.

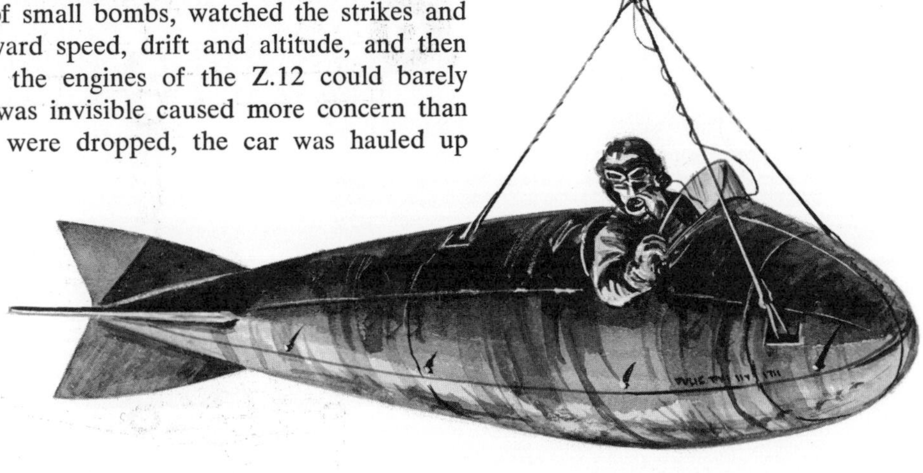

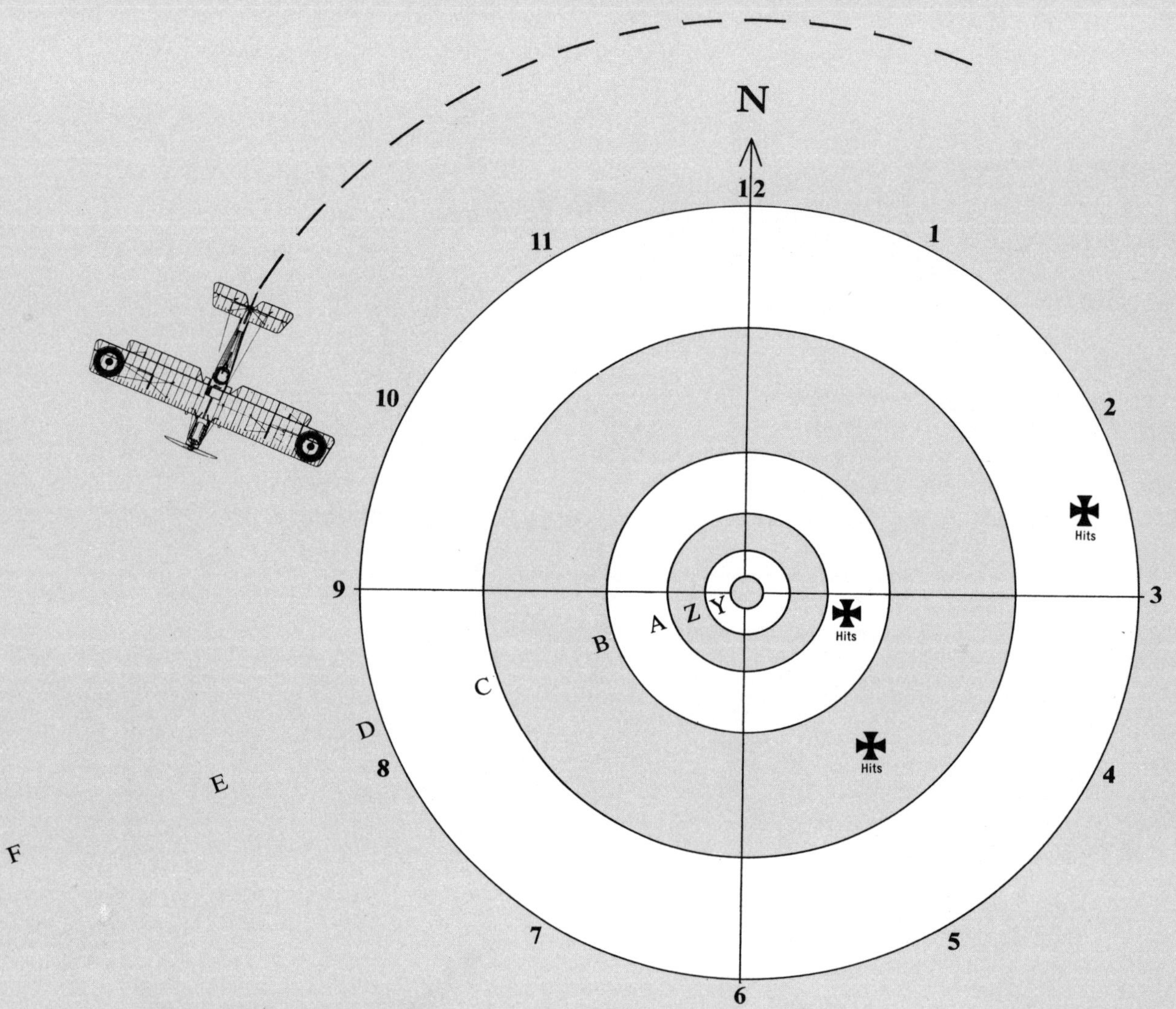

ARTILLERY-SPOTTING developed rapidly once the front began to stabilize—within two months of the outbreak of war in some sectors. The early use of wireless telephony speeded it in the British Royal Flying Corps. The early wireless reports to battery commanders were sometimes quite informal while the war was for the most part regarded as a huge lark: "Your last shot in the middle of three batteries in action. Search all round within 300 yards . . . and you have them."

A formal and less colorful method of "art-obs" was put into practice early in 1915 and remained in use for the rest of the war. Called the "clock code," it was at once graphic and flexible for it depended on unvarying values which were almost impossible to misinterpret—the dial of a clock and true north. The target was considered to be the center of a dial; twelve o'clock was understood to be true north from the target, and the other hours in their proper positions round the dial. These values remained the same regardless of which direction the battery was shooting. Thus, a shot that landed due south of the target was said to land at six o'clock; a shot that landed due west of the target, nine o'clock. Imaginary circles were drawn around the target to represent ranges of 10, 25, 50, 100, 200, 300, 400 and 500 yards. These ranges were identified by code letters: Y, Z, A, B, C, D, E, E and F respectively. Thus a shot that landed ENE and 200 yards from the target was signalled "C 1" in Morse code.

Pre-arranged signals were made to the observers in the aeroplanes from the batteries, or any ground post, with strips of canvas stretched on the ground.

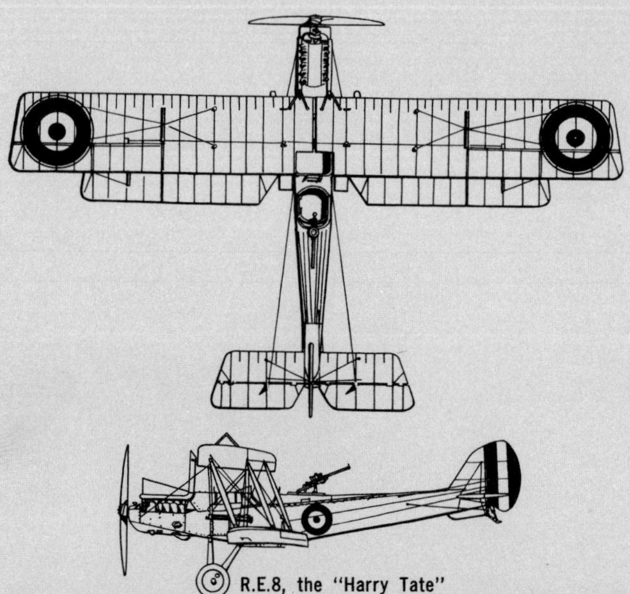

⑥ R.E.8, the "Harry Tate"

NATIONAL MARKINGS were not used before the outbreak of the war, and not for some time after. Not until it became apparent that such markings were vitally necessary to prevent aircraft being shot down by their own side, was any movement in this direction made. One German army Zeppelin, the Z.VIII, crashed in the forest of Badonviller in France on 23 August 1914, after having been damaged by French ground fire and finished off by German ground fire. Over-zealous German troops mistakenly opened up on it as it drifted overhead, disabled. The Germans were not the only ones to be fired on by their own infantry. During the retreat from Maubeuge to Mons, the British Tommies, disgruntled by the continual retreating without having been beaten, vented their feelings by firing furiously at anything that flew over—British, French or German.

The ground crews of the Royal Flying Corps turned to and painted large Union Jacks on the bottom wings of all the aeroplanes in the hope of reducing the amount of British fire the machines had to weather. Unfortunately, the Union Jack, except in the most favorable conditions, was liable to resemble the German Cross. On 26 October 1914, two men named Hosking and Crean, of No. 4 Squadron, R.F.C., were shot down in flames by British troops who apparently mistook the Union Jack for the Iron Cross. Shortly thereafter, the R.F.C. adopted a French-type roundel, reversing the colors to maintain national distinctions.

Some form of roundel was the basis of the insignias of all the Allied air services. The French used blue, white and red (reading from the center), the stylized poppy cockade that had been a French tradition since the Revolution. The British used red, white and blue. When the Americans finally arrived on the scene they used white, blue and red; the Belgians used black, yellow and red; the Italians used red, white and green (or green, white and red). The Russians used rings of blue and red, separated by thin rings of white, around a white center.

Turkey, alone among the Central Powers, used a color other than black for her aero insignia. During 1914 her aircraft bore a red square with a white star and crescent. From the beginning of 1915 she too used black, the design being a solid black square outlined in white.

Germany, Bulgaria and Austria-Hungary used the black Iron Cross or a straight-sided version of it. At the start of the war, the aeroplanes that bore any kind of national marking had a handpainted Iron Cross of odd proportions (see illustration, pages 18–19). Until uniform templates came into general use, the crosses had non-regulation arms because it was difficult to render them correctly owing to the large radii involved.

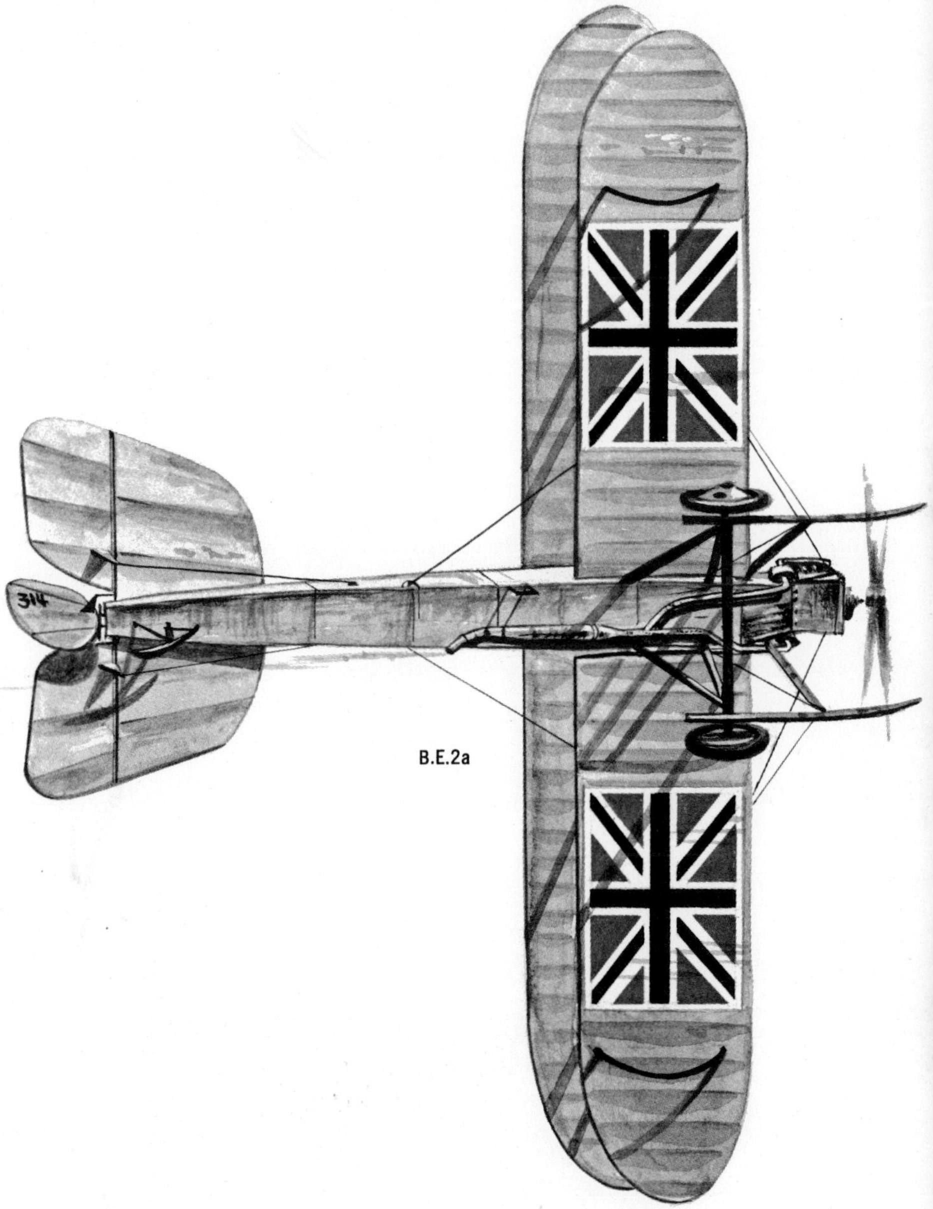

B.E.2a

1

2

3

4

5

6

THE CENTRAL POWERS 1/Germany 1914-1915 2/Germany 1915-1917 3/Germany 1917-1918 4/Germany 1918 5/Turkey 1915-1918 6/Bulgaria 1914-1918 (The aero insignias of Austria-Hungary followed German practice)

1

2

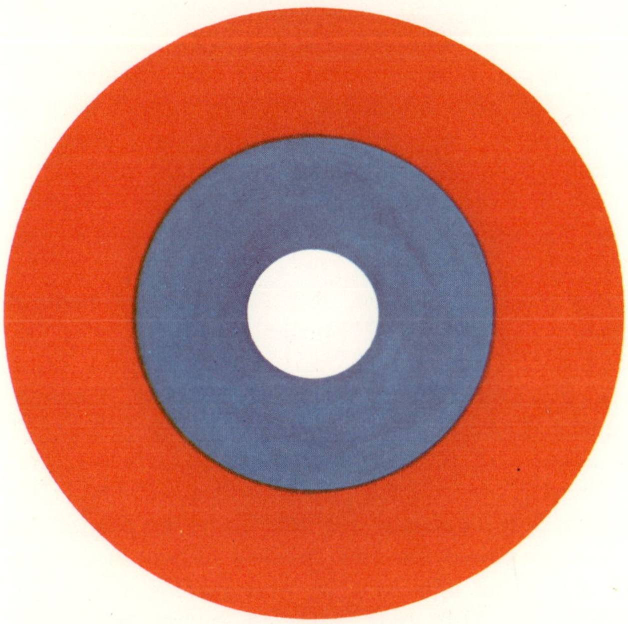

3

4

5

6

THE ALLIES 1/Great Britain, 2/France, 3/United States, 4/Italy, 5/Belgium, 6/Russia

ZEPPELINS LZ.37, LZ.38 and LZ.39, stationed in the Bruges area, set out after dusk on Sunday, 6 June 1915, to bomb London. Over the Channel they were advised that weather conditions were unsuitable, so they turned back in the general direction of Calais to bomb the railroads. British radio receiving stations on the East Coast picked up the German transmissions and telephoned the Admiralty, who in turn telephoned the information to the Dunkirk squadron with instructions to intercept the Zeppelins as they descended to make their way back.

The "Dunkirk squadron" was No. 1 Squadron, R.N.A.S., under Squadron Commander Arthur M. Longmore (an Air Chief Marshal in World War II). It had been stationed in Dunkirk since February. The aeroplanes of the squadron were the usual heterogeneous collection of those days—the Voisin, Farman, Blériot, Avro, Curtiss, Morane and Vickers.

Longmore received the call about half past midnight and dispatched several aeroplanes. One of them, an Henri Farman F.22 pusher armed with four 20-pound bombs, was piloted by Flight Sub-Lieutenant J.S. Mills, who headed for the Zeppelin sheds at Evere. As he approached the field, he was caught by several searchlights. He promptly flashed a signal light as if he were coming in to land, and the ground gunners held their fire. Mills then proceded to drop his bombs from a fairly low altitude and succeeded in hitting the LZ.38 inside its shed. The Zeppelin blew up in a column of smoke and flames. Mills escaped and returned to Dunkirk.

Meanwhile, another of the aeroplanes, a Morane-Saulnier *Parasol* piloted by Flight Sub-Lieutenant R.A.J. Warneford, approached the LZ.37 south of Bruges. Warneford spotted the airship in the vicinity of the coast at Ostend, and had been stalking it as it flew toward its shed at Gontrode, a few miles southeast of Ghent. The gunners aboard the airship fired occasional bursts at Warneford, forcing him to keep his distance and preventing him from closing in to launch an attack. His *Parasol* was not armed with a machine gun but instead carried six 20-pound bombs in a improvised rack under the fuselage. Unless Warneford could get close above the Zeppelin, there was no way for him to attack it, save by ramming. As the stalk continued with Warneford unable to close in and the

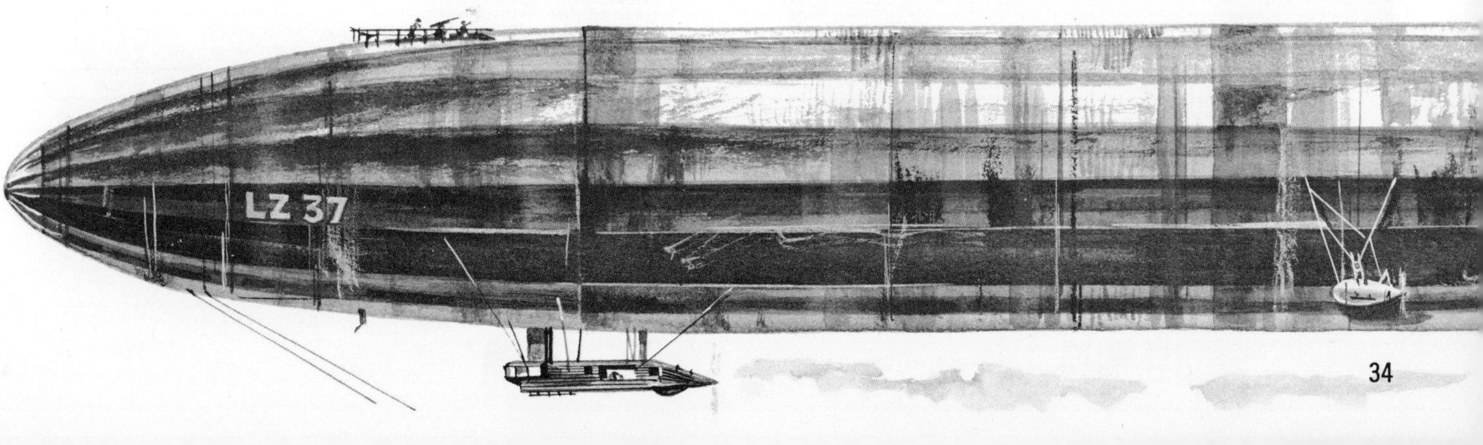

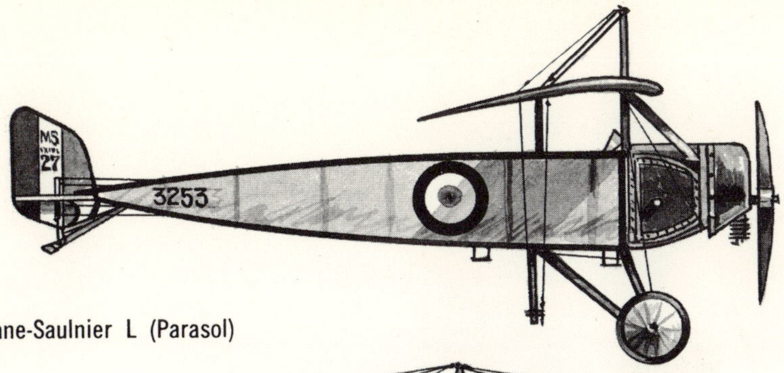

Morane-Saulnier L (Parasol)

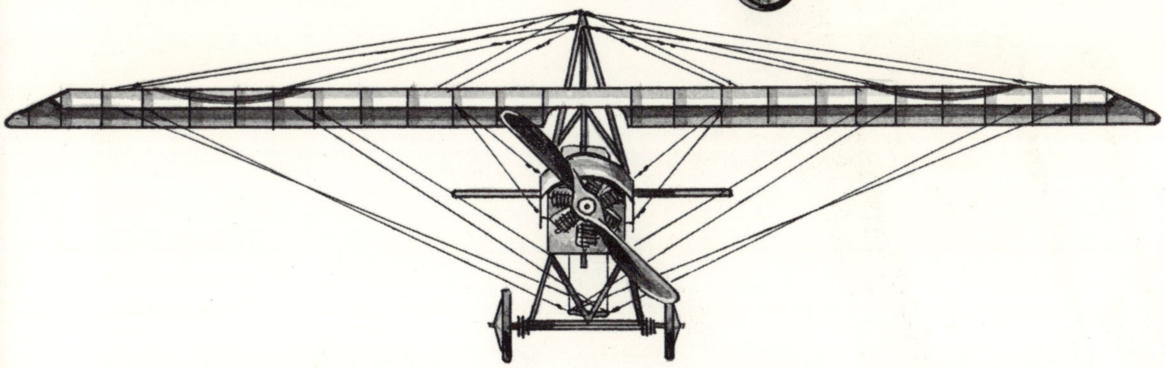

crew of the airship keeping a wary watch out against any tricks, the two machines passed over Ghent and the Zeppelin came within minutes of its base at Gontrode. The airship's skipper, *Oberleutnant* Otto van der Haegen, hoping to draw the *Parasol* into the range of the antiaircraft guns at the field, gave the order to descend. It was a mistake, for he thereby lost the one advantage the airship had over the aeroplane—height. At 11,000 feet Warneford watched the huge shape ahead of him settle gently toward the earth. He put his nose down in a shallow dive, swooped over the Zeppelin, and dropped his six bombs at one salvo when he was 150 feet above her. The sixth bomb hit her square in the middle and instantly there was a tremendous explosion. The *Parasol* was tossed like a leaf in a storm. Warneford was upside down when he caught a glimpse of a shower of flaming fragments falling all around. The wreckage of the LZ.37 landed in a suburb of Ghent, killing four persons on the ground and injuring many others. One crew member survived. He fell all the way to earth trapped in the cabin, went through the roof of a convent, and landed senseless on a bed in the dormitory.

Warneford regained control of his wildly tumbling *Parasol* and was setting a course for home when his engine conked out. He glided down in darkness, straining his eyes for a look at the ground. It was the gray half-light before dawn, but by some miracle he landed safely in a field. He was somewhere behind the German lines but he did not know exactly where. He climbed out of his machine and looked around. He decided to burn the *Parasol* and clear out. He listened for the sound of German patrols coming to pick him up, but it was very still and he concluded that his silent landing had gone undetected. In the dark he found the engine trouble with his nose—a broken fuel line. He effected a temporary repair and managed to swing the prop by himself, start the engine, climb in, and take off. He reached the Allied lines with no further trouble.

Late the following evening he received a telegram from King George V informing him that he was to be awarded the Victoria Cross. On Friday, 18 June 1915, Warneford took off in a new Henri Farman pusher for a short morning flight. A few hundred feet off the ground he made a sharp turn and the tail collapsed. He was hurled out of the machine. He landed in a cornfield and died on the way to the hospital.

THE SOPWITH BABY, a descendant of the Tabloid, was flown by many early R.N.A.S. pilots on coast defense patrols. It was powered by a 110 (or 130) h.p. Clerget rotary engine which gave it a top speed of about 100 m.p.h. Babies operated from seaplane carriers in the North Sea and the Mediterranean, and from the seaplane station at Dunkirk until the spring of 1917.

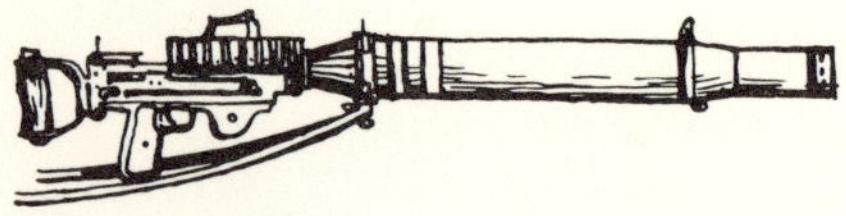
Lewis (Great Britain)

Lewis

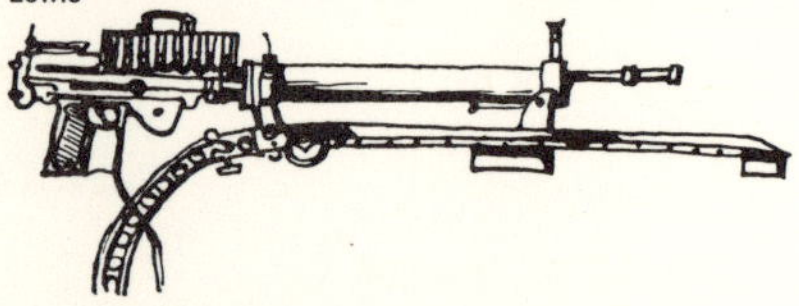
Lewis

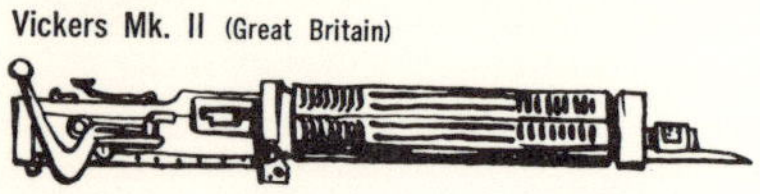
Vickers Mk. II (Great Britain)

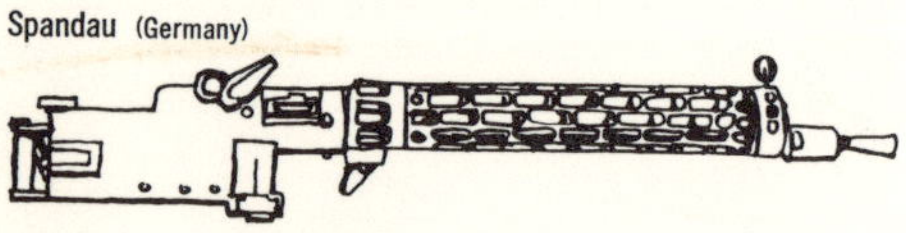
Spandau (Germany)

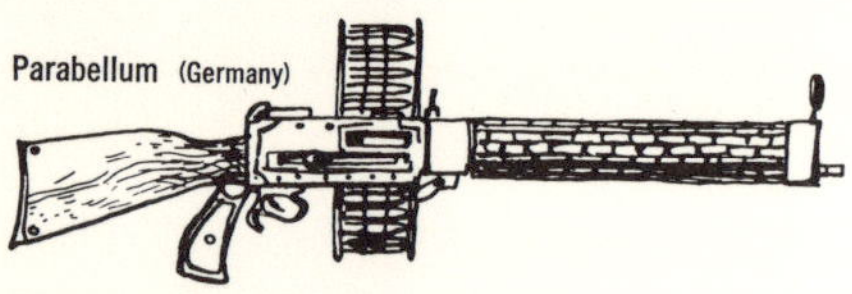
Parabellum (Germany)

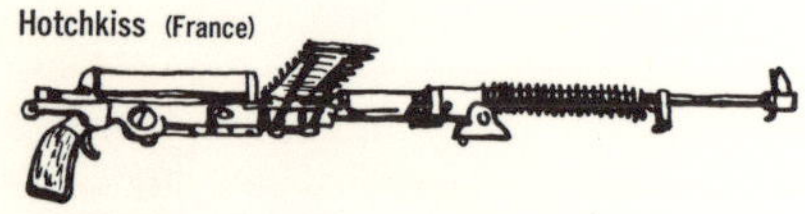
Hotchkiss (France)

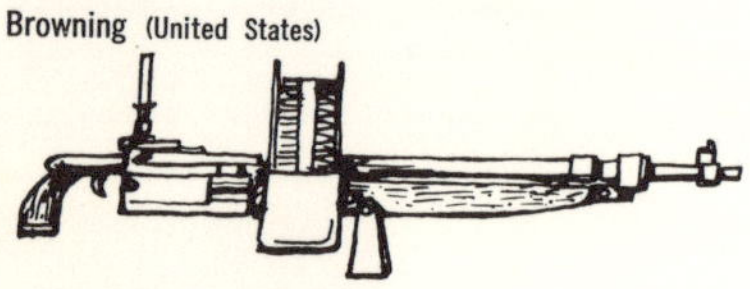
Browning (United States)

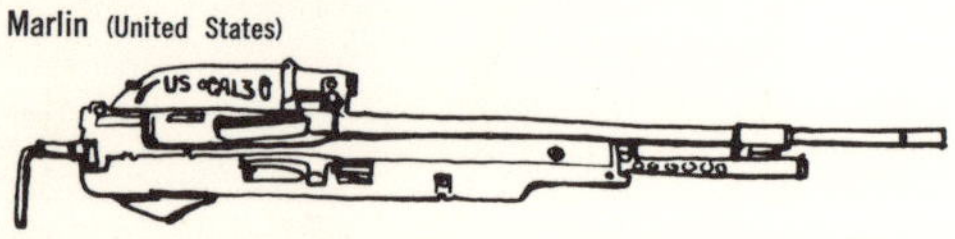
Marlin (United States)

THE FIRST TIME ONE AEROPLANE brought another one down was on 26 August 1914. Three Austrian aeroplanes bombed a Russian aerodrome in Galicia, where the XI Corps Air Squadron under Staff Captain Petr N. Nesteroff was based. Nesteroff, another of the small band of pre-war aviation pioneers, took off in his Morane-Saulnier scout in pursuit of the Austrian machines. Climbing to their altitude and overtaking the slower two-seaters, he drew up parallel with the lead machine flown by *Leutnant* Baron von Rosenthal. The Austrian pilots made no effort to escape as no aeroplane at that time was armed with anything other than a rifle; it was nearly impossible for a pilot to fly and fire a rifle accurately. Nesteroff, however, did not plan to shoot down his man—he was unarmed. He flew straight at von Rosenthal's machine and rammed it. The wrecks fell to the ground and both pilots were killed.

Such suicidal tactics were the exception rather than the rule, and until the arming of aeroplanes became standardized, a number of victories were scored by the "nearly impossible" method of shooting with a hand gun. Group Captain R.J.F. Barton of No. 4 Squadron, R.F.C., and *Capitaine* Félix Brocard, later to command the Stork Group, both shot down German aeroplanes by shooting at them with revolvers at close range.

Another unorthodox method was the "anchor" of the Russian ace, Staff Captain Alexander A. Kazakov. A six-footer with quiet, mild manners, Kazakov carried an icon of St. Nicholas with him when he flew, and whenever possible attended the funerals of enemy aviators he had shot down. At the beginning of the war, he was a cavalry officer; he switched to the aviation service toward the end of 1914.

On 18 March 1915, he was flying a Morane-Saulnier scout in an army cooperation squadron when the report came in of an Albatros two-seater that was spotting for the German artillery. Kazakov went hunting for it in his Morane equipped with the anchor. The idea was to get close to an enemy machine, snag some fragile part of it with the hook, and tear it up. He found the Albatros and closed with it, but whether the technique worked is not known for he also rammed the machine in the process. The Albatros fell out of control and was destroyed; Kazakov managed to crash-land safely.

Rifles and pistols aside, the first weapon regularly taken up was the Hotchkiss machine gun, a clip-fed piece barely larger than a rifle. It was the weapon used by the French on the Moranes (see pages 40–41) and on the Voisin pushers (see page 92). Hotchkiss guns were mounted on the pushers at the initiative of Gabriel Voisin himself, working with the French officer *Capitaine* André Faure, the C.O. of V.B. 24. On 5 October 1914, two men of that squadron scored the first aerial victory of all time. On a bombing mission in the vicinity of Rheims, *Sergent* Joseph Frantz and *Caporal* Quénault shot down an Aviatik in flames after a short chase, Quénault standing up in his seat to do the shooting.

The Lewis gun, with or without its air-cooling jacket, was the standard observer's gun in the Allied air services. It was fed from a revolving drum whose capacity was increased from 47 to 97 rounds in 1916. It was mounted either on a ring in the rear cockpit of two-seaters or atop the upper wing for the pilots. In this position it was fixed to fire over the propeller.

A light model of the Parabellum, the standard infantry machine gun, was used by German observers. The Parabellum was a Maxim gun as was the so-called "Spandau" gun. These designs originated in the Prussian state arsenal at Spandau, Berlin, and while the name was universal among the Allies, the Germans never called any gun a Spandau. It was simply the LMG.08 or LMG.08/15—the aviation model of the 1908 Maxim gun or the 1915 revision of it.

In Britain, the Maxim gun was manufactured by the Vickers company and was known as a Vickers gun.

The American guns, Colt and Browning, were used during the war as was the Marlin, an improved version of the Colt.

A variety of other guns was used at one time or another during the war, such as the Italian Revelli or the Austrian Schwarzlose, but the most important from the point of view of numbers used were the Lewis, Vickers, Parabellum, and "Spandau."

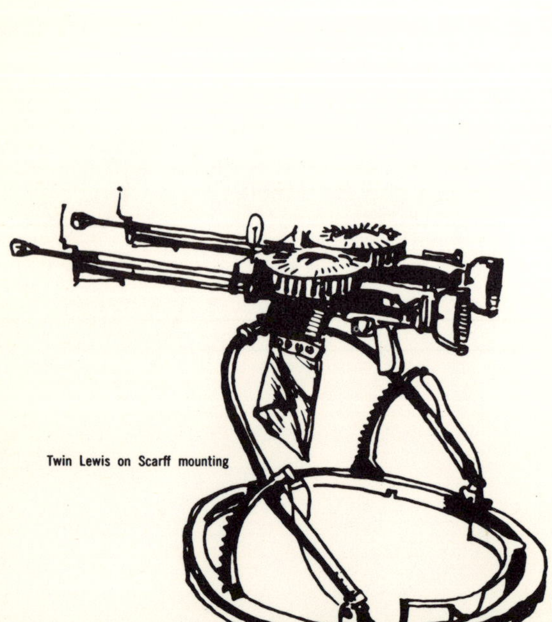
Twin Lewis on Scarff mounting

The Lewis drum was easy to handle and protected the cartridges from oil and dirt—on the ground. In the air, it was difficult to handle because it weighed several pounds and one had to fight the slipstream to keep the drum from being wrenched from one's grasp. Changing drums while fighting was something no one liked to think about.

The Lewis ejected its spent cartridges to the right from the rear of the receiver group. On a wing-top mounting this was satisfactory, but in pusher aeroplanes it was necessary to catch the cases in a canvas bag lest they foul the propeller. The other three weapons, Vickers, Parabellum and Spandau, all ejected spent cartridge cases to the left. They were fed by belts entering the right side. The belts at first were made of canvas, but as these belts caused jams through slip-stream deformation or wet weather swelling, they were replaced with flexible disintegrating link belts.

Various dampers were devised during the war, their function being to retard the escape of combustion gases and so speed up the action of the guns. The rate of fire of the standard guns could be increased from 500–600 rounds per minute to almost 1,000.

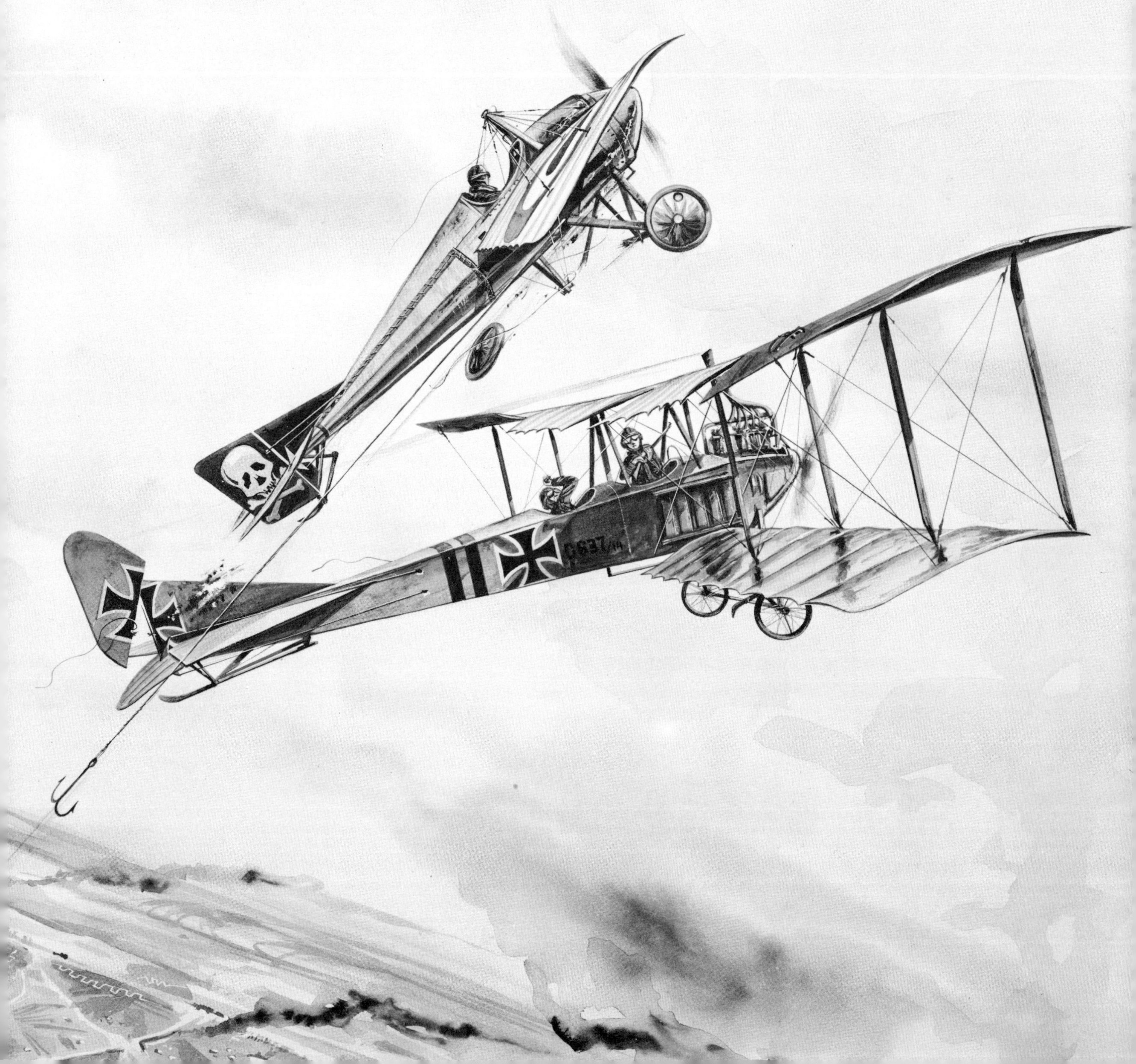

ROLAND GARROS was born in 1888 on the island of Réunion off Madagascar in the Indian Ocean. His father was a well-to-do lawyer and his parents were cultured people who wanted him to study music. Sent to Paris about 1909 to begin his studies, he met Alberto Santos-Dumont and became interested in flying instead. Santos-Dumont agreed to undertake to instruct him in flying and Garros proved an able student. He soon became an exhibition pilot, winning the Paris-Rome race in 1911, and on 23 September 1913, successfuly navigating the Mediterranean Sea for the first time in an eight-hour flight from St. Raphaël to Bizerte. On the outbreak of war he volunteered for the French air service and was assigned to M-S 23, attached to the Entrenched Camp of Paris.

In the same outfit was another pre-war pioneer named Eugène Gilbert, a native of Auvergne. In 1913 Gilbert had made two record-breaking 1,000-kilometre flights—Paris to Spain and Paris to Pomerania. In M–S 23 Garros and Gilbert worked together on various attempts to arm aeroplanes in order to be able to fight with them. Toward the end of 1914 Garros was given leave to report to the Morane-Saulnier aeroplane company at Villacoublay near Paris to take up the problem with Robert Morane.

It seemed natural to begin with the premise that straight ahead was the way to shoot when attacking another aeroplane. The problem was how to mount the machine gun so that it would be within the pilot's reach for reloading and clearing, for to so mount it and still have it fire straight ahead necessarily meant that it had to fire through the whirling blades of the propeller. The solution finally evolved was not the ideal one but it was the first one that was widely used, and Garros was the one who introduced it. It was elementary, even primitive—the propeller was armored. Steel wedges were bolted to the propeller blades in line with the muzzle of the machine gun so that any bullets striking them would be deflected and the

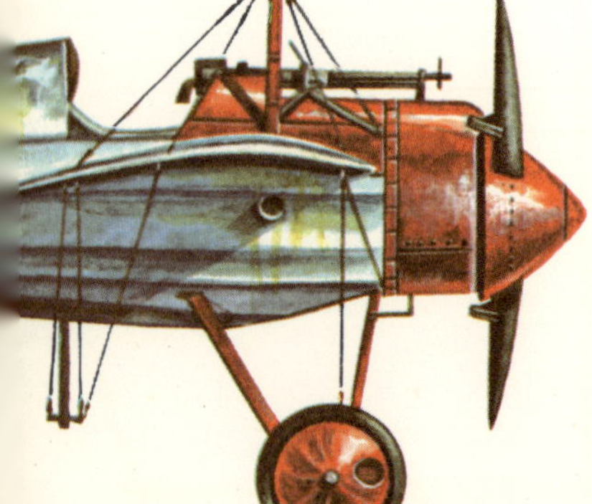

Morane-Saulnier N

blades would suffer only glancing blows. The gun was fixed firmly in position in front of the cockpit and was aimed by aiming the aeroplane. In April 1915 Garros used this device for the first time, shooting down an Aviatik in flames in the vicinity of Ostend. At the end of the same month he force-landed behind the enemy lines and the "deflector gear" thus fell into the hands of the Germans.

At Schwerin near the Baltic, 60 miles east of Hamburg, was a ramshackle group of buildings known as the Fokker Aeroplane Works. It was said of Anthony H.G. Fokker that he built beautiful aeroplanes in ugly buildings. At Schwerin his employees were turning out a line of single- or two-seater monoplanes used as scouts by the German army. Fokker was a Dutch national (he adopted German citizenship during the war) who had found his first commercial success in Germany before the war and had remained there, encouraged to hope for better things by modest government subsidies. When Garros' Morane-Saulnier scout was examined by the Germans, they saw that the deflector gear was no secret weapon to be feared, in fact it was so simple that it could be duplicated in quantity overnight. When they tried the gear with steel-jacketed German ammunition, however, the propeller blades were shattered, so selecting the German aeroplane that came closest to matching the Morane, Fokker's, they requested deflector gears just like the captured one. Instead, Fokker's staff designed a "synchronizing gear;" the propeller itself—through a simple mechanical linkage—fired the gun when the blades were clear. Fokker single-seater scouts equipped with the new gear and labelled E I (for *Eindecker*—monoplane) were issued in ones and twos to the two-seater squadrons to act as armed escort to the unarmed observation machines. The inevitable next step was to use the Fokkers to attack Allied observation machines. In the last half of 1915 it became almost impossible for the British and French to fly over the German lines. It was the period of the "Fokker scourge."

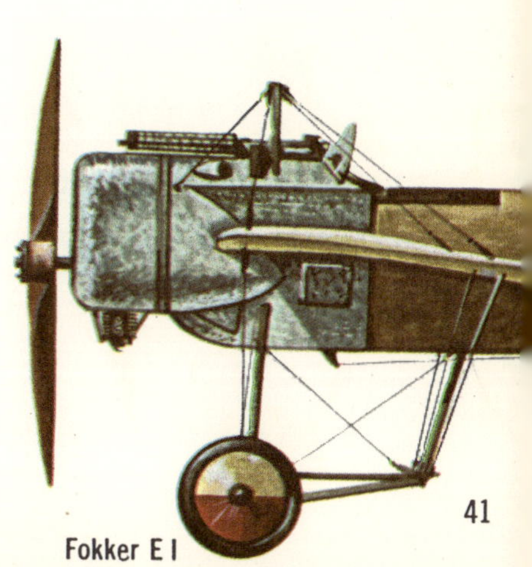

Fokker E I

THE STRATEGY AND TACTICS OF AIR WAR

was a relatively straightforward business in the 1914–1918 war. Strategy can be defined as the most effective maneuvering of units before a battle —outthinking the enemy; tactics, the most effective maneuvering of units once battle is joined—outfighting him. A strategic air concept would be the bombing of supply dumps so the enemy is short of ammunition before an attack. A tactical concept would be the securing of a height advantage over an enemy squadron so that the initial pass could be a fast diving attack, because a diving attack confers extra speed and allows the pilot to zoom or continue diving, in either case to get away or return to the attack with the advantage unimpaired.

In the 1914–1918 war, all flying had the same purpose—to support the armies, to lend a hand to the infantry. The ideas were there, but the air services were too small to have any significant effect on the outcome of the war or even the battles. It was not until World War II that air power succeeded in doing what the infantry had always done—take ground (the island of Pantelleria, 11 June 1943).

In the war that was once naively called the Great War, the two-seaters were by far the most important class of aeroplanes. Most air fighting was a direct result of efforts to protect or destroy them. Their jobs were contact patrol, observation, artillery-spotting, reconnaissance, and photography, plus a handful of odd-jobs including bombing, trench-strafing, and spy-dropping. Without the two-seaters there would have been no need for the fighters.

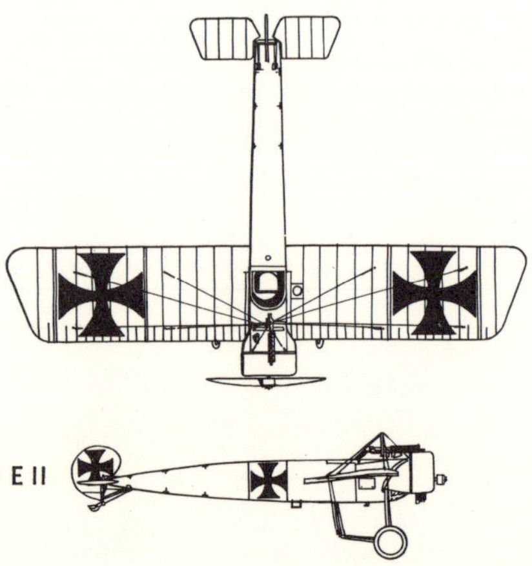

Fokker E II

Reconnaissance means spying out new developments behind the enemy lines, observation means

keeping a watch on them. Photography is a supplementary method of observation, and it is also a useful means of pinpointing targets for an attack. Contact patrol is a means of keeping a watch on your own troops. Aeroplanes on contact patrol fly back and forth between the front and headquarters and signal the progress, or lack of it, to headquarters so that the commanders have a realistic picture of the situation. (Artillery-spotting has been discussed on page 30.)

Air-ground co-operation worked both ways. Warning systems were developed by both sides early in the war. Troops in the forward lines reported all sightings of enemy aircraft; these were telephoned to appropriate squadron headquarters where the necessary action was taken—pilots on stand-by were sent up to intercept, for example.

The Germans, outnumbered three to four by the British and the French on the Western Front, were careful in their use of aeroplanes. A large part of their artillery-spotting was done by balloons and they did not formulate, as did the Allies, an offensive policy whereby all flying was to be done across the enemy lines. The Allies required that in addition to escort and defensive interception missions, the fighters should also fly offensive patrols, which meant literally to go out looking for fights. There is an element of waste in assigning men to general rather than specific duties, but both sides subscribed to the principle of non-specific patrols. They sent out flights or squadrons to find enemy machines and shoot them down. The difference was that the Allies did their hunting on the German side of the lines. The Germans simply waited for them.

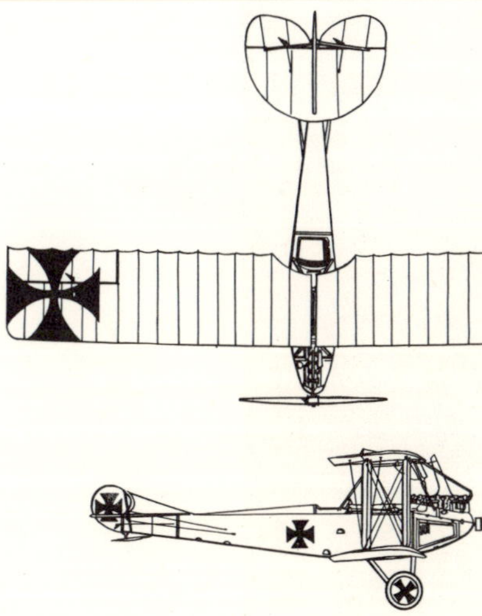
Aviatik C I

Pfalz E I

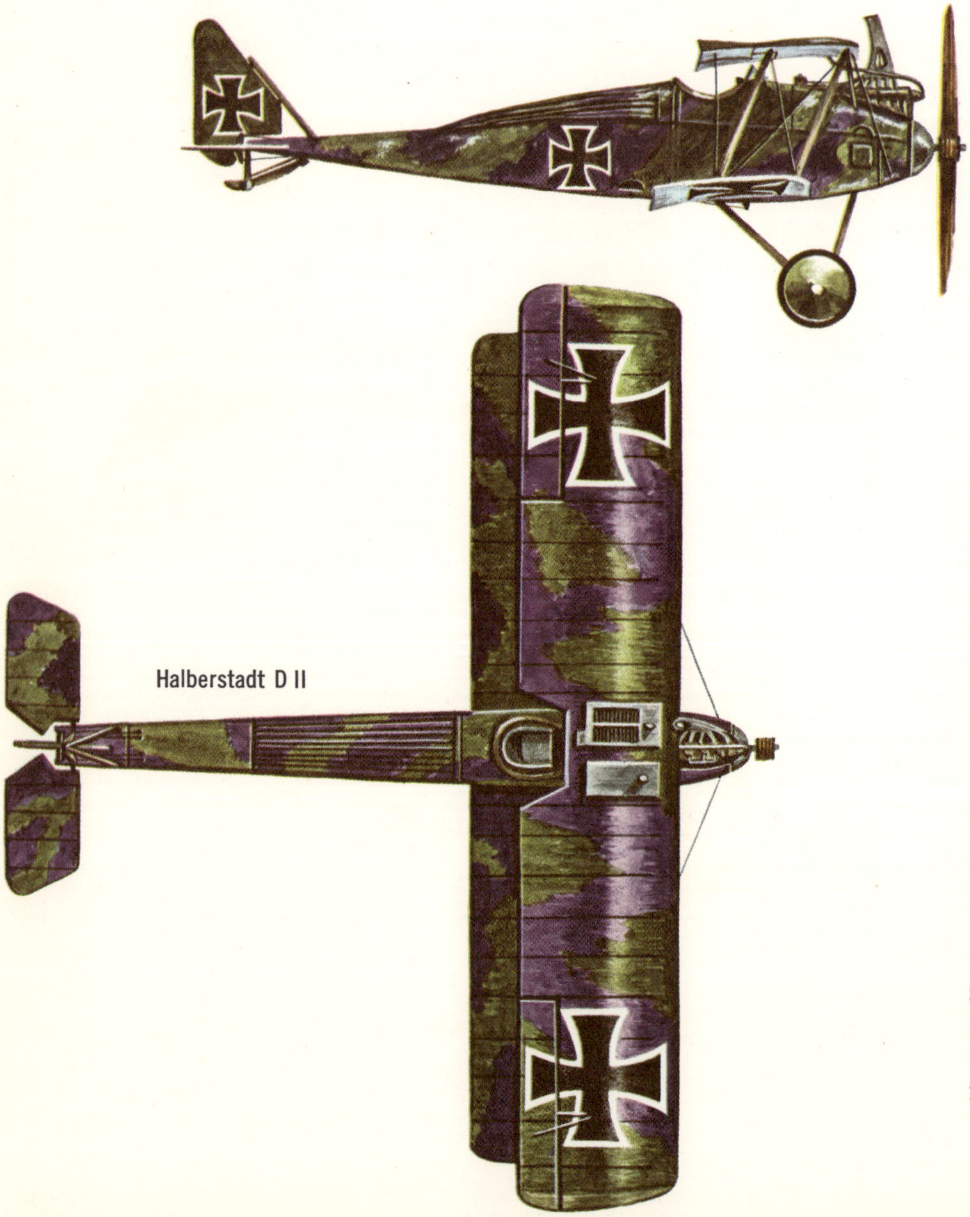

Halberstadt D II

When the Fokker *Eindeckers* proved a success as armed escorts for the two-seaters of the *Fliegerabteilungen*, several other types were pre-empted for the same role. The Pfalz *Eindecker* was one. Similar in appearance to the Fokker, the Pfalz was quite different structurally, being constructed of fabric and wood throughout as opposed to the welded steel tubing construction of the Fokker. It was powered with an 80 or 100 h.p. Oberursel rotary engine. The Pfalz monoplanes were usually classed as "Fokkers" by Allied airmen; Fokkers served on both the Eastern and Western Fronts throughout the summer of 1916 when they were outclassed by the new Allied Nieuports and D.H.2s. Another machine was the Halberstadt D II, a biplane single-seater developed from a conventional two-seater and powered with a 120 h.p. Mercedes engine. Built by the Halberstädter Flugzeug-Werke which was originally a branch of the British and Colonial Aeroplane Company of Bristol, the D II was very maneuverable and strong enough to sustain long steep dives. Both the Pfalz and the Halberstadt were equipped with the Fokker interrupter gear and a single Spandau machine gun.

By the end of 1915 there were over 100 German single-seaters on the Western Front. Their activities were co-ordinated by the establishment of several *Kampfeinsitzer-Kommandos* or K.E.K. — Combat Single-seat Commands. The K.E.K. grew out of the temporary groupings arranged on their own initiative by a few air service officers, groupings which permitted single-seaters to operate on their own from time to time instead of being tied to two-seaters. Such famous aces as Boelcke, Immelmann, Buddeke and Berthold started their combat careers with the various K.E.K. and it was from such units that the first German fighter squadrons were formed.

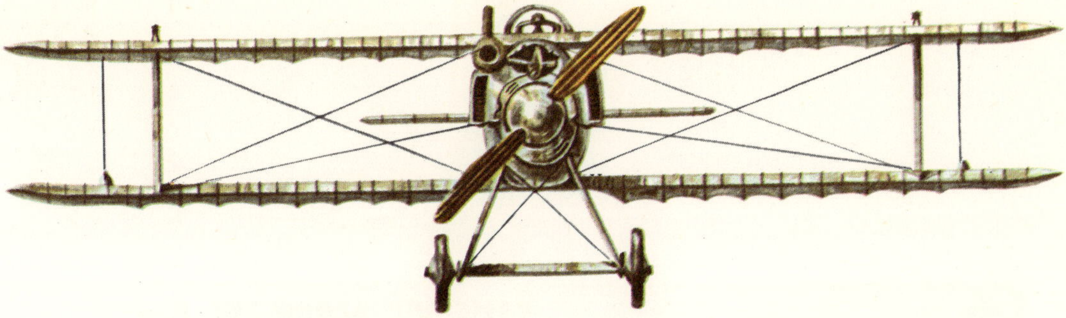

L.F.G. Roland C II

TYPE	SPAN ft. in.	LENGTH ft. in.	WEIGHT (gross)	SPEED m.p.h.	ENGINE h.p.
Pfalz E I	36 8	22 6	1250	90 to 105	80 Oberursel
Halberstadt D II	28 11	23 11	1606	90	120 Mercedes
Roland C II	33 8	25 2	2825	103	160 Mercedes

The Flying Whale, the L.F.G. *Wahlfisch,* was one of the revolutionary types of the war. Designed in 1915 and test-flown in the fall of that year, it reached the front early in 1916 and served throughout the year. Its chief function was reconnaissance, and as it was one of the first two-seaters to be armed with a forward-firing gun, it was common for "Whales" to fly escort for "Whales."

The L.F.G. company was formed in 1912 by a consortium of German industrialists and financiers. In 1915 a designer named Tantzen joined the firm and the *Wahlfisch* or C II was his creation. Tantzen's original thinking on the C II was motivated by the ideals of streamlining and good visibility, and for a 1915 design the C II succeeds remarkably well in attaining these advantages. Drag was much reduced by the clean fairing of the I-type interplane struts, the elimination of center section struts and bracing, and by the smoothness of the plywood covered fuselage. While the downward view was restricted, generous cut-outs at the wing roots remedied the situation somewhat. The droop snoot gave the pilot a good view forward and down and both pilot and observer had an uninterrupted view upward and to the sides.

The fuselage of the C II, an early example of semi-monocoque construction, was a type of shell, formed of thin strips of ply wound around a wooden skeleton. The several layers of this external skin was almost paper thin and wound with their grains in opposition, which gave great strength for surprisingly little weight.

The constructional methods used in the *Wahlfisch* were to have considerable influence on air warfare when utilized by the Albatros company in its series of fighters which appeared in the summer of 1916.

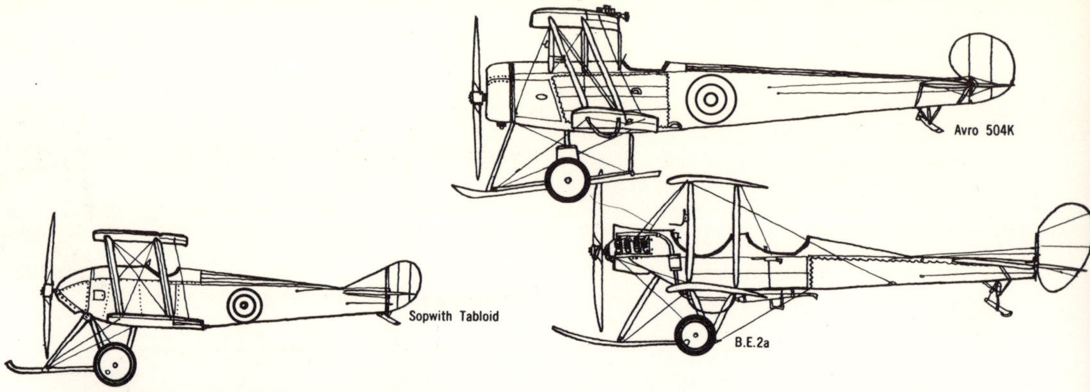

SAMSON'S AEROPLANE PARTY is the comic opera name by which the British remember the first Naval Air Unit, formed at Eastchurch in November 1911. On 27 August 1914, the unit went to Ostend under Squadron Commander (later Air Commodore) Charles Rumney Samson to furnish air co-operation for a brigade of Royal Marines. It was suggested before the fly-over that Samson's squadron should tie Union Jacks to the struts of the aeroplanes. This was not done and Samson was shot at by over-eager Marines. Not because he failed to fly the Union Jack: British ground troops probably would have fired at him even if the entire aeroplane had been painted red, white and blue.

The force remained at Ostend for a few days only, then was ordered to return to England. Because of a haze over the Channel, they landed at Dunkirk instead of flying home, and were subsequently ordered to remain there and operate against the Zeppelins. They didn't see any Zeppelins, but while they were there, they wrote a fantastic chapter in the history of the Royal Naval Air Service with their forays in armored cars. Using automobiles that had been armored by boiler plate at the Dunkirk shipyards, the pilots, armed with rifles and one Maxim gun, drove out to reconnoitre as far as Cassel and Bruges. On some occasions they were escorted by one of their number in an aeroplane who swooped low and fired Very lights to signal the presence of enemy troops. Once "Samson's Aeroplane Party" fought a pitched battle in the streets of Douai, holding off German troops who were occupying the town, providing a distraction which enabled 2,500 French troops to escape an encirclement.

On 12 September the aeroplane party was put out of action by a squall which smashed the aeroplanes, sending them cartwheeling across the beach where they had been staked down.

With new aeroplanes and a new name—No. 3 Naval Sqdn.—Samson took his flying-infantry-armored car-sailors to the Dardanelles to join the Gallipoli expedition in March 1915.

At about 10:00 a.m. on 19 February 1915, a squadron of British and French battleships opened fire on the Turkish forts guarding the straits and pounded them heavily through the day. Answering fire was weak and in the next two weeks the bombardment was resumed at intervals. Landing parties of Marines and sailors were put ashore to roam the tip of the Gallipoli peninsula. They were abruptly driven off by the rallying Turks at the end of the first week of March, and for six weeks thereafter the operation was stalled. The Allies were forced to concede that battleships could not rush the straits alone and "take" Constantinople. An amphibious expedition was organized under General Sir Ian Hamilton consisting of 75,000 men —30,000 Australians and New Zealanders in two divisions, the 29th British Division of 17,000 men, one French division of 16,000, and a Royal Naval Division of 10,000.

The landings took place on 25 April 1915. About 29,000 men got ashore on six different beaches. Losses to both sides were heavy. The Allied force lost perhaps 15,000 men. By the end of the first week of May, they had lost another 5,000.

On 19 May the Turks launched a violent offensive to drive the Anzacs into the sea. They lost 10,000 men by tea-time that afternoon. A truce to bury the dead was arranged for 24 May. The burial parties of both sides fraternized in no-man's-land while the job was done. Then the slaughter resumed.

So it went through the summer and fall. When it was hot it was unbearably hot; when it was cold it was unbearably cold. Flies and dust made the men miserable in the summer; after a blizzard in November, sentries were found frozen to death at their posts, their weapons in their hands. And all the time there was the killing.

The only British airship at the beginning of the war to be armed—it carried a single Hotchkiss gun—was Naval Airship No. 3, the Astra-Torres, purchased from France in 1913. It flew anti-submarine patrols over the Channel from the outbreak of the war and was based for a time at Dunkirk with Samson's Aeroplane Party.

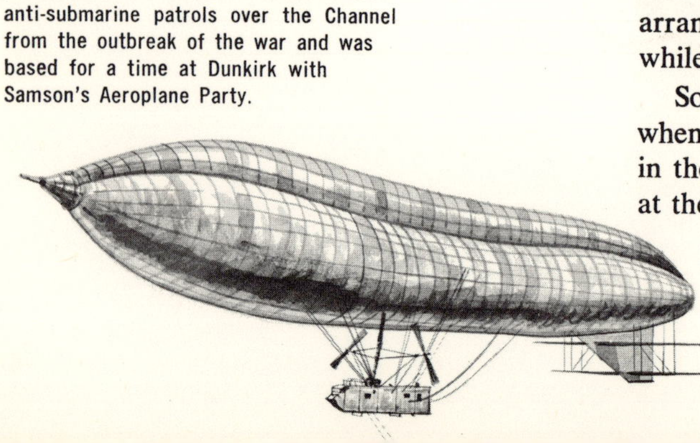

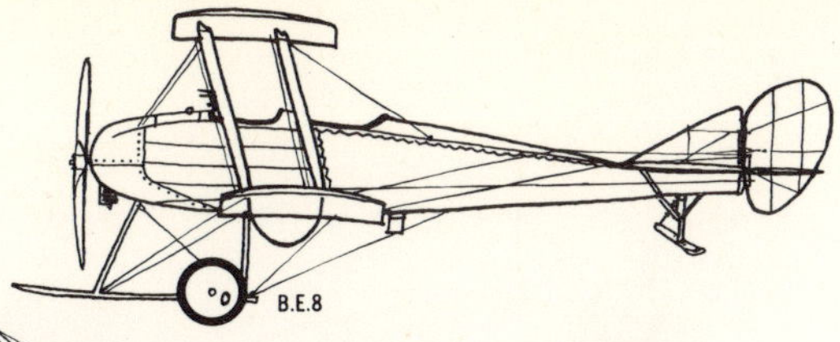

B.E.8

B.E.2c

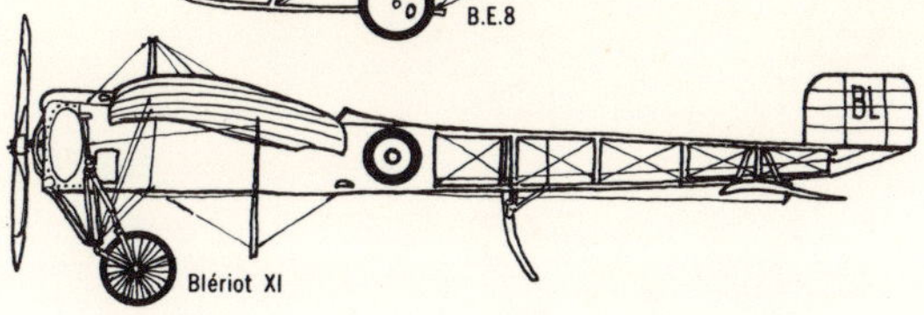

Blériot XI

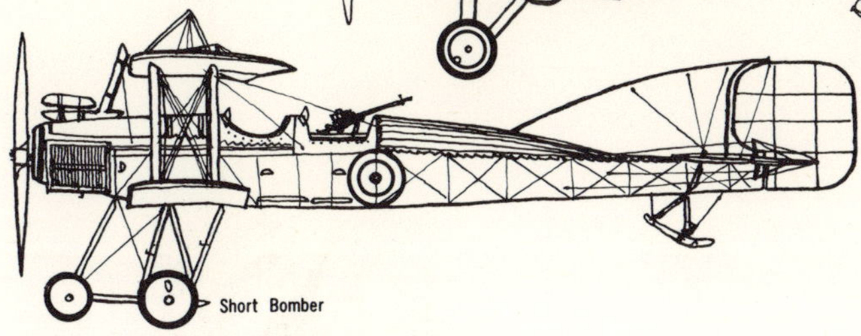

Short Bomber

The incredible folly of attacking dug-in machine guns with infantry charges across open country was practiced at Gallipoli as on the Western Front—only at Gallipoli, the open country was mostly rocky mountainsides.

When the Allies finally decided to abandon the expedition at the end of 1915, they had lost a quarter of a million men. The Turks had lost about the same. The Turks at least had the satisfaction of seeing the Allies withdraw and knowing that they had stood up to a major invasion and held fast.

Far from reaching Constantinople, the Allies had remained pinned to the toeholds on the beaches they had taken the first day. If the initial invasion force had been anything like the force that was eventually expended just to hold the beachheads, they probably would have been in Constantinople in two weeks as planned; the Russians could have been kept supplied through the shipping route Mediterranean—Sea of Marmora—Black Sea (the objective of the whole campaign); the collapse of the Russian armies in the field might not have occured; and the Russian Revolution that followed the collapse might not have taken place.

No. 3 Wing under Samson did valuable work during the campaign—chiefly artillery-spotting for the fleet's guns and photography. Mosaic photographs, pieced together from many overlapping photographs, were made to show virtually the entire peninsula, as the Western Front was eventually photographed in its entirety. Samson himself did a great deal of flying, and on one occasion spotted and strafed an enemy staff car in which Mustapha Kemal was riding. The future first President of the Turkish Republic barely escaped with his life.

The first successful torpedo attack was made at Gallipoli against a Turkish ship, and among the strange duties of the naval pilots at Gallipoli was a "distraction patrol"—flying low over the Turkish batteries along the Straits, they would distract the gunners while British submarines sneaked through into the Sea of Marmora.

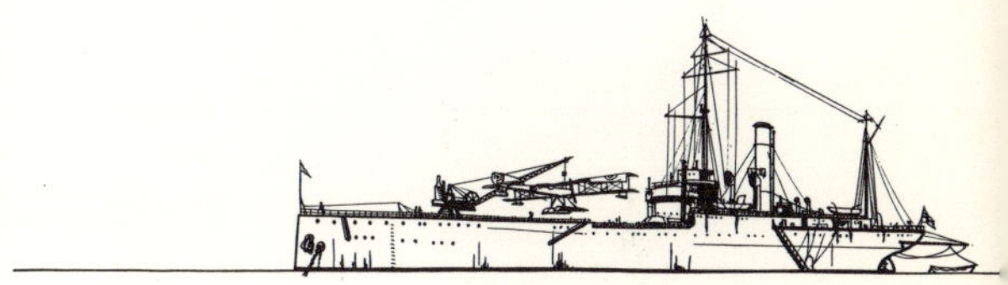

Samson and his squadron were established on the island of Tenedos early in April 1915 and the seaplane tender *Ark Royal* joined the fleet. The problems of maintenance were brutal. When the aeroplanes were uncrated, only five out of the 30 were serviceable. The airfield itself had been laid out where a vineyard once stood and had been rolled more or less flat by Greek workmen using empty oil drums filled with cement. In July Samson moved to a forward airstrip on Cape Helles where the Anzacs were fighting to hold their beachheads. Here he was under the Turkish guns and was forced to run the gauntlet of their shelling every time he took off or landed. After a time he abandoned the airstrip, leaving a dummy aeroplane behind to give the Turks something to shoot at.

Among the aeroplanes flown at Gallipoli was the Nieuport Type 10 or 12 two-seater. The first batches of these machines were purchased from the French for the R.N.A.S., but the type was later manufactured under license in Britain. They were flown as two-seaters on photography and artillery-spotting missions, and as single- or two-seaters for armed escort missions. On occasion, the single-seater version was flown as a bomber, the weight saved by leaving the observer home allowed 200 pounds of bombs to be carried.

Lieutenant Richard Bell Davies (later a Vice Admiral) was one of the original members of "Samson's Aeroplane Party." He had flown over to Ostend on 27 August 1914, taking part in the adventures there and at Dunkirk. On 19 November 1915, while on a bombing raid against Ferejik Station in southern Bulgaria, he displayed uncommon gallantry when he landed under fire and rescued the pilot of a Henri Farman which had been disabled by antiaircraft fire. He was awarded the Victoria Cross for his act.

The courage and devotion of the land, sea and air forces of both sides at Gallipoli were unsurpassed—only the blunders of high command were unworthy of them.

A567

THE EAGLE OF LILLE was the name given by the German public to a young Saxon aviator named Max Immelmann. The Allied two-seater crews in Flanders said he flew an aeroplane that could stay in the air for a week at a time. As there were only a handful of *Eindecker* pilots on the Western Front at the end of 1915, Immelmann was the whole "Fokker scourge" almost by himself. He had gone to the front as a two-seater pilot in *Fliegerabteilung 62,* formed at Döberitz, Berlin, in May 1915 under *Hauptmann* H. Kastner. In the same unit, also serving as a two-seater pilot, was a former member of the Prussian Cadet Corps, Oswald Boelcke, who had been in flying training when the war started and soloed 15 August 1914, just as the air services were suffering their first casualties.

In June 1915 Tony Fokker and *Leutnant* Otto Parschau arrived at the *Fl. Abt. 62* airfield at Douai to demonstrate the *Eindecker* and its new armament. *Hauptmann* Kastner was an experienced pilot and it was he who first flew the *Eindecker* for escort with flights from *Fl. Abt. 62*. Fokker instructed Boelcke on the machine and Boelcke instructed Immelmann. On 1 August 1915, Immelmann scored the first victory with an *Eindecker,* a British machine that had taken part in a bombing raid on the Douai airfield. He and Boelcke flew alternately the *Eindeckers* and the two-seaters until the formation of the K.E.K. Immelmann was put in command of the K.E.K. at Douai, Boelcke was transferred to Sivry, about twelve miles north of Verdun, to command the K.E.K. there.

By the summer of 1916 the Allies, shocked out of their complacency by the onslaught of a handful of Fokker pilots, had developed aeroplanes that were a match for the *Eindeckers,* no matter how great the skill of their pilots. After fifteen victories, Max Immelmann met a sudden end on 18 June 1916, just one year after he had been taught to fly an *Eindecker* by Oswald Boelcke. During a fight near Lens, his *Eindecker* was seen to attack an enemy two-seater, an F.E.2b of No. 25 Squadron, then dive out of the fight and break up in the air. The British credited his death to the F.E. crew—Second Lieutenant Waller, pilot, and Corporal McCubbin, gunner. The Germans announced after an investigation that the machine had collapsed as a result of previous damage by enemy antiaircraft fire. A third opinion, still current, was that Immelmann's synchronizing gear malfunctioned and he shot his propeller off, the vibrations set up by the shattered propeller tearing the aeroplane apart. It had happened before to both Immelmann and Boelcke, though without such consequences, for they had succeeded in landing safely each time. Whatever the cause of Immelmann's death, it was the culminating death in a depressing series that signaled the end of the Fokker's usefulness. Almost none of the *Eindecker* pilots lived to the end of 1916. It was a gloomy time for the German air service.

By the beginning of 1916 both Immelmann and Boelcke had scored eight confirmed victories, an unusual accomplishment for the time, and were awarded Germany's highest award for valor, the *Pour le Mérite* or "Blue Max."

During the summer of 1915 when the *Eindeckers* were first beginning to interfere with the Allied two-seaters, a number of future aces made their debuts. Boelcke and Immelmann, of course, were the leading *Jagdfliegern,* or fighter pilots, but there were others whose unusual careers merit mention. Hans Joachim Buddeke was a regular army officer who transferred to aviation when the war began and first served at the front as a two-seater pilot in *Fl. Abt. 23*. When an *Eindecker* was issued to the unit, he was one of those pilots selected to fly it. At the end of 1915 he was transferred to Turkey where he continued to fly an *Eindecker* and was called "The Shooting Hawk"—*El Schahin.*

Rudolph Berthold, the "Iron Knight," also began his flying career in *Fl. Abt. 23*. He flew an *Eindecker* from the beginning of 1916 and scored five victories to become an ace during the spring of that year. He was wounded several times, resumed flying before he was fit, and when his right arm became permanently disabled, flew anyway with special controls installed in his machine. He achieved a score of forty-four victories, and won the *Pour le Mérite*.

The *Eindecker* pilots were the first of the German aces, and their techniques laid the groundwork for the development of such famous fighter formations as the "Circuses." The pilots who followed them had the advantage of better aeroplanes, but the skill and daring of the first generation were never surpassed.

Max Immelmann, Der Adler von Lille

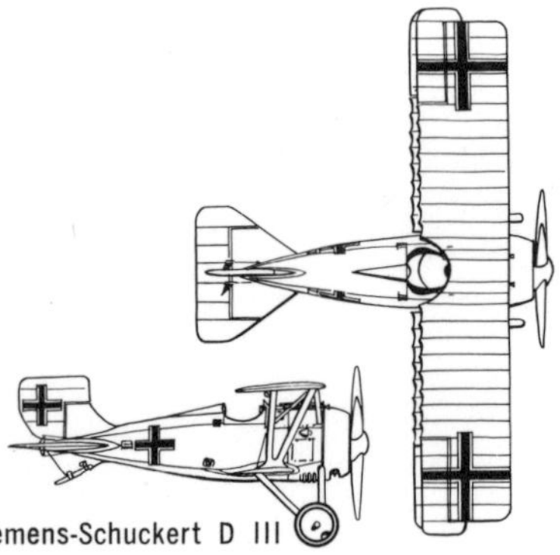
Siemens-Schuckert D III

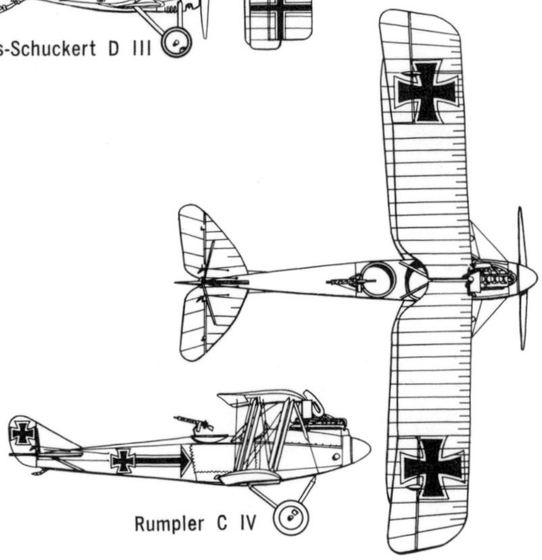
Rumpler C IV

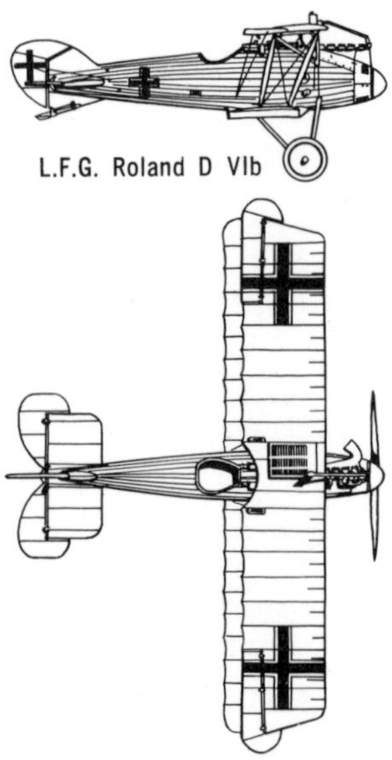
L.F.G. Roland D VIb

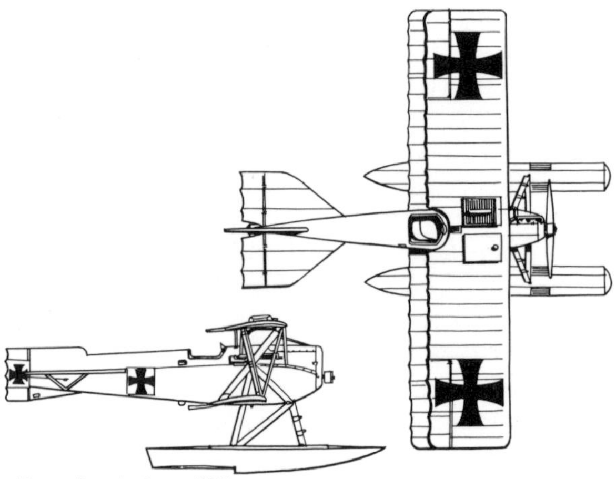
Hansa-Brandenburg KDW

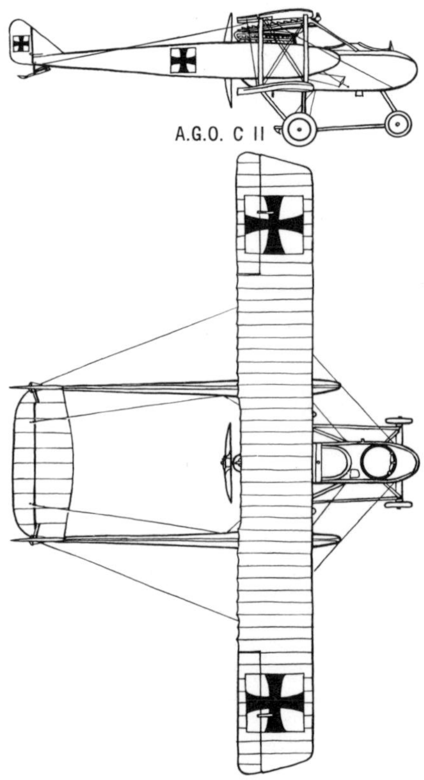
A.G.O. C II

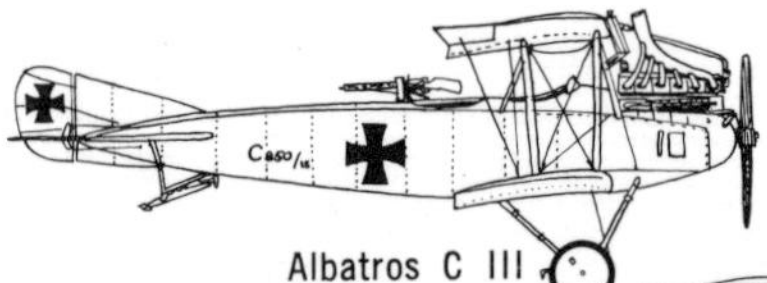
Albatros C III

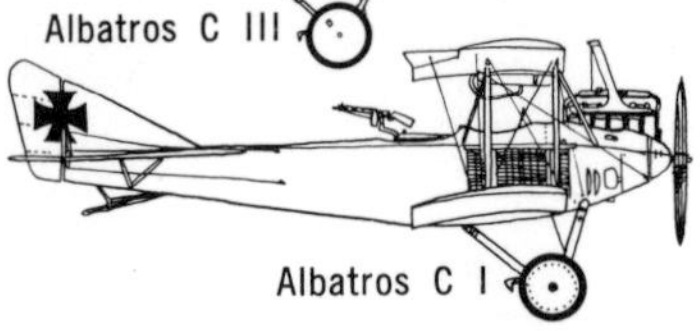
Albatros C I

Albatros C VII

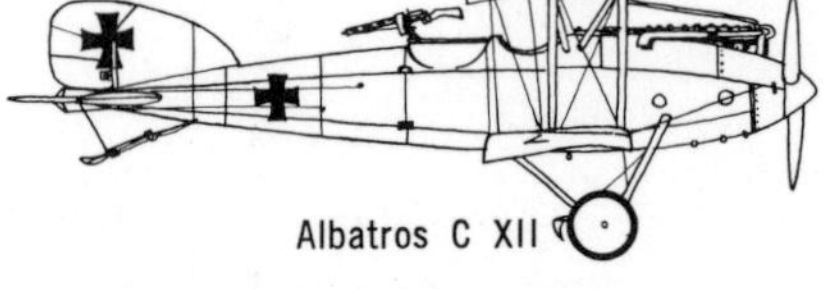
Albatros C XII

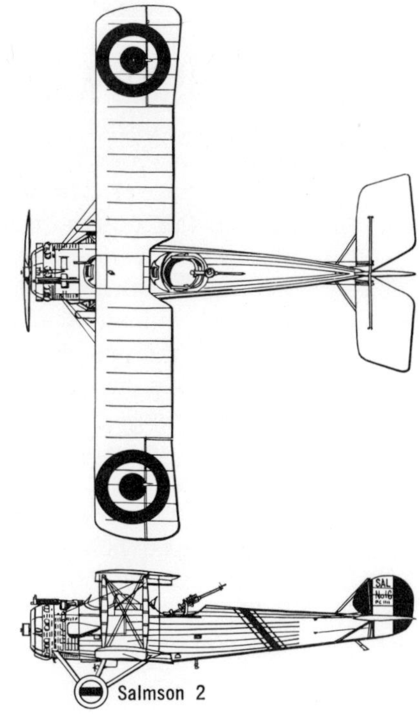

Salmson 2

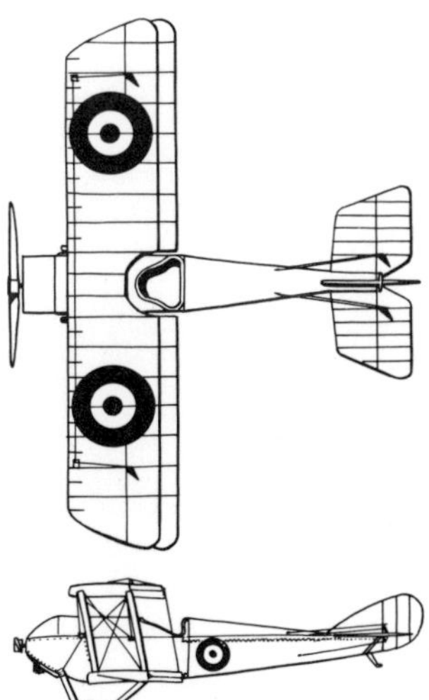

Martinsyde S.1

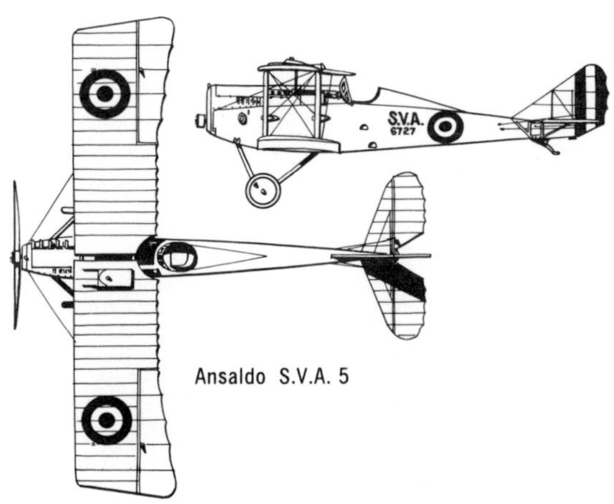

Ansaldo S.V.A. 5

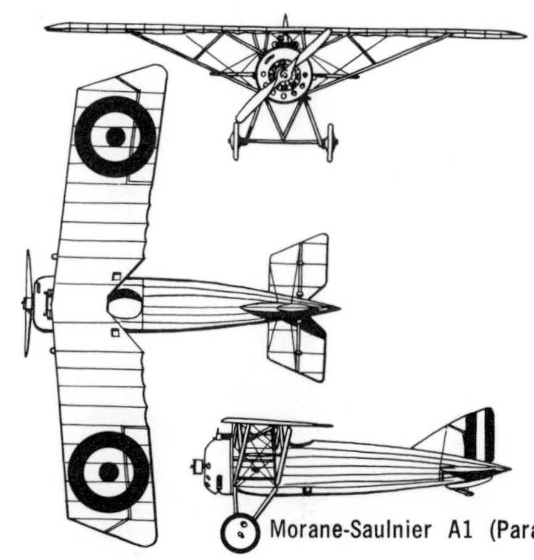

Morane-Saulnier A1 (Parasol)

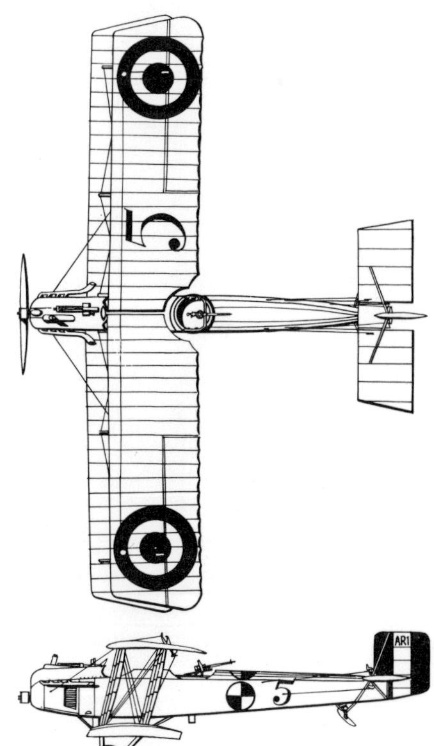

Dorand AR.1

THE PUSHER AEROPLANE, like the triplane, is a type characteristic of the 1914–1918 war. A number of both types were developed before and during the war, but were rarely seen after it. One reason the pusher was considered so important during the war—and virtually the only reason—is because it was possible to mount a gun on it to fire forward without having to resolve the problem of shooting through the propeller. Since the Germans had quickly standardized an interrupter gear for a forward-firing gun, they had no need of pusher types, but the Allies, slower to grasp the significance of this innovation, persevered doggedly with the pusher. It is regrettable but true that the Allies often lagged behind the supposedly unimaginative Prussians.

The pusher invariably suffered one drawback because of its configuration, and that was that it could never be aerodynamically clean. It was always slower than contemporary tractor aeroplanes. Further, with its center of gravity located somewhere in the middle of its length, it was less stable fore and aft than a tractor, and some pusher types were prone to easy and dangerous spins. In a crash there was the danger that the motor would crush the pilot who sat in front of it.

Some pushers were for a time successful. The F.E.2b and 2d, although based on a pre-war design, were able to hold their own against the *Eindecker*. The gunners of F.E.2 machines claimed Max Immelmann and wounded Manfred von Richthofen.

The D.H.2 defeated the *Eindeckers* on the British front, but in the spring of 1917 the new German Albatros fighters had no trouble dealing with the D.H.2 (opposite page).

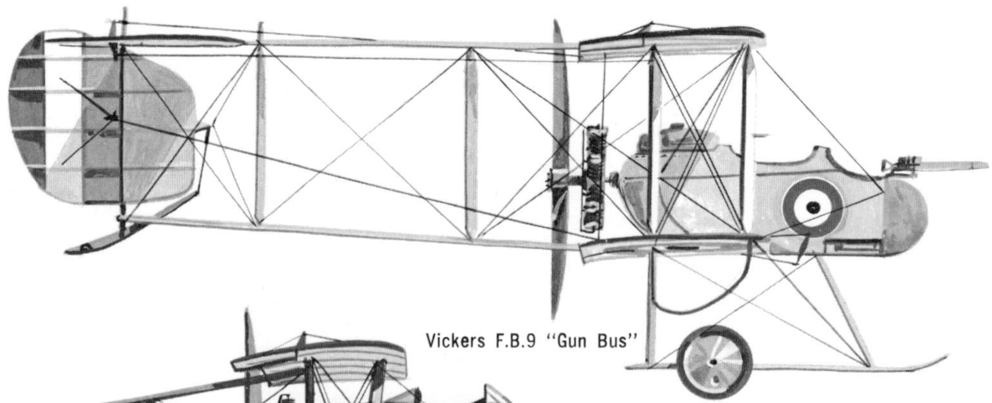

Vickers F.B.9 "Gun Bus"

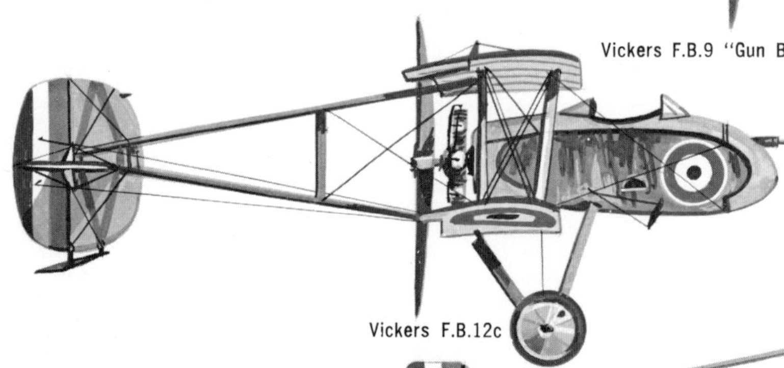

Vickers F.B.12c

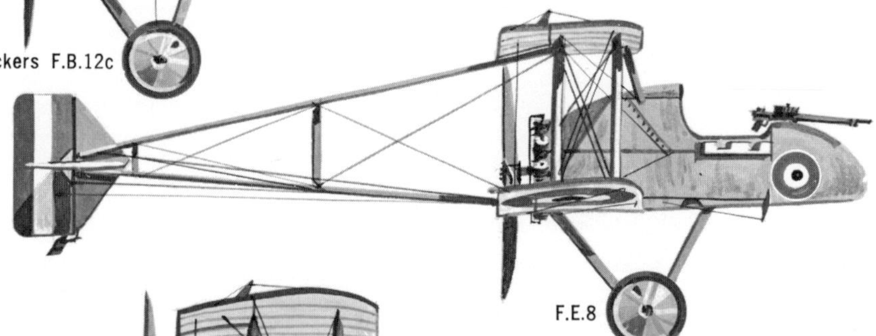

F.E.8

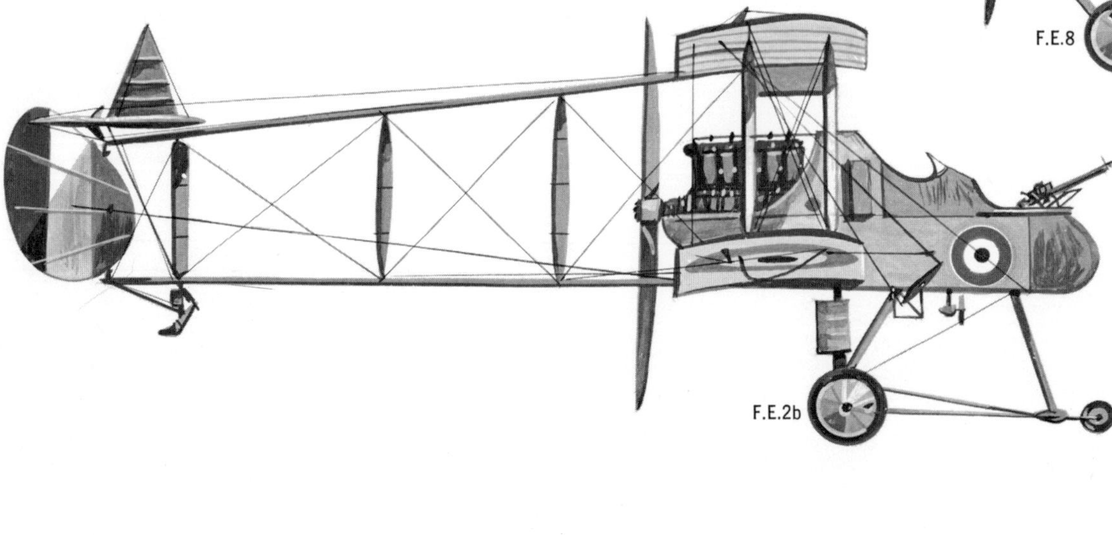

F.E.2b

5964

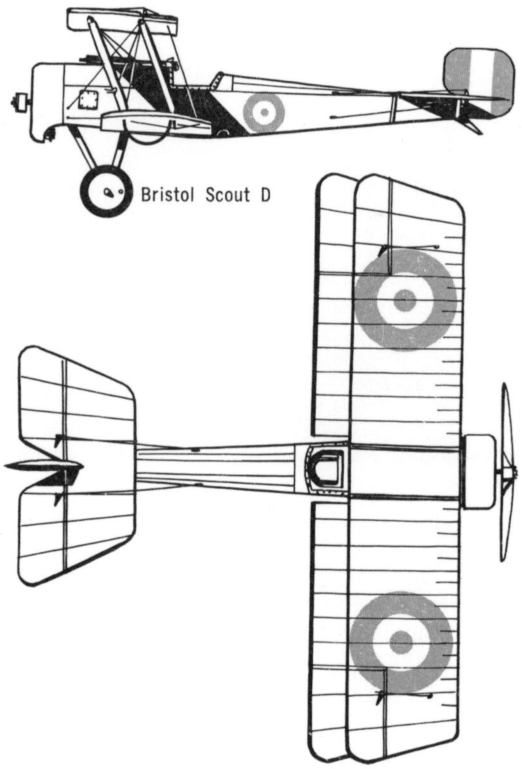

Bristol Scout D

ALBERT BALL was a native of Nottingham, the seat of Robin Hood country. He shared with the legendary archer one outstanding characteristic—he was an uncanny marksman. Ball joined the Sherwood Foresters on the outbreak of the war, but quickly requested a transfer to aviation after a visit to the R.F.C. station at Hendon where he saw flying for the first time. He was sent to France early in 1916 where he served as a B.E.2c pilot in No. 13 Squadron. In the spring of the year No. 13 was still flying an odd assortment of aeroplanes. It was not until well on in the year that it was uniformly equipped with one type—the B.E.2e. On the squadron strength in the spring was a trim biplane called the Bristol Scout. It was a single-seater type that had been developed before the war as a racer like the Sopwith Tabloid, and most of the R.F.C. squadrons had one or two or three for fast scout duties. At first the Scouts carried no armament unless the pilot took a pistol or revolver with him, later a rifle or a Lewis or Vickers gun was mounted on the side of the fuselage and fixed to fire diagonally forward to clear the propeller. Still later, some Scouts were armed with a Lewis gun mounted on the top wing and sighted to fire straight ahead over the propeller. It was with a Scout armed in the latter style that Ball first flew as a fighter pilot. His headlong impetuosity in trying to attack German aeroplanes while flying a slow B.E. two-seater led his C.O. to send him up on free-lance patrols in the Scout. If he managed to shoot down any Germans, excellent. If not, at least he would not get himself and an observer both killed. Ball shot down several enemy aircraft that were not officially credited to him by the time of the opening of the battle of the Somme. His method was always the same—to plunge straight into enemy formations. There was no jockeying for position with Ball. In a sense, he was the worst air combat tactician of the war. No one with any sense would rush alone at the enemy with the thought that once in the middle of a gaggle of enemy ships he would be safe from their fire and be able to shoot them all down at point blank range. Such were his nerve and marksmanship that it worked.

He flew successively a Bristol Scout, a Nieuport 17 and an S.E.5, and of them all his favorite machine was the Nieuport in which he brought to a high point of development the attack he had originated in the Scout. He would dive under the tail of an enemy ship and tear off a burst with the top wing Lewis pulled back. It required split-second timing and deadly accurate aim, both of which Ball had.

He was one of the early high-scoring aces—when he disappeared in May 1917, his score was forty-four. Only Boelcke and Guynemer had achieved such scores at that time. Ball was twenty-one when he disappeared, and the manner of his death has never been discovered. During a fight in the evening of 7 May 1917, he was seen to dive into a cloud. He never came out.

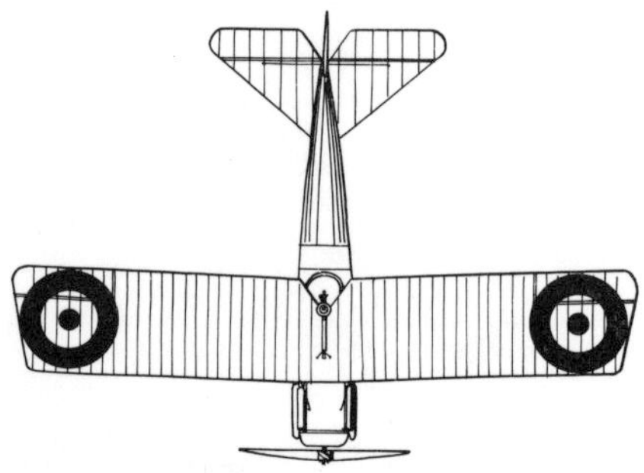

Early in 1916 while Ball was still a two-seater pilot, he presented his C.O. with some ideas for an aeroplane that would be "heaps better than the Hun Fokker." Apparently nothing survives of whatever sketches he may have made, and the project was not pursued. Late in the same year, however, when he had become a competent and experienced fighter pilot he visited the Austin Motor Company, Ltd., of Birmingham, and consulted extensively with the technical and design staffs who were building a new fighter around the geared 200 h.p. Hispano Suiza engine. The A.F.B.1, the result of the collaboration, bore at least one unmistakeable sign of the influence of Ball—the top-wing Lewis gun. The A.F.B.1 was a clean design, capable of a top speed of 138 m.p.h. and a climb to 15,000 feet in sixteen minutes. It was not ready for testing until the summer of 1917, several months after Ball had been reported missing. By that time, production of the S.E.5 was in full swing, and as available supplies of the Hispano Suiza engine were thus pre-empted, the A.F.B.1 was abandoned.

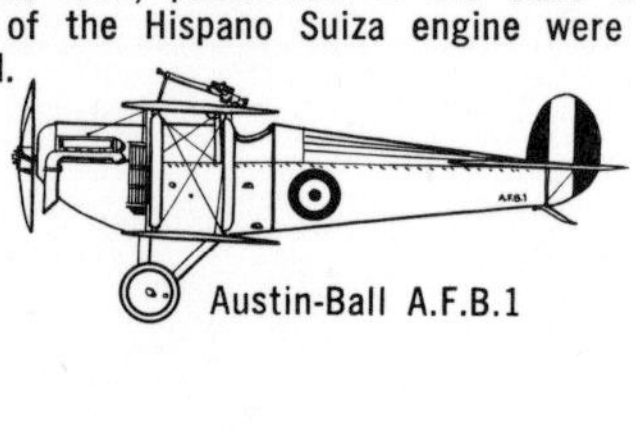

Austin-Ball A.F.B.1

Albatros D I 391 /₁₆ *(Leutnant Büttner, Jasta Boelcke)*

THE ALBATROS COMPANY of Johannisthal, Berlin, was well established before the war as the manufacturer of a sturdy line of two-seaters. Located on the Johannisthal aerodrome, the company also sponsored a flying school which was rapidly expanded after the outbreak of the war. Thousands of pilots went through the Albatros school and flew Albatros aeroplanes at the front.

The Albatros two-seaters were the backbone of the German air service and the B II was the backbone of the company. The B II was a pre-war design that was manufactured and used as an *ab initio* trainer right up to the end of the war. The B II was strong, easy to fly and dependable, its plywood body being famous for its ability to absorb the shocks of rough handling by students.

From its beginnings the Albatros company used plywood in a variety of techniques, and these were to some extent passed on to other aero constructors who built Albatros machines under license. At one point the flow reversed course, for the Albatros fighters of 1916 were much influenced by the revolutionary L.F.G. Roland C II.

Before the *Eindeckers* began to be submerged by the new Allied fighters, the Albatros design team, led by two men named Thelen and Schubert, began work on a true modern fighter—the D I. With its plywood body, powerful engine (150 h.p. Benz or

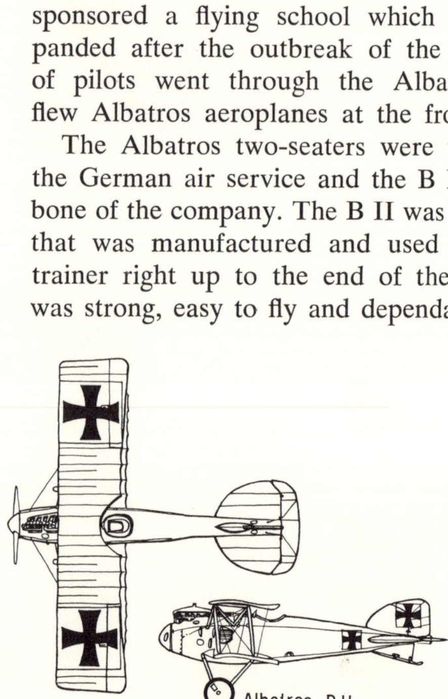

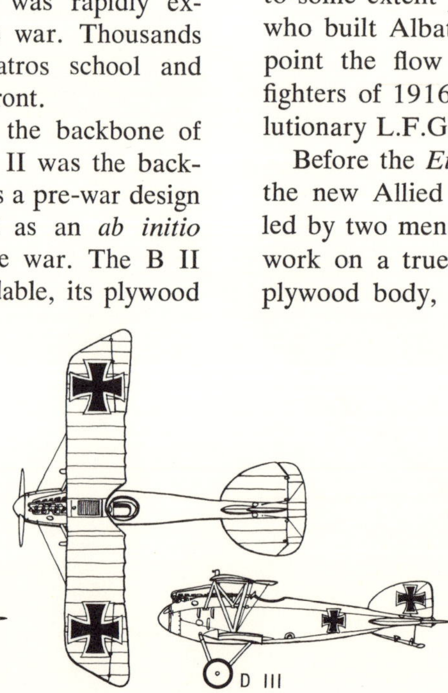

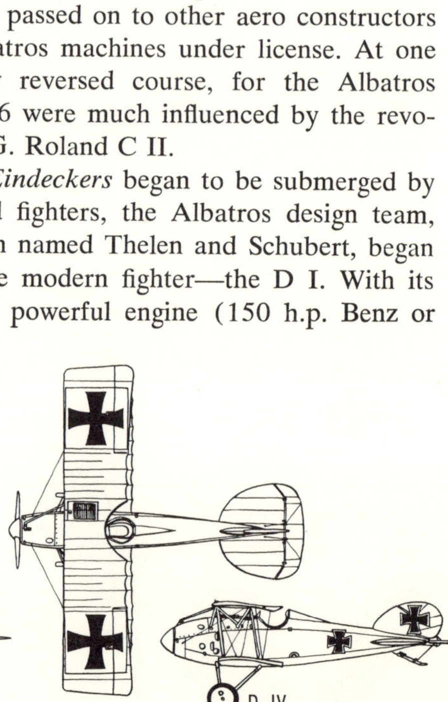

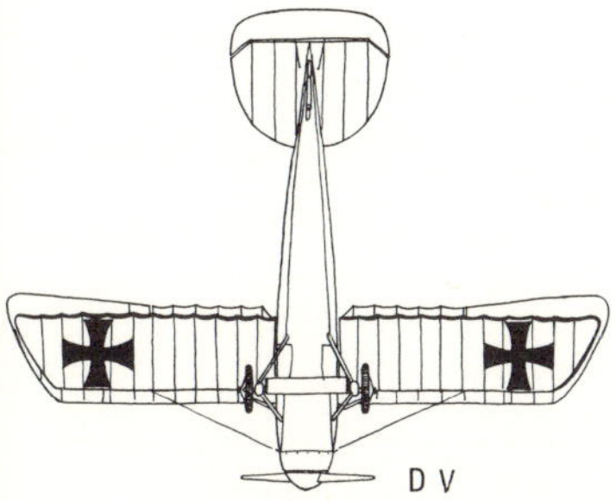
D V

160 h.p. Mercedes) and two guns—it was the first twin-gun fighter—it was just the machine with which to replace the existing single-seaters.

The fuselages of all the Albatros fighters were covered by pre-formed slabs of plywood screwed to a skeleton of plywood "O" formers and light wooden stringers.

The first of the line, the D I, began its operational career in September 1916, the D II following quickly. Over 200 D II's were operating on the Western Front in January 1917. The D I and D II, because of their roughly equal wings, were called "German Spads," a name that was commonly misunderstood because it was also applied, incorrectly to the D III, which bore no resemblance to the Spads. The D III was the first of the "V-Strutters." In the fall of 1917 there were between 300 and 400 regularly in service on the Western Front. Over 1,100 of the D V and D Va types were in service in May 1918.

The D III and D V were plagued with one serious problem—that of structural failure in the bottom wing. Because of the placing of the spar, the narrow bottom wing sometimes vibrated severely under stress, as for example in a prolonged dive, and on occasion collapsed. A temporary solution was effected in the D III and D V by the fitting of a short auxiliary strut to the leading edge, but in the D Va the problem was resolved by redesign.

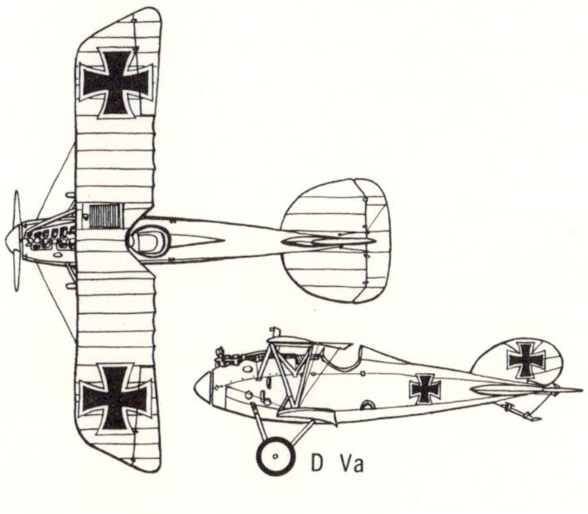
D Va

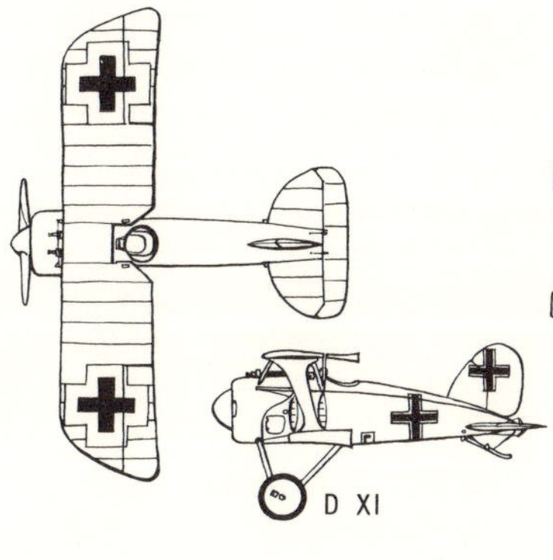
D XI

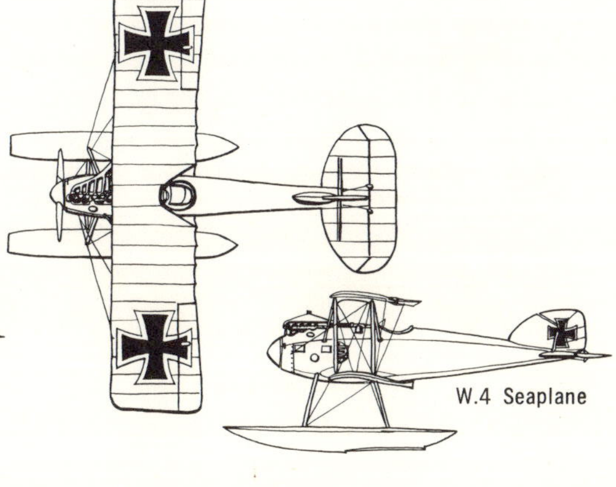
W.4 Seaplane

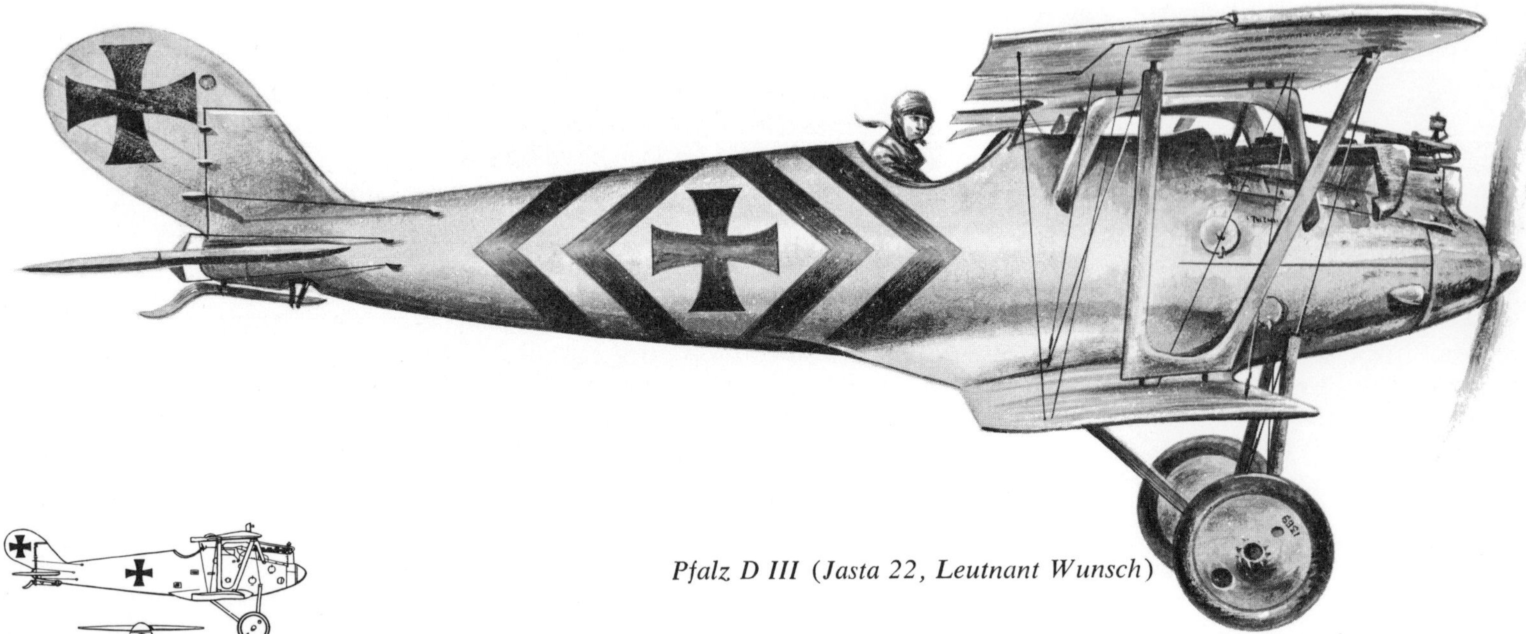

Pfalz D III (Jasta 22, Leutnant Wunsch)

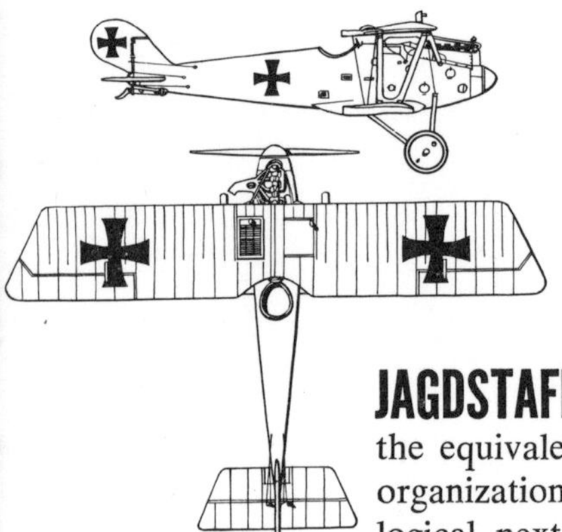

JAGDSTAFFEL, literally "hunting echelon," was the equivalent of "fighter squadron," and in the reorganization of the German air service was the logical next step after the *Kampfeinsitzerkommandos*. The decision to reorganize had not come with overnight revelation, but rather had grown slowly along with the necessary expansion of the air service. The innovations in the field, such as the K.E.K., had been worked out by a few imaginative officers who were ready to assume responsibility for their actions and to defend them with the evidences of positive results. High-level support was forthcoming from no less a personnage than Quarter-Master General Ludendorff, Field Marshal von Hindenburg's right hand man, who was firmly in favor of the air service's being recognized as a separate but integrated service like the infantry, the artillery, the cavalry and the engineers. The Kaiser gave his approval and the new service was placed under the command of a cavalry general named Ernst von Hoeppner. Oswald Boelcke, a good organizer as well as a good pilot and a good shot, met in a series of conferences with the *Feldflugchef* (Field Flying Chief), or Chief of Staff, Major Hermann von der Lieth-Thomsen, to air his practical views on organization and function. The *Jagdstaffeln* were the outcome of these conferences. The basic establishment of a *Jagdstaffel* (usually shortened to *Jasta*) was fourteen aeroplanes, later increased to eighteen, but rarely in practice what it was supposed to be on paper. The *Jastas,* whatever their prescribed numerical strength, were more often than not smaller than Allied fighter squadrons. The British squadrons, for example, consisted of twelve aeroplanes in three flights of four until the spring of 1916, but from then on were enlarged to eighteen aeroplanes in three flights of six.

The German air service, having attained its independence, was baptised with an official name, *Luftstreitkräfte,* or Air Combat Force; General von Hoeppner was styled *Kommandierender General der Luftstreitkräfte,* a title that was shortened in everyday speech to *Kogenluft*. One of the common denominators of English and German is the proclivity to shorten long words or expressions. Antiaircraft artillery was called *flak* by the Germans (and in the 1939–1945 war was so called by both the Germans and the British). It comes from *Flieger Abwehr Kanone,* or aviation defense gun. An army chaplain was called a *Sak,* for *Sünde Abwehr Kanone,* or anti-sin gun.

Staffel, meaning literally "echelon," was the standard combining form for several aviation unit names. Two-seaters such as the L.F.G. Roland *Wahlfisch* were assigned to protection squadrons called *Schutzstaffeln,* or *Schustas.* Two-seaters assigned to ground attack duties formed battle squadrons called *Schlactstaffeln,* or *Schlastas.*

The reorganization was to become effective in October 1916, and the machinery was being put in motion from the summer on. The initial strength of the fighter service was seven *Jastas,* the command of *Jasta 2* falling to Oswald Boelcke. Although his outfit was the second in numerical order, it was the first to be formed and the first in action, and considering the material contribution he had already made with his suggestions on tactics and organization, there was every justification for Boelcke's being given the unofficial title of Father of the German Fighter Service.

During the summer of 1916 Boelcke traveled to the various fronts on an inspection tour of the air service and at the same time recruited pilots for his own *Jasta.* Among the promising candidates was a young Silesian cavalryman, Baron Manfred von Richthofen, the son of a professional army officer.

Baron, or *Freiherr,* von Richthofen was a lieutenant in the First Regiment of Uhlans when the war started. He transferred to aviation in May 1915 when it became apparent that the cavalry had no place in the war, and was posted to *Fl. Abt. 69* on the Russian Front in June to serve first as an observer. In August he was sent to the Western Front where he flew as observer, gunner, and bombardier after which, in November, he was posted to Döberitz, Berlin, to train as a pilot. He soloed on Christmas Day 1915.

When Boelcke's "cubs" began to assemble at the *Jasta 2* field at Douai in northern France at the end of August and the beginning of September 1916, the British on that part of the front had defeated the *Eindeckers* with their famous pushers, the D.H.2 and the F.E.2b. Boelcke lectured his men and demonstrated his techniques for them, taking them up for intensive drilling in formation flying and team tactics. He was determined they would be ready when the test of actual operations came, for the goal of the *Jastas,* and indeed of the entire reorganization, was nothing less than the winning of aerial supremacy.

Manfred von Richthofen was Boelcke's finest pupil. It is worth noting that his first victory, on 17 September 1916, was an F.E.2b, the same type of aeroplane as the one Max Immelmann had died attacking.

With the introduction of the Albatros fighters in Boelcke's *Jasta 2,* the Royal Flying Corps was plunged into a second and more severe trial than that of the earlier "Fokker scourge." The slow two-seaters such as the B.E.2c machines of the Royal Aircraft Factory were easily shot down by the Albatros pilots. A desperate attempt to put more fighters at the front was made by the British when they introduced the B.E.12, a single-seat version of the B.E.2c. The chief difference between the B.E.2c and the B.E.12 was that the B.E.12 was twice as easy to shoot down. Of his first ten victories, von Richthofen downed five B.E.12's.

On 23 November 1916, von Richthofen had his first fight that tested his ability against that of another fighter pilot when he duelled successfully Major L.G. Hawker, V.C., the commanding officer of No. 24 Squadron. Hawker's D.H.2 had superior maneuvrability, but von Richthofen's Albatros had superior speed and firepower. After a long tailchase during which the two aeroplanes drifted over the German lines and dropped from 8,000 feet down to 3,000, Hawker made a sudden break and dived for the British lines. Doggedly pursuing, von Richthofen finally shot Hawker down as he zig-zagged for the lines at tree-top height. At no time during the fight had von Richthofen tried any maneuvres other than simple chasing. He was not a born pilot, and never attempted to develop flashy stunt flying. He was conservative, even cautious, in his flying and was without romantic notions about the wind in the wires and the rest of it. He was a professional, unswerving in his devotion to duty. His duty, as he saw it, was to shoot down enemy aeroplanes and anything that was not directly connected with performing that duty was a waste of time.

'The Red Knight'

Oberleutnant Lothar Freiherr Von Richthofen

Leutnant Josef Mai

Leutnant Max Ritter Von Müller the second 'Eagle of Lille'

Eduard Ritter Von Schleich 'The Black Knight'

Rittmeister Manfred Freiherr Von Richthofen 1892-1918

AIR MARSHAL WILLIAM AVERY BISHOP

V.C., C.B., D.S.O. and Bar, M.C. and D.F.C., was the one who said it most unequivocally: "It was the mud, I think, that made me want to fly." He said it in his wartime autobiography, *Winged Warfare*. Bishop, a native of Owen Sound, Ontario, Canada, went to England with the Seventh Canadian Mounted Rifles in June 1915, and had enough of mud while stationed at Shorncliffe camp near Folkestone without even going to France. He applied for the R.F.C. and was accepted for training as an observer. He first went to France with No. 21 Squadron in the fall of 1915 and served as an observer until the beginning of May 1916. He was unlucky at all times except under fire. He was in auto crack-ups, aeroplane crack-ups and things fell on him. Once he nearly suffered a fractured skull when a steel cable hit him on the head as he stood in a hangar. He was unconscious for two days. Enemy bullets came close but never touched him. When he finally went to the hospital, it was to recover from the knocks of bad luck, not as a result of enemy action.

Through the intercession of an influential patroness, Bishop won a chance to train as a pilot. He came through with colors not exactly flying, but with himself and most of his aeroplanes in one piece. He was never a brilliant pilot, and at times he was barely adequate, but when it counted most, in closing with German fighters, he suddenly became magnificent. Perhaps he was not interested in flying for its own sake and did not really try to fly unless it was for the immediate purpose of shooting down an enemy machine.

He returned to France in March 1917 as a member of No. 60 Squadron and was soon promoted to the command of "C" Flight. He was known as a wheel-smasher in the unit because of his frequent bad landings, but by the end of the first week of May when he went on a two-week leave he had nineteen confirmed victories.

Albert Ball had hunted up Bishop just before he disappeared and suggested that from what he, Ball, had heard about him, Bishop was just the man he was looking for to join him on a private little adventure. He had the idea that a couple of single-seaters could slip over the lines at dawn and shoot up a German aerodrome and get away before the Germans knew what hit them. It was the kind of show that appealed to Bishop, so like Ball in temperament. Both were pilots of indifferent skill, moody and depressed after a victory, whose sole tactic was to rush straight in and blaze away at point blank range.

Bishop was shocked at the news of Ball's disappearance, and soon after returning to duty with No. 60 Squadron decided to go ahead alone with the show he and Ball were to have staged together. He took off before 4:00 a.m. on 2 June, a morning of cloud and rain, and headed toward Cambrai. The aerodrome he came across was the base of *Jasta 5* at Estourmel, south-east of Cambrai. He dived on the field in the first light of dawn and fired his first burst at a string of machines lined up before the tent hangars. Four Albatros pilots tried to take off to get at him. He shot one of them up as its wheels left the ground. He turned back over the field and fired at a second one. He missed, but the pilot crashed anyway. The other two Albatros took off in opposite directions, one of them flying away and one of them scrapping with Bishop for a moment before being shot down near the field. Bishop got away from the fourth machine and cleared out.

Ball had erred on the side of optimism when he calculated that the Germans would be so surprised at this kind of an attack that they would not be able to put up any resistance. Bishop had had his hands full for a few minutes. But that was when he flew best—when he was thinking about shooting, not flying.

B1566
2
3
4
F
A
E

MILITARY AEROBATICS

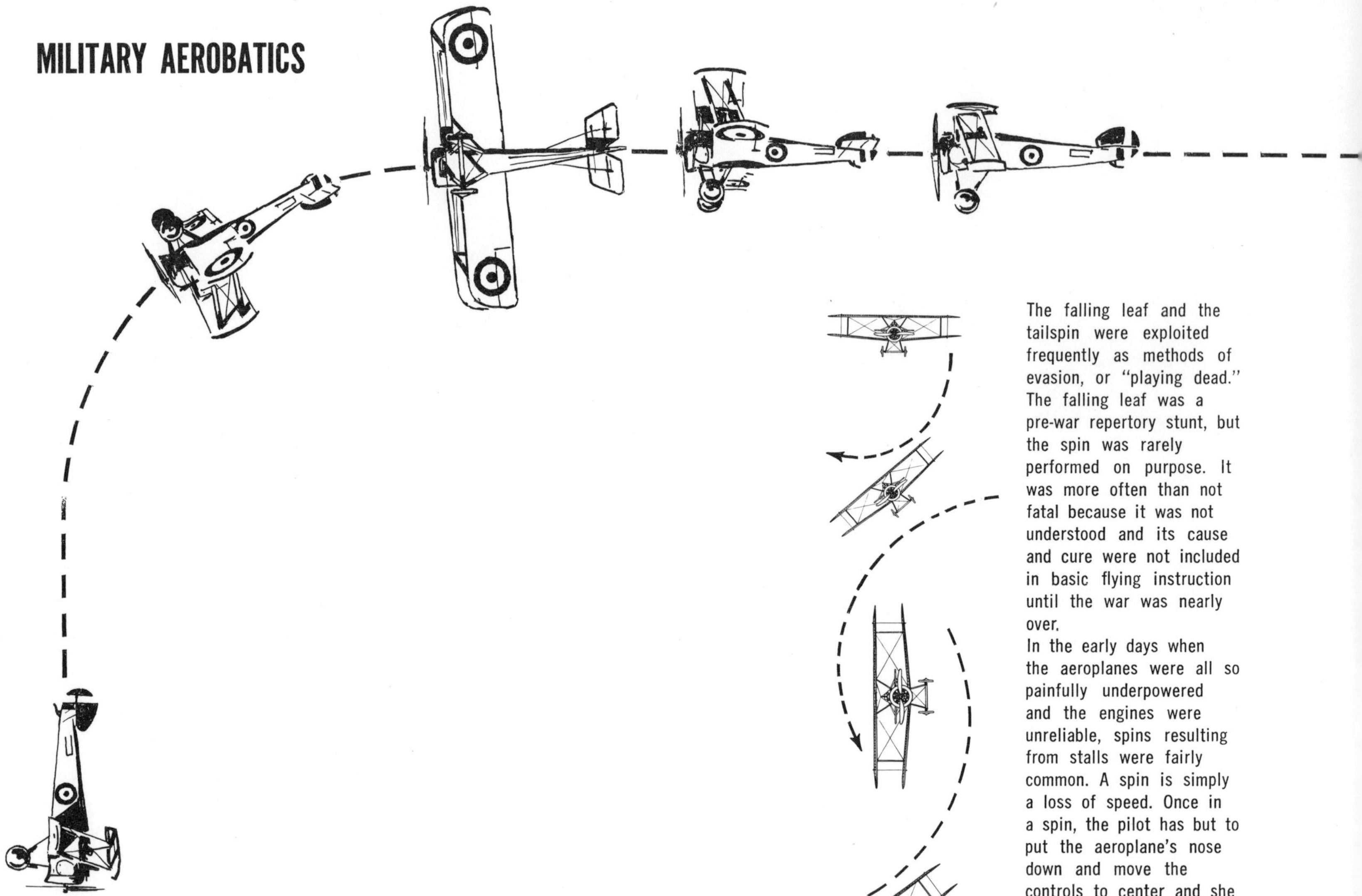

The split-S was a means of diving that was brisk and to the point. Along with the wingover, it is the preferred means of diving because, unlike the simple maneuver of abruptly dropping the nose, it does not subject either the pilot or the aeroplane to the "unnatural" stresses of negative g's. Pushing the nose down hard tends to throw the pilot out of his seat, but in a wingover or a split-S centrifugal force keeps him firmly in place. Moreover, in the case of a pilot wishing to dive toward a point below him, the wingover and the split-S allow him to keep that point in view as he enters the dive.

The wingover is a bank with the stick forward. The aeroplane curves smoothly around and down and ends up going down as steeply as you wish. The split-S is beautifully simple. The pilot rolls his machine on her back and pulls the stick into his stomach. It's rather like going through the last half of a loop. Depending on how well a machine can roll—and the Sopwith Camel, for example, could flip over like a tiddely-wink—the split-S is one fast way to get from up here to down there.

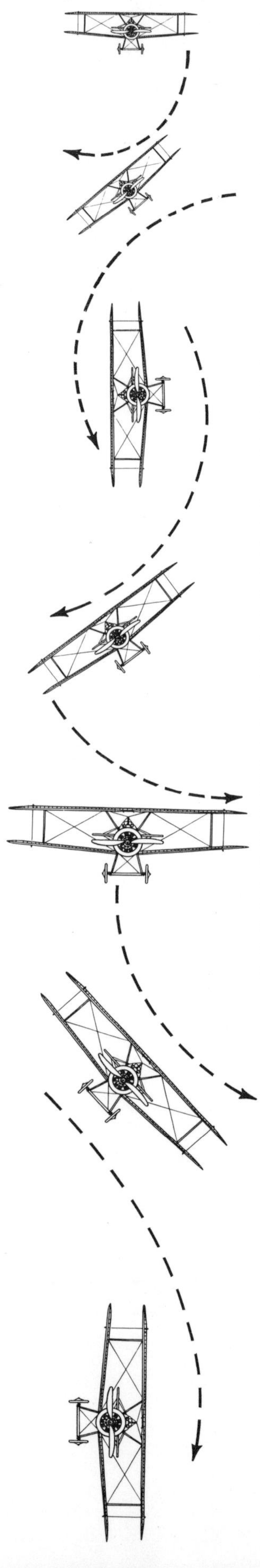

The falling leaf and the tailspin were exploited frequently as methods of evasion, or "playing dead." The falling leaf was a pre-war repertory stunt, but the spin was rarely performed on purpose. It was more often than not fatal because it was not understood and its cause and cure were not included in basic flying instruction until the war was nearly over.

In the early days when the aeroplanes were all so painfully underpowered and the engines were unreliable, spins resulting from stalls were fairly common. A spin is simply a loss of speed. Once in a spin, the pilot has but to put the aeroplane's nose down and move the controls to center and she will come out of it by herself as soon as she has regained flying speed. Most inexperienced pilots tried to bring the nose up but this only made the spin worse and they went right into the ground.

When systematic flying instruction and engineering progress made better pilots and stronger aeroplanes, such violent maneuvers as spins, falling leaves, and split-S's became a necessary part of every pilot's survival equipment.

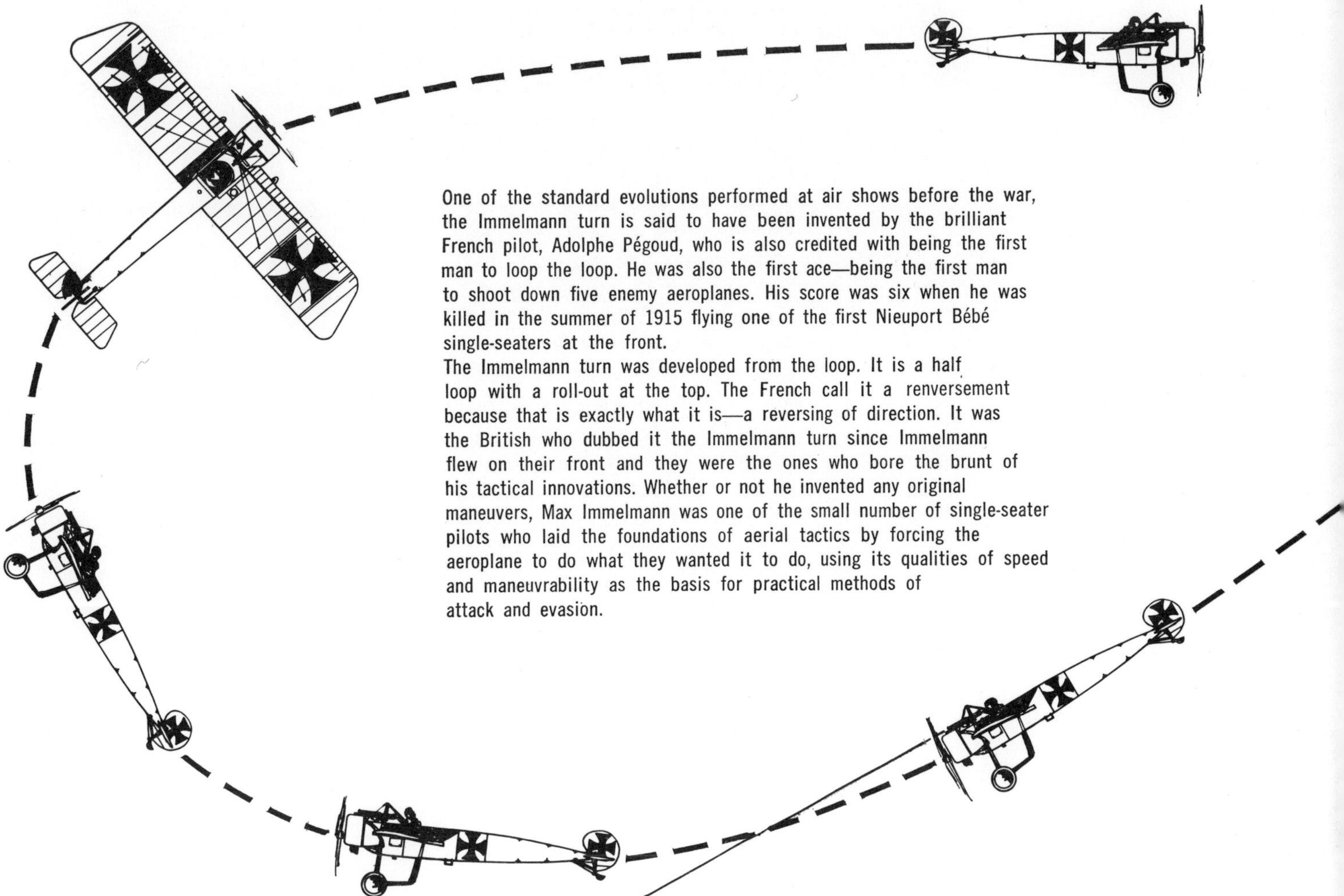

One of the standard evolutions performed at air shows before the war, the Immelmann turn is said to have been invented by the brilliant French pilot, Adolphe Pégoud, who is also credited with being the first man to loop the loop. He was also the first ace—being the first man to shoot down five enemy aeroplanes. His score was six when he was killed in the summer of 1915 flying one of the first Nieuport Bébé single-seaters at the front.

The Immelmann turn was developed from the loop. It is a half loop with a roll-out at the top. The French call it a renversement because that is exactly what it is—a reversing of direction. It was the British who dubbed it the Immelmann turn since Immelmann flew on their front and they were the ones who bore the brunt of his tactical innovations. Whether or not he invented any original maneuvers, Max Immelmann was one of the small number of single-seater pilots who laid the foundations of aerial tactics by forcing the aeroplane to do what they wanted it to do, using its qualities of speed and maneuvrability as the basis for practical methods of attack and evasion.

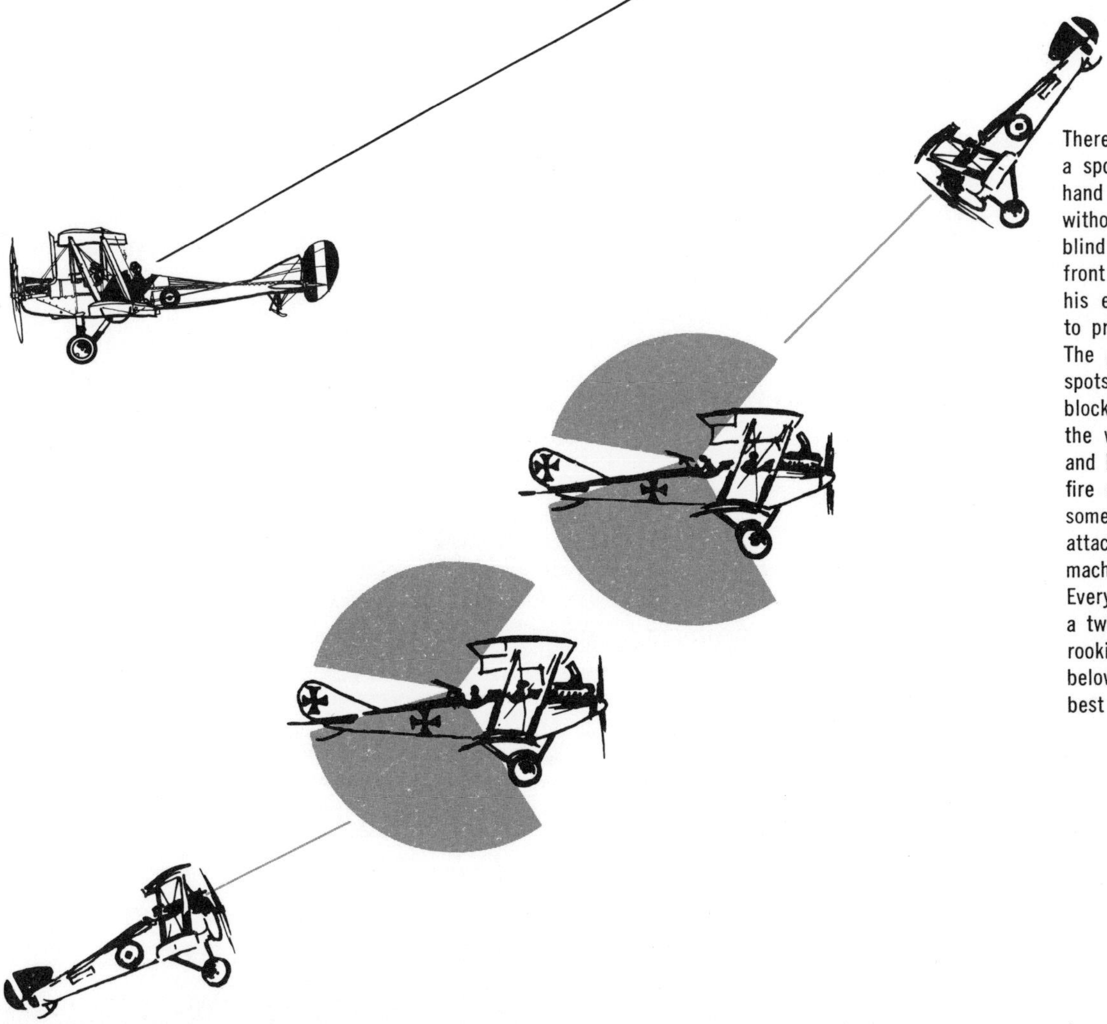

There has to be a blind spot in every defense, a spot where an experienced eye and a fast hand can see and deliver a telling blow without undue risk. For the single-seaters, the blind spot was everywhere save directly in front of the gun. The fighter pilot had to keep his eyes open and swivel his head continuously to prevent being surprised.

The gunner in a two-seater had three blind spots to watch: below, where the fuselage blocked the view, diagonally forward, where the wings stretched across the field of fire, and behind the tail, which blocked the field of fire aft. An experienced fighter pilot could sometimes exploit a careless enemy formation, attacking from such an angle that the enemy machines masked each other's fire.

Every successful fighter pilot who tangled with a two-seater gave the same advice to the rookies—come at them fast, behind, and below. Fancy maneuvers and tricky angles were best left to the experts.

THE GERMANS OPENED THE BATTLE OF VERDUN on 20 February 1916, with a tremendous artillery bombardment. They employed four *Fl. Abt.* and fourteen balloons for artillery spotting, and some twenty *Eindeckers* to protect the two-seaters. Included as targets for the artillery were the French aerodromes, which were systematically destroyed and the French air service was driven back from the Verdun front.

The task that faced the *Service d'aéronautique* when General Pétain issued his famous order to seize and hold aerial supremacy was no easy one. At the end of February, Colonel Barès took command of the French aviation at Verdun and ordered that its strength be increased to eight reconnaissance, two artillery and six fighter *escadrilles,* or about 120 aeroplanes. Commanding the fighters was Major Tricornot de Rose, a pre-war aviator who held the first military pilot's brevet in the French air service. Major, or *Commandant,* de Rose was famous for his huge, drooping moustache and his cool daring, and had a reputation as a great pilot and an experienced leader. At Verdun he led the fighters himself on patrols and escort missions, and inaugurated methods of interception. He organized the *escadrilles* into flights and introduced formation flying. He can be credited with having first wielded fighter squadrons as units in action, for prior to his innovations even homogeneous squadrons had been mere gaggles of individual aeroplanes.

The machine with which de Rose accomplished his miracles was the Nieuport *Bébé,* the first modern fighter of the war and the first in the immortal series of Nieuport "V-strutters."

Among the famous aces who served under de Rose at Verdun were Navarre, Heurtaux and Guynemer.

Jean Navarre had already been cited for the Legion of Honor when he arrived at Verdun. He had also run afoul of de Rose because of his wild antics and unmilitary behavior, but it was de Rose who had agreed to put through the recommendation. It was de Rose also who permitted Navarre to have his Nieuport painted red as a taunt and a dare to the German *Eindecker* pilots. Navarre was not the first pilot to resist military discipline, nor was he the last, and the many who had their machines painted in flashy colors were sniffed at as circus clowns by the stiff-necked army officers. But by scoring a dozen victories in a few months at Verdun, Navarre gave a boost to French morale when it was badly needed that no general since Napoleon could boast of.

Alfred Heurtaux was a cadet at St-Cyr when the war began. He was immediately commissioned a second lieutenant in the 9th Hussars, and before the war was a month old had won his first citation. At the end of four months he had won two more and had earned sufficient prestige to win a transfer to aviation against the wishes of his commanding officer who was naturally loathe to lose such a dynamic officer.

Heurtaux first served in aviation as an observer in M-S 23 with Roland Garros. Unfortunately, Garros was not his pilot. Heurtaux was assigned to a pilot who must have been one of the most inept in the service. After several crack-ups and as many close shaves, Heurtaux decided that if his neck were destined to be broken he would prefer to do it himself. He applied for pilot training. He was sent to Pau in the Pyrenees, one of the largest air combat schools in France. In the spring of 1916 he was posted to *Escadrille* N.3 flying Nieuport *Bébé* single-seaters at Verdun. There he scored his first victory, an L.V.G. two-seater down in flames on 4 May.

When the commanding officer of N.3, *Capitaine* Brocard, was promoted to *Commandant* and placed at the head of Combat Group XII, of which N.3 was one of the squadrons, Heurtaux was appointed to succeed him as C.O. of N.3.

Heurtaux was a smooth and accomplished pilot, a crack shot and an inspiring leader. Before he was seriously wounded in the fall of 1917 and forced to retire from active flying, he had scored twenty-one confirmed victories. He rose to the rank of general in the French air service, served in the *Résistance* in World War II, and lives today in retirement in Paris.

Roland Garros Escadrille M.S 23

Jean-Pierre Léon Bourjade, 28 Victories Escadrille N.152

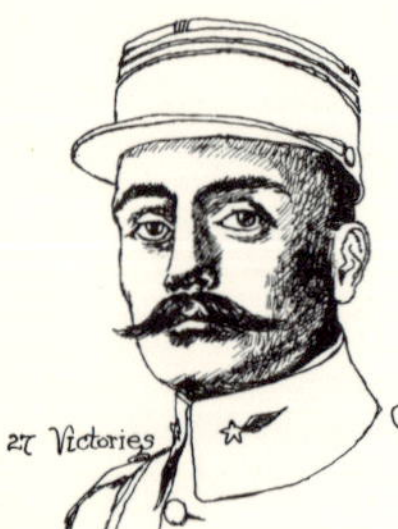
27 Victories Capitaine Armand Pinsard, Escadrille M.S 23.

Lieutenant Charles Nungesser, N.65 45 Victories

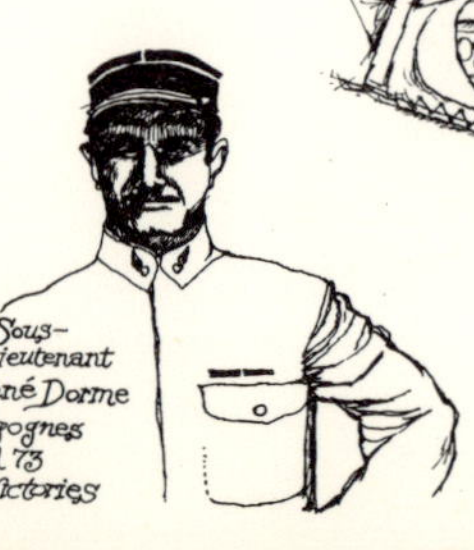
Sous-Lieutenant René Dorme Cigognes SPA 73 23 Victories

Verdun, 26 February 1916. Jean Navarre, in a wildly painted Nieuport *Bébé,* forced a German aeroplane down intact in the French lines where its crew were taken prisoner, and shot another one down on a later patrol for the first French "double" of the war. For this double victory he was mentioned in the army communiqué for that day, the first time a French fighter pilot was so cited. Navarre was also one of the first fighter pilots of the war to sport a flamboyant personal color scheme on his aeroplane.

Escadrilles SPA 26

SPA 3

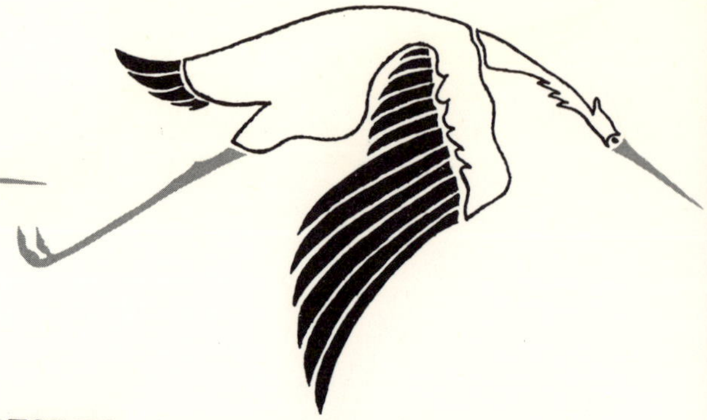

THE STORKS was the name given to four French squadrons—3, 26, 73 and 103—whose official designation was Combat Group XII. Under the command of Félix Brocard these four *escadrilles* were the highest-scoring units of the French air service. A fifth *escadrille,* 167, served with the group for a time also, but the first four were the ones that made the name "Stork" famous, and of the four, 3 and 103 were the elite.

Georges Guynemer was the leading ace of the first. It was called N.3 while it was equipped with Nieuports and Spa 3 while it was equipped with Spads. Guynemer was a frail-looking boy who twice failed to pass army physical tests—he finally got into the air service through a combination of wire-pulling, his father's influence and his own pathetic eagerness. Even after he got into the air service and became an ace, army officers would look at him and say, "My God, have we no one but children left to fight the war?" He began his flying service as the pilot of a two-seater and he and his observer/gunner scored their first victory in July 1915. Just before Christmas 1915 and his twenty-first birthday, Guynemer was awarded his fourth citation and made a *Chevalier* of the Legion of Honor, the citation describing him as: "A Pilot of great value, model of devotion and courage." Transferred to Verdun soon after the opening of the battle, Guynemer shot down a German machine en route for his eighth victory. He was shot down himself shortly thereafter, the second of seven times that this "weakling" was to be shot down and by some miracle survive. Once, when he brought his riddled crate in to a crash landing in no-man's-land, the French infantry in the front lines came charging up out of their trenches to rescue him.

He rejoined N.3 in time for the opening of the battle of the Somme, and on 23 September 1916, he shot down three enemy machines in one day and was accidentally shot down himself when he ran into a French artillery shell at about 10,000 feet. He had just begun flying one of the new Spad machines and it is possible that not even one of Guynemer's usual miracles would have saved him if he had still been flying a Nieuport. "The Spad is solid," he said simply.

In January 1917 he scored five victories in as many days; in February he was promoted to *Capitaine,* and in May he shot down four aeroplanes in one day. By that time he had forty-five victories, twenty citations and had been twice wounded.

SPA 73

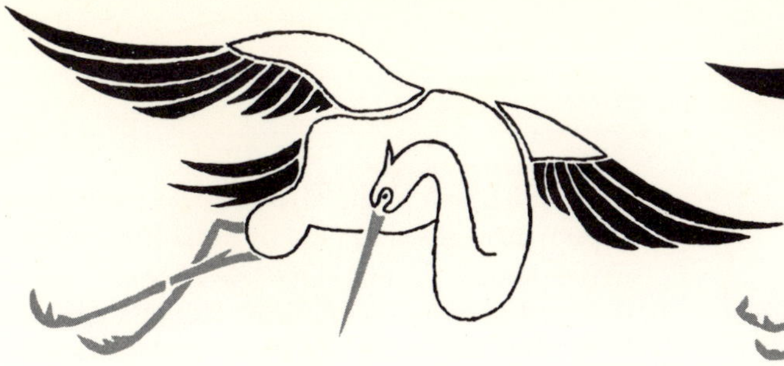

SPA 103

In September 1917, after more than 600 hours of operational flying and with his score standing at fifty-four, Guynemer vanished while on patrol. No trace was ever found of him or his Spad, and his disappearance is one of the unsolved mysteries of the war.

René Fonck was born in Alsace in 1894 and learned of the progress of aviation as a boy by reading over and over any reference to flying in newspapers and magazines. The pre-war pilots were his idols and he resolved to learn to fly. When the war began he was assigned for a time to the engineers where he spent a dreary time digging trenches. In February 1915 he finally received orders to report for flying training which he began the first of April at Le Crotoy. Assigned to a Caudron squadron, Fonck created something of a sensation when he "captured" a German aeroplane in the air by so crowding the enemy pilot that he was forced to land behind the French lines. A few exhibitions like that and it was clear that Fonck was being wasted in a two-seater squadron. He was sent to Le Plessis-Belleville aerodrome near Paris for conversion to fighters. On passing out, he was assigned to Spa 103 of the Stork group, under the command of *Capitaine* d'Harcourt.

Fonck's first victory with the Storks was not officially recorded. On 3 May 1917, while flying a patrol with a Lieutenant Gigodot, he sent a German artillery spotting machine down out of control near Berry-au-Bac. Fonck ended the war with an official score of seventy-five enemy aircraft. His own unofficial total was 127.

A cool-headed, adroit pilot who handled his aeroplane with the absolute confidence, Fonck was not a show-off. He never stunted for the fun of it, but regarded flying solely as a means of fighting. His aim was uncanny. He always scored with the minimum number of bullets—sometimes four or five sufficed—and he said that he put them into the target just as if he put them there with his hand. Once he shot down three machines with three short bursts in one pass, and all three went down together to crash within a 100-yard circle.

On 9 May and on 26 September 1918, he shot down six confirmed machines in one day, the only fighter pilot of the war to achieve such a feat.

His last victory, a few days before the Armistice, was a two-seater that had been dropping propaganda leaflets, and which crashed while a cloud of leaflets were still floating down.

Fonck died quietly in his sleep in 1953.

D.H.2. No. 24 Squadron, R.F.C.

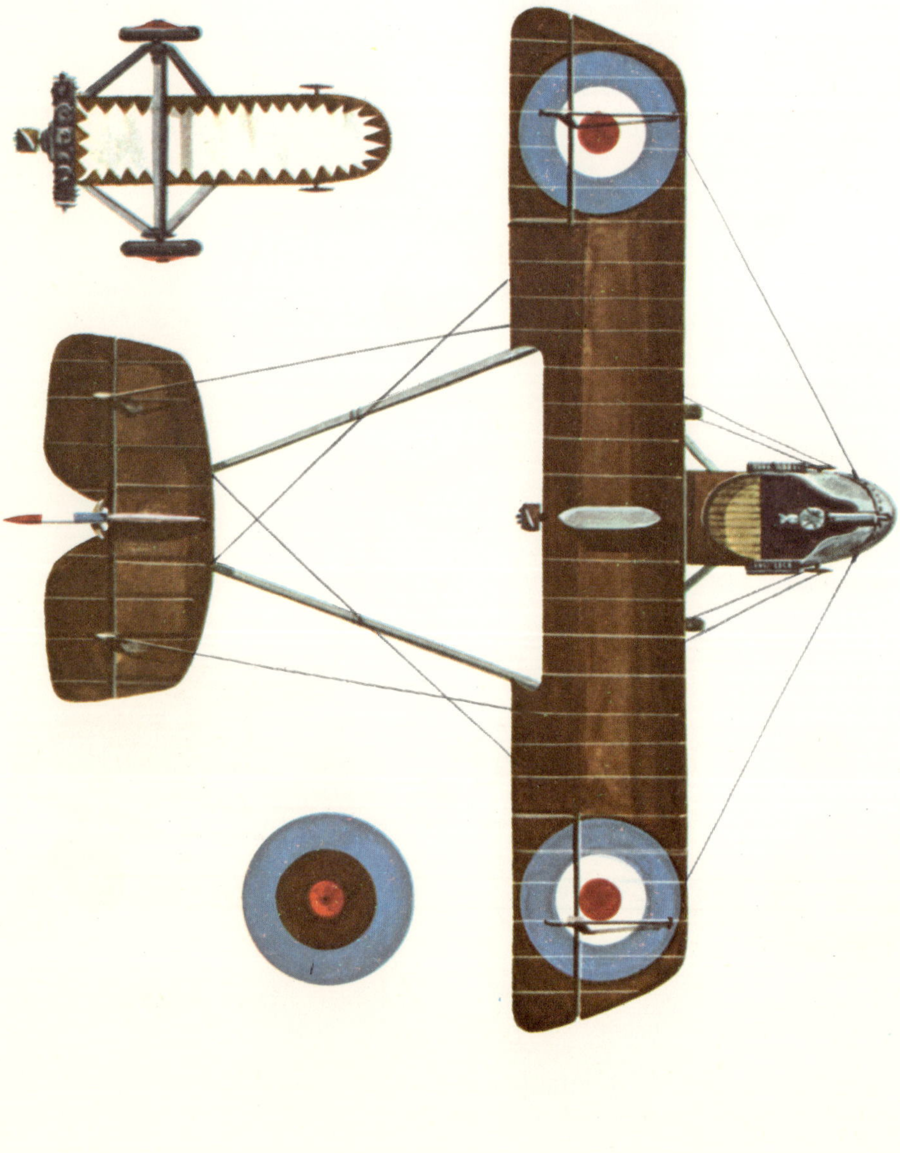

HAWKER'S SQUADRON was the name popularly given to No. 24 Squadron, R.F.C. Lieutenant Lanoe George Hawker transferred to aviation from the Royal Engineers at the outbreak of war and served in France with the earliest squadrons to reach the front. One of Britain's first aces, he won the Victoria Cross in the summer of 1915, the first man to win it as a fighter pilot. In February 1916, as Major Hawker, he brought the first British all-fighter squadron to the front—No. 24, equipped with the D.H.2 pusher.

Hawker's squadron stopped the *Eindeckers* and gave the R.F.C. two-seaters vital protection to resume their work of photography and observation.

It was in a fight with two D.H.2's of No. 24 Squadron that Oswald Boelcke met his accidental death in October 1916. Turning suddenly after an unsuccessful attack on one of them, his wing brushed the landing gear of the machine flown by a comrade who was unable to bank out of the way quickly enough. Boelcke's machine immediately began to spiral down, although it looked as if he had it under control. Suddenly the damaged wing collapsed, and the Albatros fell to the ground bearing the Father of the German Fighter Service to his death.

In November 1916 Hawker, whom the Germans called "The English Boelcke," was shot down by Manfred von Richthofen. He was succeeded in command of No. 24 by Major C.E.C. Rabagliati, formerly of the Yorkshire Light Infantry, who had flown to France on 15 August 1914, with No. 5 Squadron. He ended the war as a Lieutenant Colonel.

Leutnant Stephan Kirmaier, who was appointed to command the fallen Boelcke's squadron, was himself shot down by Captain J.O. Andrews (later an Air Vice Marshal), who was at that time the commander of "A" Flight of No. 24.

The standard factory finish of the D.H.2 was clear-doped all over, but the machines of No. 24 Squadron were repainted in France with a somewhat non-regulation color scheme. They were "coffee brown" on the upper surfaces with white on the underside of the nacelle. To render it less conspicuous, the white ring of the national roundel was sometimes painted coffee brown also—which was more than a little non-regulation.

The death of Oswald Boelcke, 28 October 1916

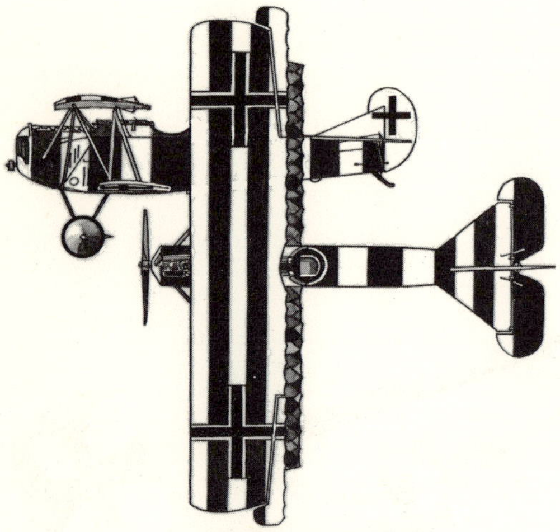

DVII. Jasta 6/JG 1

BLOODY APRIL, the April of 1917, inevitably followed the appearance of the Albatros fighters on the Western Front in the latter part of 1916 and the formation of the *Jastas*. It was the British who coined the phrase, for it was they who suffered the bloody losses. With the advent of spring, the traditional time for the opening of new offensives and the renewing of old ones, the two-seaters of the R.F.C. were called on to make intensive observation, photography and artillery-spotting operations. When their obsolete B.E.2's and R.E.8's crossed the lines in large numbers, they were cut down in large numbers.

At the beginning of 1917, Manfred von Richthofen was appointed to the command of *Jasta 11*. He was also awarded the *Pour le Mérite*. He was aware that his name was being given some prominence not only in the German newspapers, but in those of France and Britain as well, and he began to consider how he might enlarge on his prestige. A capital idea, and one that was apparently long in his mind, was to have his aeroplane overpainted with some flamboyant color so as to render it unmistakeable. He chose red. Navarre had flown a red Nieuport at Verdun during the spring of 1916, the period when von Richthofen himself had flown there as a two-seater pilot. He doubtless had heard of this extraordinary Frenchman and his antics, and he may even have seen him. Boelcke too had flown an aeroplane with a distinctive color scheme—both all-black and all-red aeroplanes are attributed to him. Thus von Richthofen is not to be credited with originating the idea of the personal color scheme, but, characteristically, with enlarging on the original idea. For no sooner had he introduced his "red bird" than he was struck by the tactical value of color-coding the entire *Jasta*. His men could spot him easily and he could keep tabs on them if their machines all had identifying marks of the "official" *Jasta* color—his color—red. The idea quickly spread to the rest of the German fighter service.

The success of the independent *Jastas* was so great in the spring of 1917 that the Germans began to search for ways to provide the entire front with air cover instead of only those sectors behind which the *Jastas* were stationed. Having developed railway organization for many years as an integral part of staff planning, and being thus railway oriented, it was natural to come up with the idea of transporting by rail fighter squadrons and all their equipment as self-maintaining units to any sector where they were needed or required. At the same time another step forward was taken in air organization by the establishment of the first permanent grouping of *Jastas* into a *Jagdgeschwader*. This was *JG 1*, composed of *Jastas 4, 6, 10* and *11*, with von Richthofen, the C.O. of *Jasta 11*, appointed to overall command.

Traveling in long trains with all their hardware, and with their aeroplanes painted in bright colors, the *Jagdgeschwadern* were soon dubbed "circuses," a name that has remained an inseparable part of aviation's lexicon.

Three more *Jagdgeschwadern* were formed, their commanders being Oskar von Boenigk, Rudolph Berthold, Bruno Loerzer and Eduard von Schleich.

Manfred von Richthofen himself was killed in action in April 1918 and was succeeded, in accordance with his will, by Wilhelm Reinhard as commander of *JG 1*. Reinhard was an artillerist who had entered the service in 1909 and was wounded while serving with his regiment in Belgium early in the war. He transferred to aviation in June 1915 and as a two-seater pilot was again wounded late in the year. Early in 1917 he transferred to fighters and was posted to *Jasta 11* in June. At the time of von Richthofen's death he was C.O. of *Jasta 6*. In June 1918 he was killed in the accidental crash of an experimental aeroplane. The command passed to *Oberleutnant* Hermann Goering, the C.O. of *Jasta 27*.

If Oswald Boelcke was the professor and von Richthofen his ambitious pupil, then surely Hermann Goering was the dunce of the class. Whereas Boelcke softened his strictness with understanding, and von Richthofen hardened his with an insistence on perfection, and both inspired in their officers obedience and a devotion bordering on idolatry, Goering was arbitrary, capricious, and a martinet who alienated the loyalty of his men. He was personally successful as a fighter pilot—he scored twenty-two victories—but his method of acquiring respect by bellowing until he was red in the face contrasted sadly with the method of Boelcke and von Richthofen, which was simply to set a noble example.

DVII. Jasta 19/JG 2. Lt. O. von Beaulieu-Marconnay

DVII. Jasta 10/JG 1. Lt. Arthur Laumann

DVII. Jasta 15/JG 2. Lt. Georg von Hantelmann

DVII. Jasta 13/JG 2. Leutnant Wolff

DVII. Jasta 5/JG 1. Lt. Josef Mai

DVII. Jasta 12/JG 2. Leutnant Greven

DVII. Jasta 64/ Vzfw. Joseph Doerflinger

DVII. Jasta 11/JG 1. Vzfw. Willi Gabriel

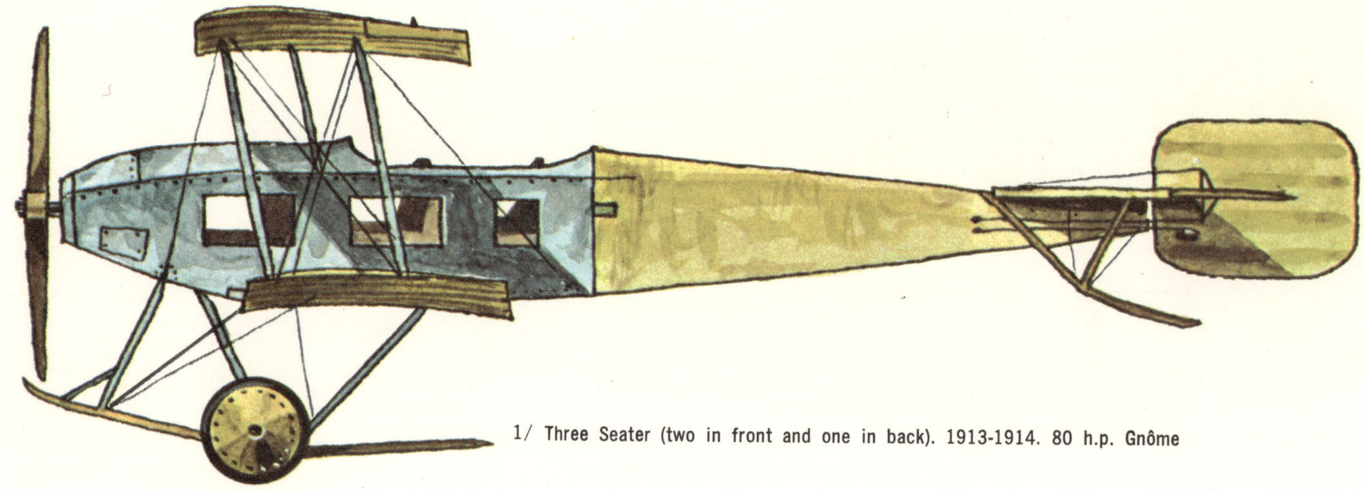

1/ Three Seater (two in front and one in back). 1913-1914. 80 h.p. Gnôme

3/ Tabloid. 1914-1915. 100 h.p. Gnôme-Monosoupape

6/ 1½ Strutter. 1916-1918. 110 or 130 h.p. Clerget

9/ Dolphin. 1917-1918. 200 h.p. Hispano Suiza

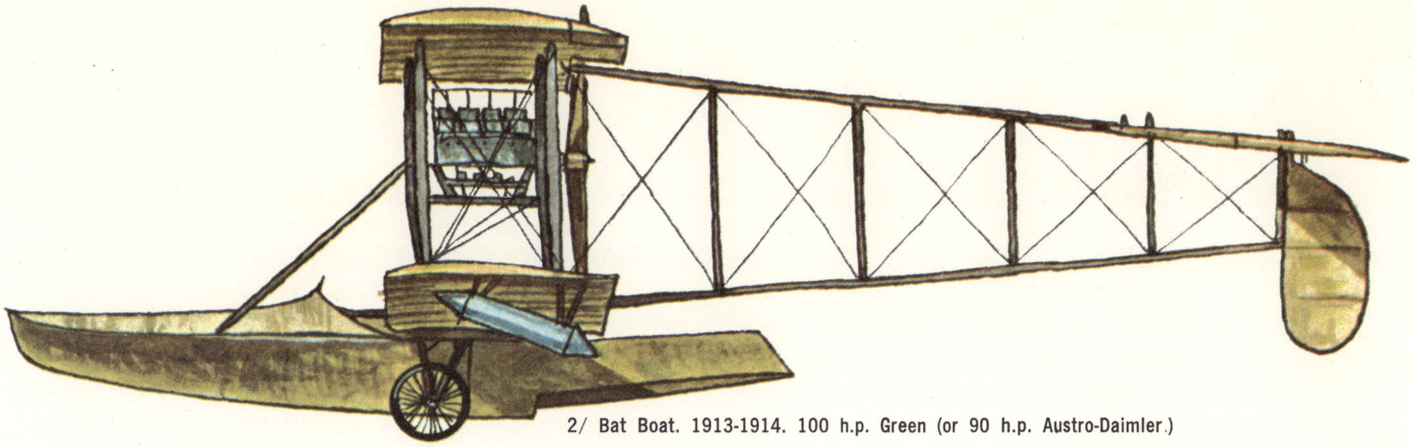

2/ Bat Boat. 1913-1914. 100 h.p. Green (or 90 h.p. Austro-Daimler.)

4/ Baby. 1915-1916. 110 or 130 h.p. Clerget

5/ Pup (R.N.A.S., fitted with deck-landing skids and arrester gear). 80 h.p. Le Rhône

7/ Triplane. 1917. 110 or 130 h.p. Clerget

8/ Camel. 1917-1918. 130 h.p. Clerget or 150 h.p. Bentley

10/ Snipe. 1918. 230 h.p. Bentley

11/ Salamander. 1918. 230 h.p. Bentley

Bentley B.R.1 9-cylinder 150 h.p.

TOMMY SOPWITH, Sir Thomas Octave Murdoch Sopwith, C.B.E., was born in 1888, and from the earliest days of aviation was one of its finest intellects. He was one of the first to repay Blériot's compliment and fly across the Channel the other way, from England to the continent (1910). He established the Sopwith Aviation Co., Ltd., at Kingston-on-Thames in 1912 and in 1913 produced the record-breaking Tabloid (3 on the previous page), a most modern machine for its time. With a top speed of 92 m.p.h. the Tabloid won handily the Schneider Trophy contest of 1914. The Baby (4) was a descendant of the Tabloid. (See pages 36–37).

The Three Seater (1) and the Bat Boat (2) were both Sopwith designs in service with the R.F.C. at the outbreak of the war, the Bat Boat being the first flying boat of the Naval Wing to be built in Britain.

The 1½ Strutter (6) entered service with the R.N.A.S. early in 1916 and was the first British machine regularly to be equipped with a synchronized forward-firing gun. It was flown both as a single-seater and as a two-seater, the former being labelled the Type 9700 and the latter the Type 9400 in the R.N.A.S. Navy nomenclature in this case (and several others) assigned a type number derived from the production batch serial numbers, the original batch of two-seaters being fifty machines series 9376 to 9425. Some 4,500 of both types were built in France under license, nearly three times as many as were built in Britain.

The Pup (5) was the only British scout in service in France at the end of 1916 and the beginning of 1917 that was capable of putting up any kind of a show against the Albatros. The Pup was a very light machine with just half the horsepower of the Albatros which, with an all-up weight of 1,950 pounds, had a 725-pound handicap. The Pup was responsive all the way up to its ceiling, which was about 17,500 feet or roughly the same as that of the Albatros. In climb the two machines were again on a par, both being able to reach ceiling in about half an hour, the Pup having a slightly slower but more steady rate of climb. As a concession to lightness, the Pup was armed with one gun as against two on the Albatros. Although this was a weight saving of fifty-odd pounds, the advantage really went to the Albatros. The best thing the Pup had going for it was its light, easy responsiveness at altitudes where the Albatros was sluggish.

The Triplane (7) and Camel (8) came out in 1917 and were both famous for their maneuverability, a Sopwith trademark. The dependable Triplane suffered the same limitation as the Pup in that it was armed with but one gun (see pages 84–85 for more on the Triplane). The Camel was the first British scout to go into action with two synchronized guns (July 1917). With a paddle-blade propeller, a rotary engine and a short fuselage, the Camel was capable of tight right-hand turns that snapped too easily into spins. Students who survived training and mastered such eccentricities found that they could turn them to advantage in combat. Only the Fokker Triplane matched the Camel's stunting qualities.

The Dolphin (9) was the biggest fighter produced by Sopwith during the war. With a wing span of thirty-two and one-half feet and a length of over twenty-two, it was almost as large as some two-seaters. It was a fast machine, its top speed being just over 131 m.p.h. Its layout was unusual, for in addition to the negative wing stagger, its cockpit was so arranged that the pilot sat with his head above the top wing. The object was to try to give him the best possible view upward and forward.

The Snipe (10) was essentially a heavier, more powerful version of the Camel. It might possibly have racked up some formidable records for itself had the war continued, but at the armistice only three squadrons were equipped with Snipes. It was a big brute, and though it was not particularly fast, it was rugged and maneuverable and its climb was as good as that of the Camel—five minutes to 6,500 feet.

The Salamander (11) was a derivative of the Snipe, although its antecedents can be seen in an experimentally armored version of the Camel. For that is what it was, an armored machine whose specific job was low-level ground attack. It was designated T.F.2, or Trench Fighter by the company. It carried some 650 pounds of armor around the cockpit and fuel tanks, in spite of which it had a top speed of 125 m.p.h. which was a shade faster than the Snipe. The difference is attributable to a cleaner design, for they both had the same engine.

In 1933, Sopwith merged with the H.G. Hawker Engineering Company to form Hawker Aircraft Limited, and in 1934 he took over the Gloster Aircraft Company. He also acquired the design services of Sir Sydney Camm, who created the immortal Hurricane of World War II. In 1936 he announced the absorption of A.V. Roe & Co., Ltd., Sir W.G. Armstrong Whitworth Aircraft Ltd., and Armstrong Siddeley Motors Ltd., and thus laid the foundations of today's Hawker Siddeley Group.

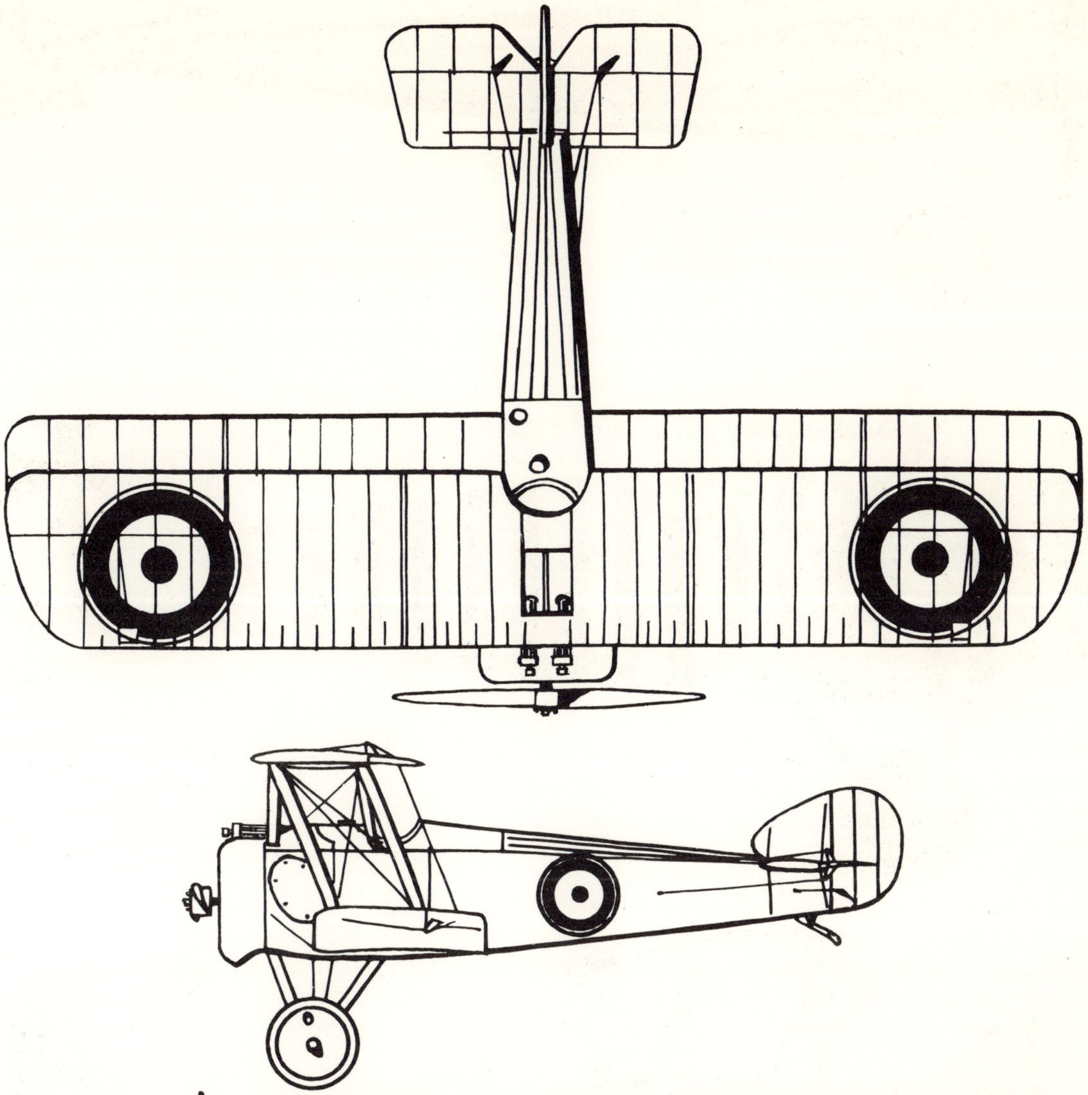

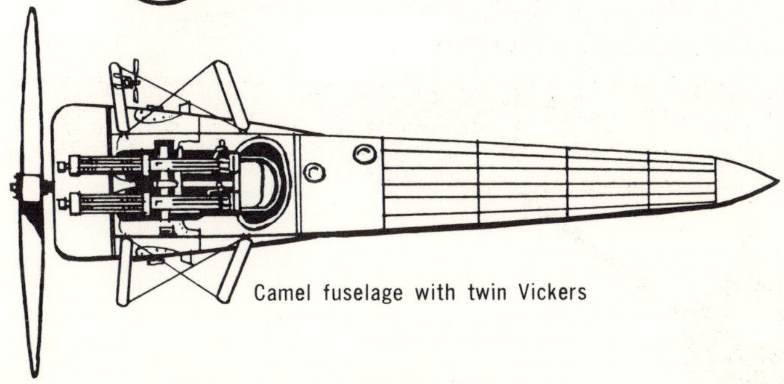

Camel fuselage with twin Vickers

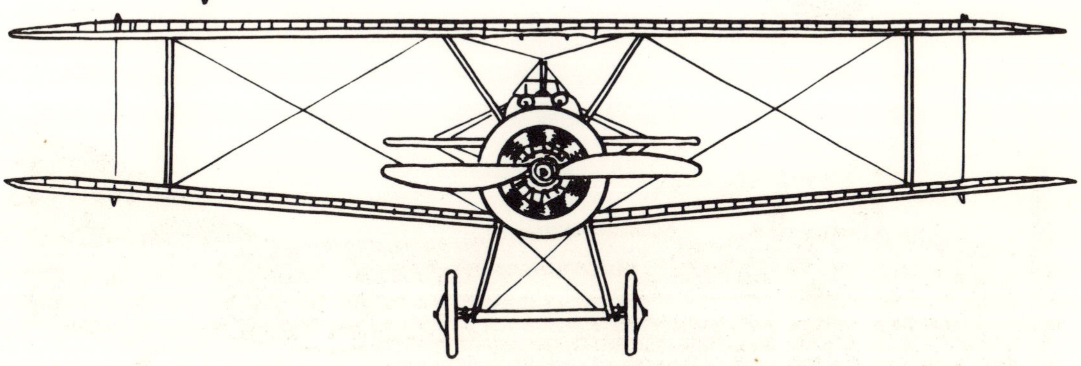

Sopwith F.1 Camel (over 5,400 built)

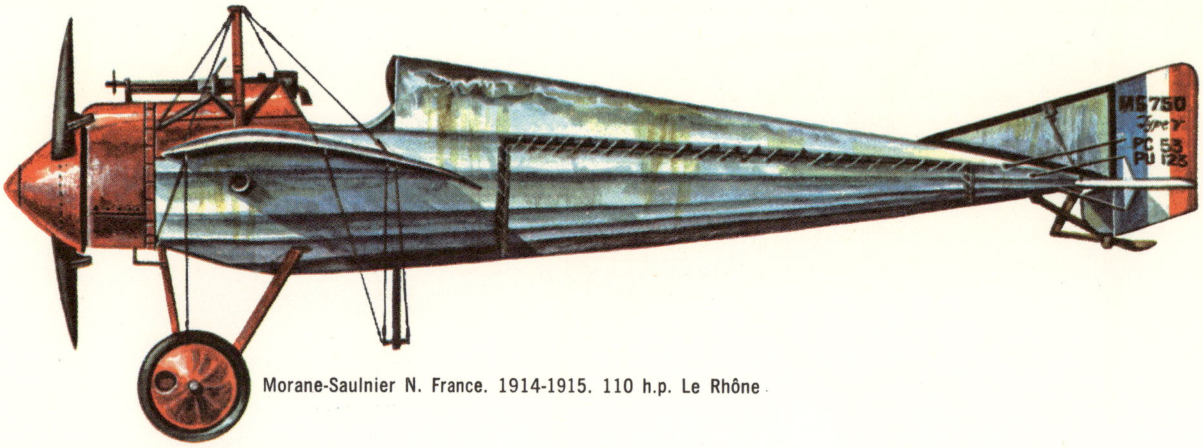

Morane-Saulnier N. France. 1914-1915. 110 h.p. Le Rhône

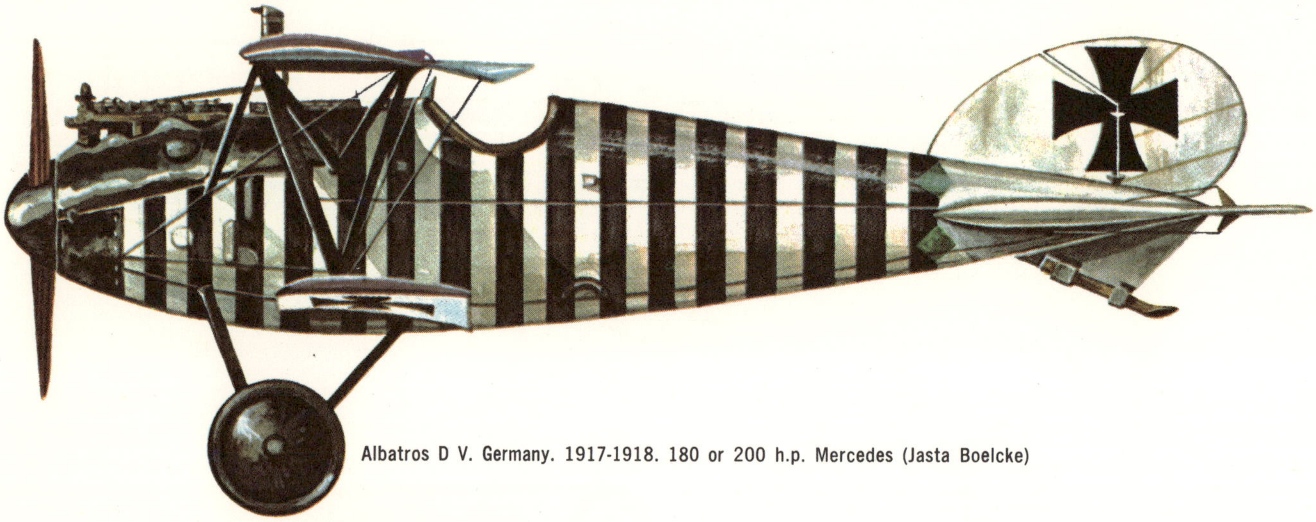
Albatros D V. Germany. 1917-1918. 180 or 200 h.p. Mercedes (Jasta Boelcke)

S.E.5a. Great Britain. 1917-1918. 200 h.p. Wolseley Viper (Captain J. T. B. McCudden, V.C., No.56 Squadron, R.F.C.)

Spad 13. France. 1917-1918. 200 h.p. Hispano Suiza (Captain E. V. Rickenbacker, 94th Aero Squadron, U.S.A.S.)

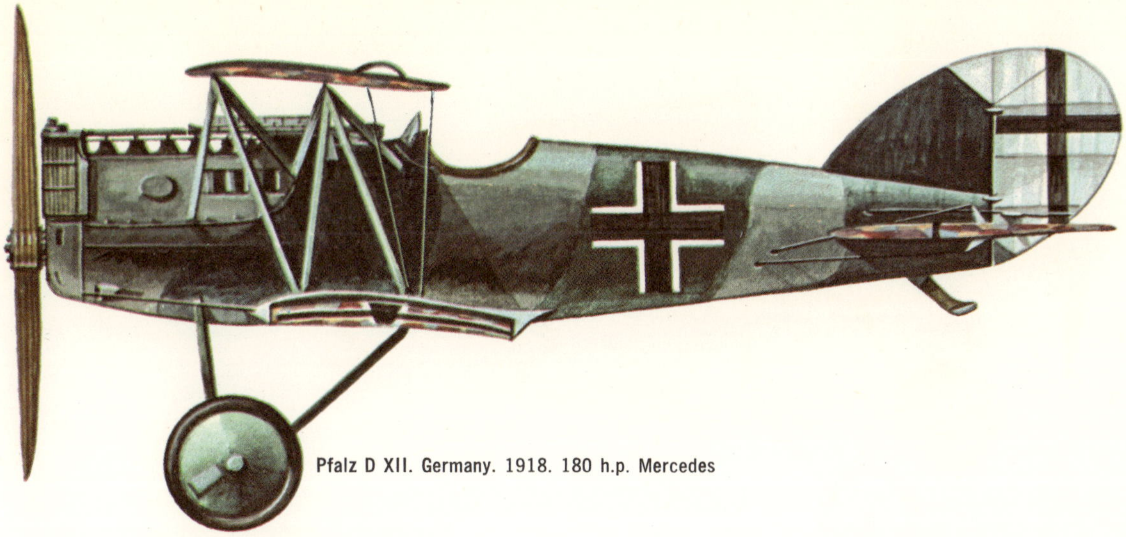
Pfalz D XII. Germany. 1918. 180 h.p. Mercedes

Sopwith 7F.1 Snipe. Great Britain. 1918. 230 h.p. Bentley. (Mayor W. G. Barker, V.C., No. 201 Squadron, R.A.F.)

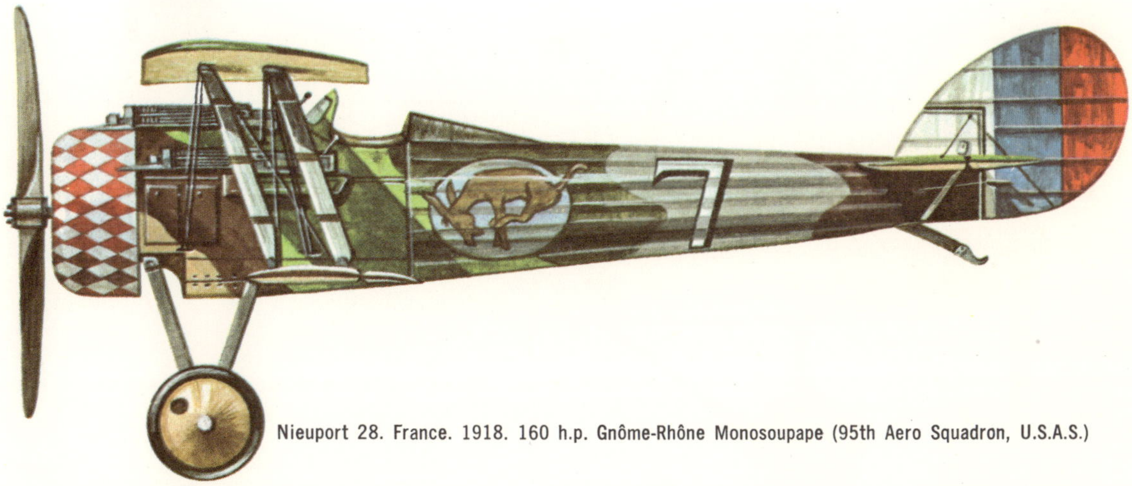

Nieuport 28. France. 1918. 160 h.p. Gnôme-Rhône Monosoupape (95th Aero Squadron, U.S.A.S.)

Phönix D III. Austria-Hungary. 1918. 230 h.p. Hiero (naval fighter squadron)

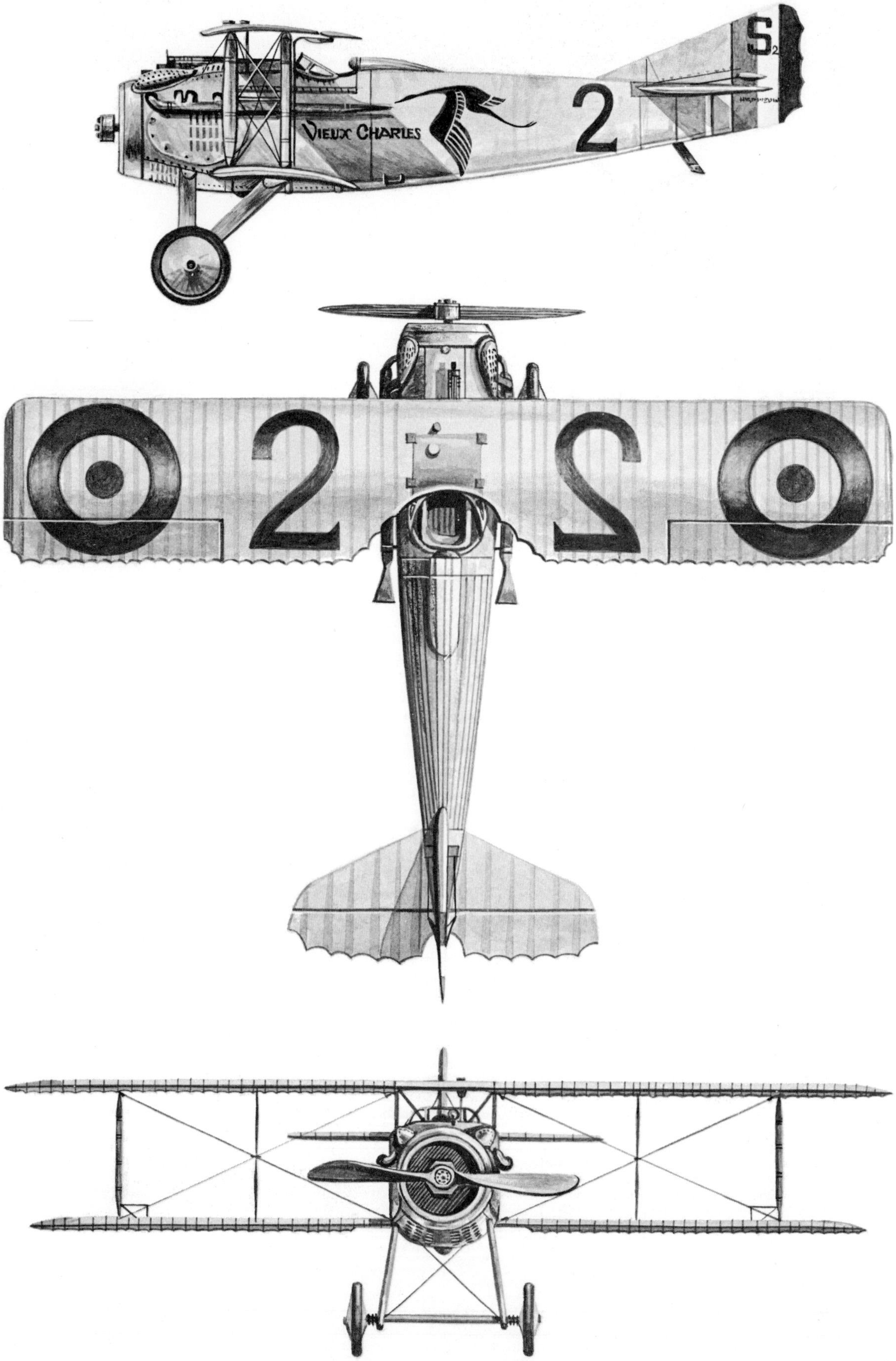

Spad 7, "Vieux Charles," flown by Capitaine Georges Guynemer, Escadrille Spa 3, 1917

S. P. A. D.

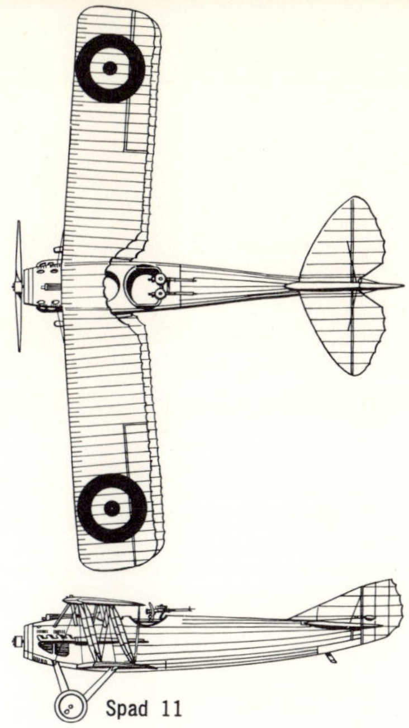

Spad 11

Apart from the Dreyfus case, the major pre-war upheavals in France were those of finance and politics whose effect was limited to the upper levels of money and power in Paris. One of the sensational financial scandals was that involving Armand Deperdussin, the director of the *Société Pour Appareils Deperdussin,* or Society for Deperdussin Aeroplanes. The Deperdussin company, also called S.P.A.D. after its initials, produced a famous series of fast monoplanes before the war that swept all the speed records for 1912 and 1913, including, in February 1912, the first official speed record in excess of 100 m.p.h. (The pilot was Jules Védrines, who during the war flew with the Storks.) The S.P.A.D. company was a successful one and it was not allowed to go down the drain just because the director was locked up. A new director was appointed, the celebrated Louis Blériot, and the company's promising future was secure. Blériot changed the name of the company to make it clear that there had been a thorough overhaul, but cannily preserved the famous initials to make it equally clear that the product would remain the same. The new name, *Société Pour Aviation et ses Dérives,* or Society for Aviation and its Derivatives, did not figure in a large way in the war in the air until the summer of 1916, but from then on dominated it. The two major Spad types, the S.7 and the S.13, were the greatest fighter aeroplanes of the war.

The S.7 was a development of the A.2, a two-seat escort fighter. The A.2, powered with an 80 h.p. Le Rhône rotary engine, represented possibly the worst attempt to solve the problem of the forward-firing gun, but except for the gunner's bizarre "pulpit" projecting forward of the motor, was a reasonably clean design. One suspects that Bécherau, who created the pre-war racers as well as the Spad fighters, must have designed the A.2 under duress. The A.2 appeared in the spring of 1915, and during the year the surprising number of about 100 was built.

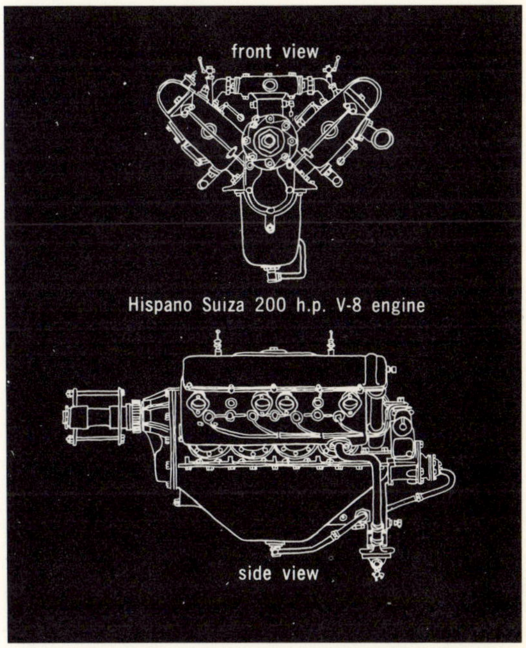

Hispano Suiza 200 h.p. V-8 engine

Fortunately, a beautiful marriage of aeroplane and engine occurred to save Bécherau further embarrassment. He had used rotary engines exclusively up to 1915, but in that year there appeared the revolutionary Hispano Suiza V–8 engine invented by the young Swiss engineer, Marc Birkigt. Birkigt, whose professional career had begun in Barcelona under the aegis of a prominent Spanish financier, was working on the engine when the war broke out. A French government technical committee was so impressed by the promise of this power plant that Birkigt was given official encouragement to speed its development.

The Spad with the Hispano Suiza engine might have been no more than a fast scout had not the French come out with a synchronizing gear at the appropriate time so that a forward-firing Vickers gun could be mounted and the awkward solution of the "pulpit" abandoned.

The Spad 7 was a small aeroplane. It was just twenty feet long and its span was twenty-five and one-half feet—several feet smaller all around and about 400 pounds lighter than the Albatros D II. With a top speed of 120 m.p.h. it was the fastest fighter at the front in the fall of 1916 and the spring of 1917. Except for the fact that it was armed with but one gun, it was never seriously outclassed even by much later aeroplanes. By the time the S.7 was in widespread use with French, British and Italian squadrons at the beginning of 1917, the next model, the S.13, was well along in development. It was armed with two synchronized Vickers guns, was powered by a 200 or 220 h.p. Hispano Suiza engine which gave it a top speed of just over 130 m.p.h., and was the standard French fighter throughout 1918.

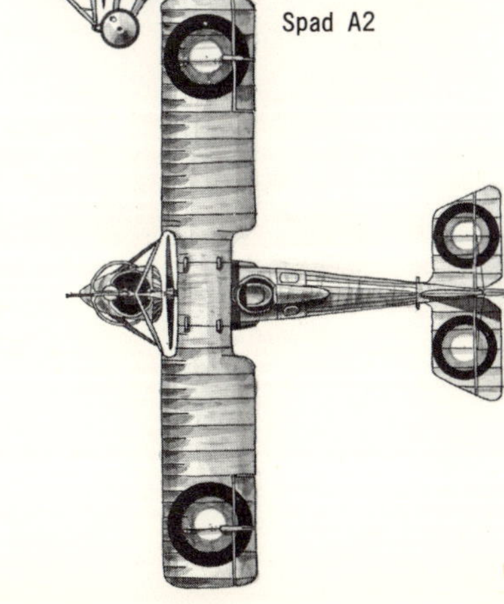

Spad A2

The Spads were not so maneuverable as the Nieuports or any rotary-engined machines, but they were handy enough for any reasonably competent pilot to keep out of trouble in them. For sheer stunting, the Fokker triplane could fly rings around a Spad, but it suffered a thirty-mile-an-hour speed handicap and wasn't a patch on the Spad for strength. The Spad could be dived hard in perfect safety while enemy pilots attempting to dive after it would suddenly find they had left their wings behind.

In the closing months of the war a third model, the S.17, appeared, powered by the 300 h.p. Hispano Suiza. Only about twenty machines had been delivered by the time of the armistice, "For which," observed *Capitaine* Madon, the forty-one victory ace who commanded Spa 38, "let the Boches be thankful."

Fok. FI 103/17
B4863
B1

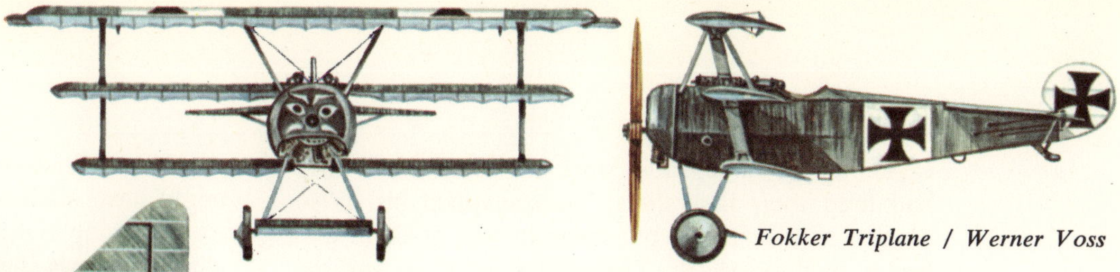

Fokker Triplane / Werner Voss

WERNER VOSS was born in April 1897 and so turned twenty during Bloody April of 1917. He was awarded the *Pour le Mérite* during Bloody April, and he was dead before he was twenty-one.

Born in Krefeld, not far from Essen, he joined a militia company, the Krefeld Hussars, and served in the trenches for the first year of the war. Like von Richthofen and Bishop and many other cavalrymen he found he could stand the war, but not the mud. He applied for aviation training and served in the German air service first as an observer, then as a bomber pilot, and finally as a fighter pilot from September 1916. He became an ace while he was still a teen-ager. He had won the Iron Cross first class while serving in the trenches, and about the only other ace who compares with him in this respect is the Frenchman *Sous-Lieutenant* Pierre Marinovitch, who scored twenty-two victories, won the Legion of Honor, and had just turned twenty-one when the war ended.

Voss was a natural pilot and handy with engines and guns. He often tinkered with his engine trying to improve its performance, and he used to spend hours going over his ammunition round by round to make sure there were no sub-standard rounds to cause jams. His shooting was as perfect as his flying and he sometimes employed his accuracy to spare men rather than to kill them. On several occasions he brought down British two-seaters by smashing their motors without hitting the crew. Having been a bomber pilot himself, he felt a certain sympathy for them.

When the Fokker company brought out its new triplane in the late summer of 1917, Werner Voss was one of the first pilots to fly it at the front, and he was the first pilot to score with it, on 29 August. Between then and 23 September when he was killed in action, he downed a score of Allied machines. The "Tripe" was a remarkably slow aeroplane, its top speed being under 100 m.p.h. regardless of the optimistic official figures which credit it with a speed of 103 m.p.h. Its poor speed was the result of an underpowered and unreliable engine, the license-built 110 h.p. Le Rhône rotary engine. What the Tripe did have in its favor, and what a pilot like Voss was ideally suited to exploit, was the combination of a good rate of climb and exceptional maneuverability.

Voss was in the habit of going out on voluntary patrols after regularly assigned duties had been fulfilled. On the evening of 23 September 1917, he was out alone when he came across a flight of S.E.5a's from No. 56 Squadron led by Captain J.T.B. McCudden.

The S.E.5a's had the height advantage and they all dived on the lone Tripe

S.E. 5a / J. T. B. McCudden

expecting to make short work of him. Before they had fired their first shots, Voss snapped his Tripe around to face them, put holes in two of them and broke up their attack. They closed in again and the same thing happened. Before the fight was over, Voss had scored hits on all of them and had sent one S.E.5a limping for home. His flying was later described as unbelieveable and wonderful to behold. An Albatros jumped into the fight for a time and tried to stay with the Tripe to cover his tail. A flight of six Albatros were also on the scene, but before they could intervene a formation of French Spads appeared and kept them occupied. The Albatros was forced to clear out and Voss again faced the S.E.5a's alone. He was doing things with his machine that the British had not seen done before. He could make it turn without banking by means of what McCudden described as a flat half-spin.

Voss was also taking it as well as dishing it out, for at one time his Tripe was on the receiving end of burst from five S.E.5a's at once. By that time he must have been hit himself, and the final burst took him or his machine while he was flying almost straight and level. By that time the fight had worked down to a fairly low altitude and the Tripe had a short dive into the ground where it smashed so hard it disintegrated.

Exactly who was in the fight and who actually shot Voss down has been the meat for many arguments since. Possibly it can never be proved conclusively that such and so was the way it was and no other—but on one point there seems to be almost universal agreement. This was one of the most extraordinary aerial combats in the Great War.

The Sopwith and Fokker triplanes made a large impression on other aero constructors in 1917. Many of them climbed on the bandwagon with improvised triplane rigs for existing biplane designs. Most of these were poor aeroplanes. The odds are 100 to one against such improvisation producing worthwhile results. On the other hand, there is no justification for ridiculing the constructors—aeronautical engineering may be quite advanced today, but in 1917 much basic research had to be carried out on the principles of instinct and (for want of a better term) taste. It was a true saying that aeroplanes that looked right, flew right.

The Albatros and Nieuport triplanes were morphologically eccentric because three wings had been arbitrarily grafted on an airframe designed for two. One and a half, in fact. They looked awful and that is precisely the way they flew. Neither of them was ordered into production. The Pfalz concern produced a triplane along more considered lines and had the 160 h.p. Siemens-Halske geared rotary engine not had so many bugs to be ironed out, it might have made a better showing. When everything was working right, the Pfalz triplane had a rate of climb that was slightly superior to that of the Fokker triplane, but front-line pilots such as Manfred von Richthofen and Eduard von Schleich were displeased with the general handling qualities of the machine when they test-flew it. It was not ordered into production.

A hemisphere away, America was dimly beginning to grasp the fact that she didn't really know what was going on "over there." Right up to the armistice, Americans, even those whose responsibility it was to know, supposed that the U.S. could wade right in and walk over the opposition.

One of the few machines produced in America during the war that bore any relation in its performance to the standards of the front was the Curtiss S–3 scout of 1916. With a 100 h.p. Curtiss V–8 engine, it had a top speed of 112 m.p.h. An attempt was made to arm the machine in March 1917 when twin Lewis guns were fitted to fire over the propeller.

The Austin Osprey was an attempt by a British company to come through with a new winner for 1918 the way Sopwith had in 1917. The Osprey was a fairly sound design when it was originated late in 1917, but its 230 h.p. Bentley rotary engine was not delivered until the beginning of 1918 and the aeroplane was not officially test-flown until March, by which time the Sopwith Snipe was well along. As the Snipe proved to be superior, and since it required the same engine, the Osprey was shelved.

An astonishing series of multi-winged experiments appeared after the successful introduction of the Sopwith triplane. There had been some efforts with this configuration before the war, but the monoplane and biplane had swept the field and until the Sopwith designers revived the concept, there were no multi-winged machines worth mentioning.

Caught up in their enthusiasm, however, after the debut of the Sopwith, some constructors produced real freaks, interesting only because they are such marvelous examples of a good idea carried to absurdity. Tony Fokker insisted, to the despair of his designer Reinhold Platz, that if three wings were good, five ought to be better. Against his will, Platz produced a quintuplane according to Fokker's specifications. The monster had such terrible handling qualities that even Fokker had trouble flying it and Platz himself is said to suffer excruciating embarrassment to this day. Fokker tried to save the machine with a few modifications, but it was hopeless and after one last flight he had it quietly rolled into a hangar and forgot about it. By tacit understanding, the subject of three-, four- and five-wingers was dropped and Platz was allowed to resume his own line of creative thinking.

Pfalz D I

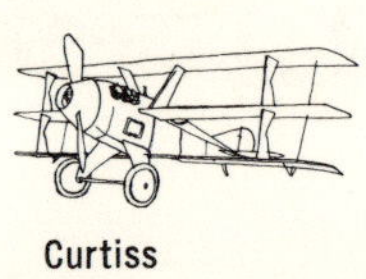
Curtiss

Austin A.F.T.3 Osprey

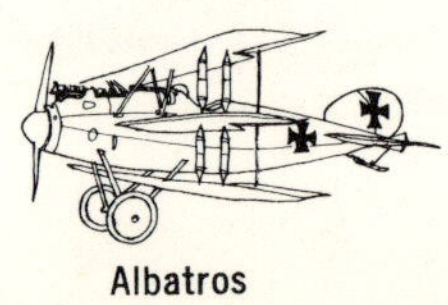
Albatros

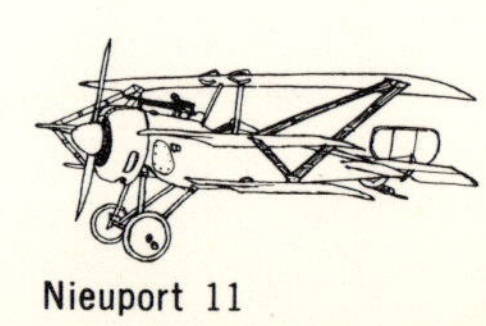
Nieuport 11

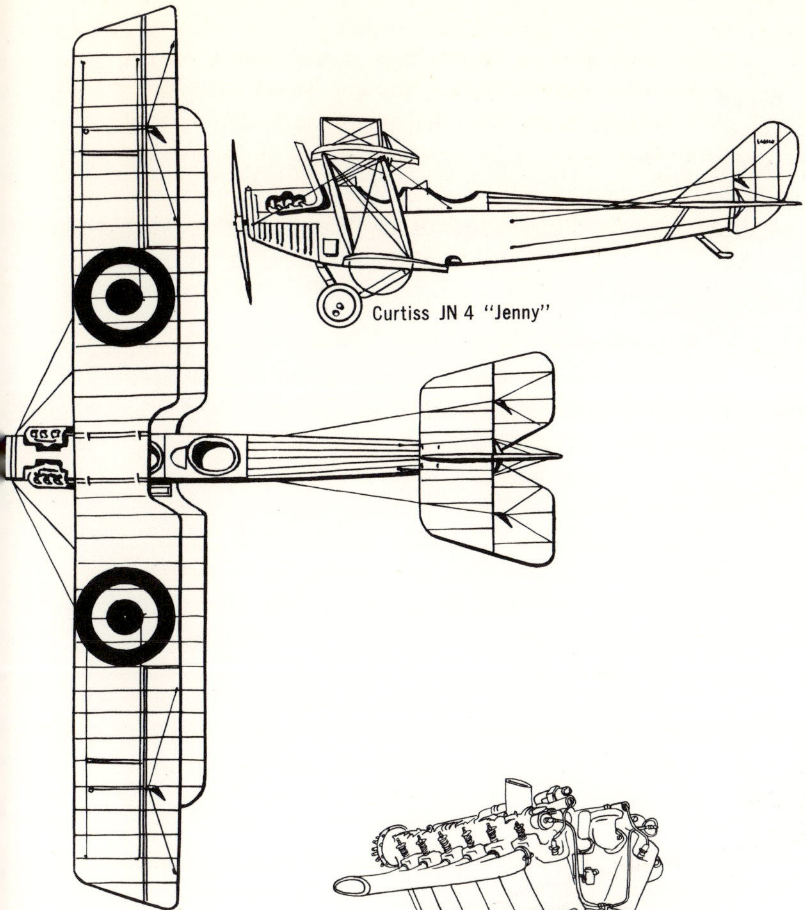

Curtiss JN 4 "Jenny"

THE UNITED STATES' AIR SERVICE did not begin to make a showing until April 1918—one year after the U.S. declared war. A great deal of fault-finding went on both during and after the war as a result of a general compulsion to hang the blame on somebody, but one of the main reasons the U.S. lagged behind the principal combatants of Europe in aero design, engineering and production was because strict censorship in Europe had prevented Americans from knowing and understanding what was happening. Many persons in authority had no idea of the importance the war in the air had assumed or how its technology had progressed.

There was only one aircraft factory in the U.S. worthy of the name—Curtiss—and a number of small shops, most of which were incapable of fulfilling large military contracts. There were a handful of qualified aero engineers in industry and the government, and it was they who made the one technical contribution to the Allied war effort—the Liberty engine. Designed, according to legend, in a Washington, D.C., hotel room, the Liberty was originally a 300 h.p. V–8 engine when its plans were unveiled before an official committee in the spring of 1917. By summer the first handmade samples had been tested and their horsepower found insufficient. After redesign, the Liberty emerged as a 400 h.p. V–12, which, once the bugs were ironed out, proved to be a fine engine. It was shipped to the front in large numbers in the last few months of the war, and remained in production in the U.S. for several years after the war.

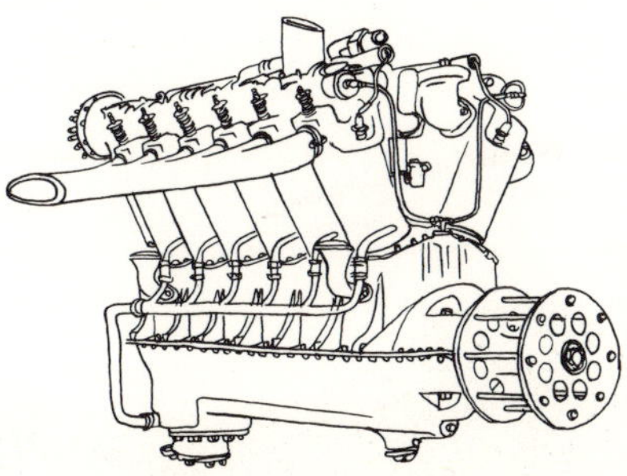

Liberty 400 h.p. V-12 engine

The American automobile and machine industry which had altogether lacked direction, found it in the Liberty and rapidly organized mass-production, but there was no established industrial reserve ready to take on the production of airframes. Expansion to war-time standards was slow. The Curtiss JN 4 "Jenny," the classic barnstormer's crate, the Thomas-Morse Scout, and the Standard E-I were the only American machines mass-produced during the war and they were used only as trainers. (At that, the Thomas-Morse was designed by Englishmen living in America.) Several European designs, such as the D.H.4, the Handley-Page 0/400, and the Italian Caproni Ca. 46 trimotor bomber, were eventually produced in the U.S., but only the D.H.4 reached the front in any quantity. Something over 4,000 had been completed by the time of the armistice.

For the most part, American aviators in the war flew French, British or Italian aeroplanes purchased by the American government.

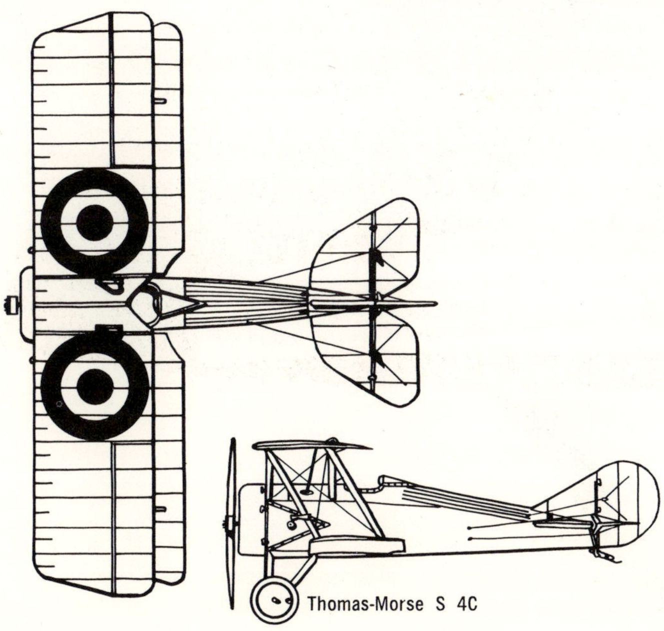

Thomas-Morse S 4C

JN 4 "Jenny"

THE SOPWITH TRIPLANE was evolved by the Sopwith designers in answer to the need for a maneuvrable machine with a good rate of climb. It was felt that by reducing the length and width (span and chord) of the wings and making up the necessary supporting surface with an extra wing, a satisfactory result could be achieved. They were right. The Triplane was a sound design, very maneuverable and with a good climb, and the only criticisms that could be made against it were that it was underpowered and underarmed. It had a 110 or 130 h.p. Clerget rotary engine and bore one synchronized Vickers gun. Yet, its deficiencies were to a large extent overcome by the remarkable R.N.A.S. pilots who flew it on the Western Front. The R.F.C. was so badly pressed that it was obliged to ask the navy for help, and in answer to the plea the navy detached eight squadrons to operate with the R.F.C. as land-based squadrons. From February to November 1917 Sopwith Triplanes were flown by pilots of

Flight Lieutenant Raymond Collishaw's Sopwith Triplane, "B" Fli

Naval 1, 8 and 10 Squadrons in Flanders.

The machine illustrated is one of "B" Flight of Naval 10, sometimes called "Black Flight" under the command of Flight Lieutenant Raymond Collishaw. Between May and July 1917, Collishaw and his men destroyed eighty-seven enemy aeroplanes. By the end of the war, Collishaw's own score was sixty confirmed victories, and today he is (a retired Air Vice Marshal of the Royal Canadian Air Force) the highest-scoring surviving ace of World War I.

Naval 10 Squadron

Seminole Insignia used until April 1917

Sioux Insignia used from April 1917

THE LAFAYETTE ESCADRILLE is possibly the most misunderstood military unit of the war. The magic name "Lafayette" is popularly supposed to be synonymous with "ace," and the extraordinary deeds attributed to the Lafayette pilots would cause them to squirm with embarrassment if they could hear them. Literally thousands of men, some of them World War I veterans, claimed to have been Lafayette pilots. Some *were* Lafayette pilots, but not all of them were veterans of the *Lafayette Escadrille* proper. The confusion was sometimes the result of innocent ignorance, for the public did not realise there were two Lafayette outfits—the *Lafayette Escadrille* and the Lafayette Flying Corps. The *Lafayette Escadrille* was the name of one French air service squadron, number 124, called N. 124 or Spa 124 depending on whether it was equipped with Nieuports or Spads. There were more volunteers than could be absorbed into one squadron, but the French government accepted all volunteers who qualified for service and assigned them to squadrons where replacements were needed at the time and transferred them into N. 124 when there was an opening—if the men wanted to go. Many American pilots who started out in French squadrons preferred to remain with their French comrades rather than transfer into a squadron of strangers even if they were Americans. To acknowledge the service of all American volunteers, whether they served in the *Lafayette Escadrille* or not, the French referred to them collectively as the Lafayette Flying Corps.

Sixty-five members of the Lafayette Flying Corps died in the war, and of the thirty-eight Americans who served in the *Lafayette Escadrille,* nine were killed in action and one, Paul Pavelka, died as the result of a fall from a horse at Salonika.

The squadron had four French officers, not including Nungesser who was attached to the squadron for a month in the summer of 1917; three of them were killed and the fourth, *Capitaine* Georges Thénault, the commanding officer, survived the war.

The *Lafayette Escadrille* achieved a score of thirty-eight victories, Raoul Lufbery accounting for nearly half of those. Lufbery was one of the old style soldiers of fortune. He was born in France, raised by relatives, struck out to see the world as a teenager, served in the American army before the war (his father was a naturalized citizen), and joined up with a French barnstormer in the Orient. When the war began, Lufbery's partner, Marc Pourpe, joined the aviation service and was killed before Christmas 1914. Lufbery served in the aviation service first as a mechanic, then as a pilot in a Voisin squadron, and had been asked to join the *Lafayette Escadrille* on the strength of his stretch in the American army. He scored seventeen confirmed victories (it is said his unconfirmed score must be around twice that), and transferred to the U.S. Air Service at the beginning of 1918 at which time the *Lafayette Escadrille* was absorbed as the 103rd Aero Squadron, U.S.A.S. Lufbery was assigned to command the 94th Aero Squadron, and before he was killed in May 1918, he had tutored the new men who were to become some of America's top aces—Eddie Rickenbacker, Douglas Campbell and Reed Chambers.

Commanding the 103rd Aero Squadron was Major William Thaw, who had served in the *Lafayette Escadrille* since its inception in April 1916. Thaw, a native of Pittsburgh, learned to fly before the war, and went to France to participate in the 1914 Schneider Trophy Race. When the war began, he offered his services to the aviation service; turned down because of his American citizenship, he joined the Foreign Legion. The Foreign Legion offered the solution to the problem of Americans, or anyone, who wanted to fight for France without jeopardizing their home country citizenship. The oath of allegiance sworn by Legionnaires was to the Legion, not to France, and once in the Legion the men could be transferred to any outfit for "temporary" duty. Some of the American volunteers who started out in the Legion never made it to the flying service. One of these was Dennis Dowd of New York. Dowd, a graduate of Georgetown University and Columbia Law School, was practising law in New York when the war broke out; he took the first boat to France. He enlisted in the Foreign Legion on 26 August 1914 and served over a year in the trenches before he was posted for flying training. He was killed in an accident at the flying school at Buc-St-Cyr on 12 August 1916, the first American to lose his life in this way. Another, Colonel Paul A. Rockwell, since 1916 the historian of the *Lafayette Escadrille,* was wounded in the infantry in the winter of 1914/1915 and invalided out of the service. He remained in France, accepting a position as correspondent with the Chicago *Daily News.* His brother, Kiffin, scored the first victory for the *Lafayette Escadrille* on 18 May 1916, and was shot down on 23 September.

The death of Kiffin Rockwell caused considerable newspaper comment in the United States—more than would seem likely when the papers were filled every day with accounts of battles that accomplished nothing, and the deaths ran into the scores of thousands. The reason perhaps was that Rockwell, historically, meant more as a dead American volunteer than as a living French soldier. His death proved that Americans were willing to die for what they believed in. That was the value of the *Lafayette Escadrille* and the Lafayette Flying Corps. The French were encouraged by the fact that Americans could and would fight. In the United States the publicity given the Lafayette flyers reminded the nation that Europe's war was also America's war, and she could not turn her back on the responsibility.

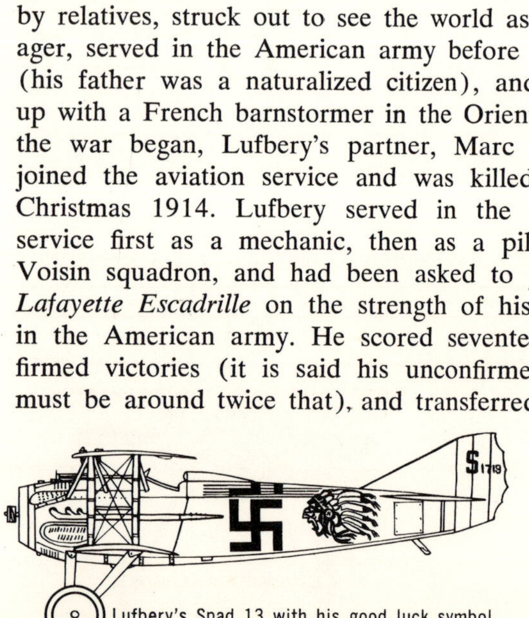

Lufbery's Spad 13 with his good luck symbol

THE FOKKER AEROPLANE WORKS, of Schwerin in Mecklenburg, was the only German company besides Pfalz (a Bavarian concern) that specialized in single-seat fighters. It was the only company whose founder and director was generally supposed to be the chief designer as well. As his home country, Holland, was neutral, it did not matter to Anthony H. G. Fokker whom he worked for; when the war was over he managed to slip across the border with sufficient finished aeroplanes and equipment to start up his business in Holland. He had made a name for himself before the war as a stunt pilot, and whatever his shortcomings as a designer, it is certain that he was one of the most gifted pilots who ever flew. He could have flown an armchair if there had been one with wings.

It was his flying school and military sales, however, that set him up in business. His early aeroplanes sold to the army, bird-like contraptions named Spiders, were not brilliant performers, but they sufficed to keep his name before the authorities. By the time the war broke out, Fokker had produced several monoplane types suited to general military reconnaissance duties. His designer at the time was Martin Kreutzer, a native of Cologne who had joined the Fokker company in 1911 and served as designer until his death in a flying accident in 1916. Kreutzer designed the famous *Eindecker* series, based originally on the French Morane-Saulnier 1912 monoplane.

The various *Eindecker* models did well enough through 1915, but from the early months of 1916 the Nieuport *Bébé* and the D.H.2 began to reverse the situation. By the time the battle of the Somme opened on 1 July 1916, the *Eindecker* had been defeated and the Germans had lost aerial supremacy. In an effort to come up with a new design that could hold its own against the Allied machines, Kreutzer and Fokker initiated a series of biplanes powered with both stationary and rotary engines. The series, D I through IV, was little more than a biplane modification of the *Eindecker* and received no very enthusiastic endorsement either from the front or from the aviation inspectorate.

The D V which followed never served at the front, but was used through 1917 and 1918 as a fighter trainer. It was an aeroplane with exceptionally fine flying qualities and possibly would have been one of the major types of the war had it not been cursed with a very poor engine—the 100 h.p. Oberürsel rotary. The D V is significant in the development of the Fokker family because it was the first design to which Reinhold Platz had been able to make a contribution.

Platz had come to Fokker as a young man in 1912. He was then, in spite of his youth, an experienced technician in gas welding. In the next few years with the company he picked up enough of aeronautical engineering and design to succeed Kreutzer a short time after his death. Platz remained with Fokker for twenty years as chief designer and technical director, and the success of the Fokker line was due to his native ingenuity. The D V was a Platz re-design of the D II. Platz' next two designs, the V.1 and V.2 were not accepted by the military, but are interesting in that they featured cantilever plywood-covered wings with rotating tips instead of ailerons.

His next design, again hampered by a mediocre Oberürsel rotary engine, was the Dr I Triplane, a light, sturdy machine whose climb and maneuvrability were unmatched in the last half of 1917. The D VI which followed was a sort of combination of the Dr I and the D VII. The D VII and the D VI were both chosen for mass production after the January 1918 fighter trials at Adlershof aerodrome in Berlin where front-line pilots such as Manfred von Richthofen and Adolf von Tutschek assembled to test the new prototypes. The D VII won so thoroughly that Albatros, Ostdeutsch Albatros and A.E.G. were ordered to produce it under license. At the fighter trials in June, the new Fokker winner was the D VIII, in which Platz had been allowed to revert to a plywood-covered cantilever wing. The D VIII was a truly up-to-date aeroplane and it was fortunate for the Allies that fewer than 100 were serving at the front by the time of the armistice. As the "Flying Razor," the D VIII had proven itself to be a very dangerous opponent. Examples obtained as reparations by Italy were still flying as late as 1925.

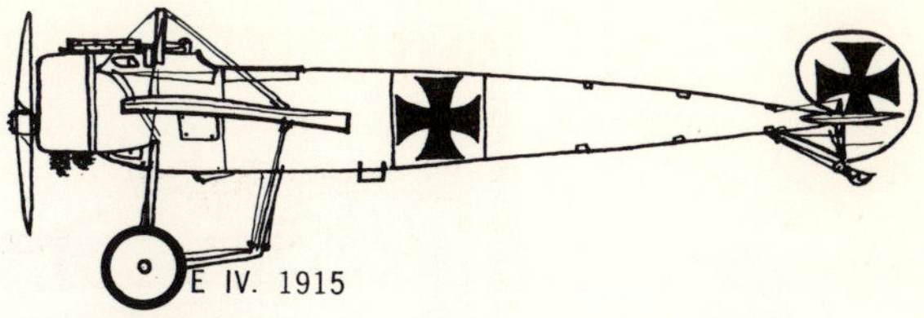
E IV. 1915

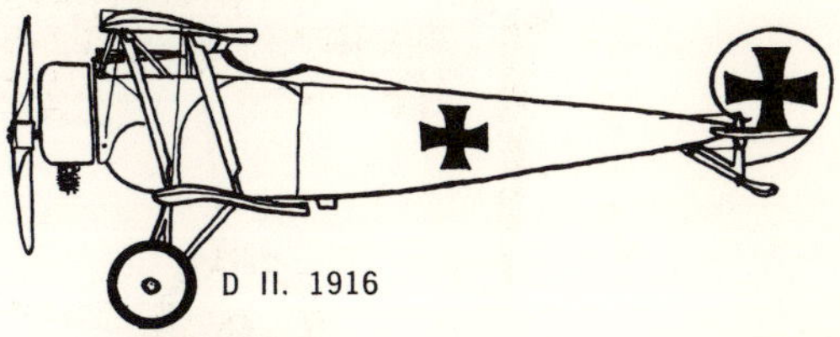
D II. 1916

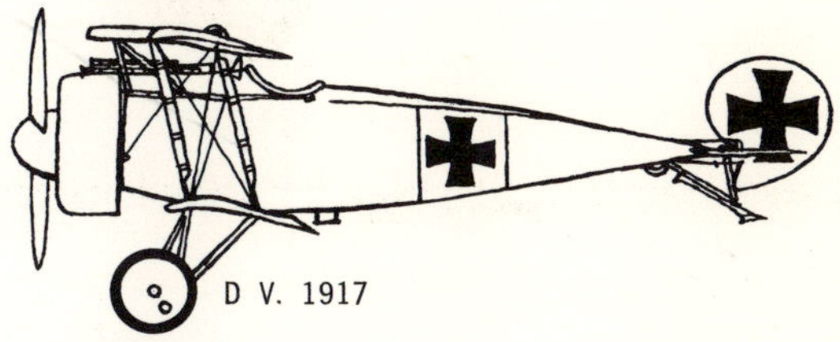
D V. 1917

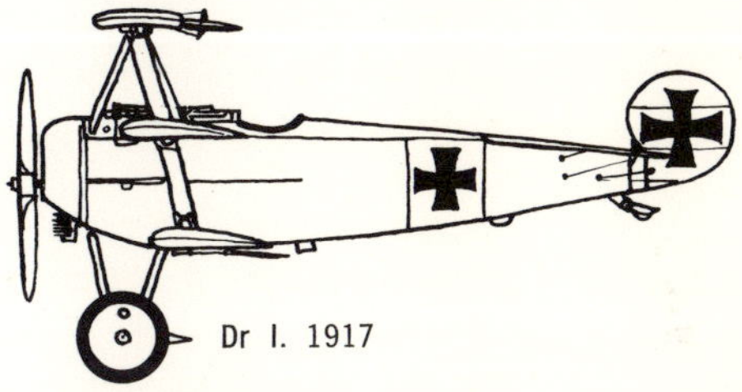
Dr I. 1917

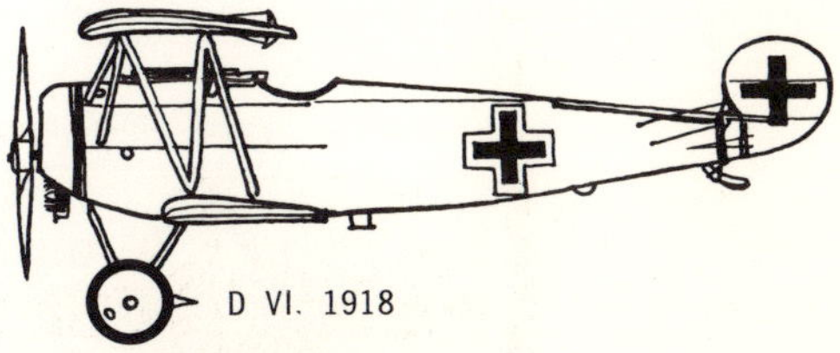
D VI. 1918

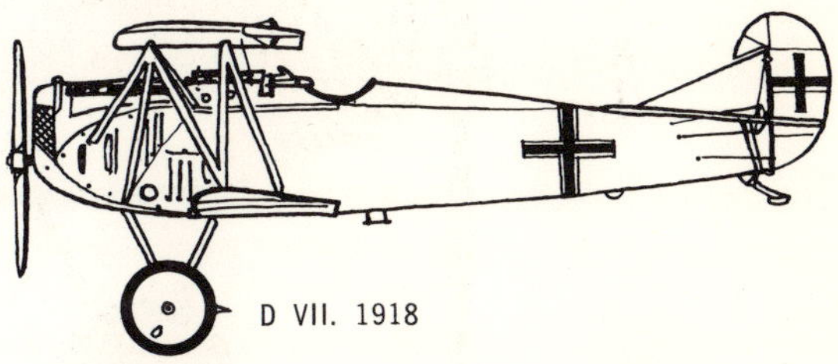
D VII. 1918

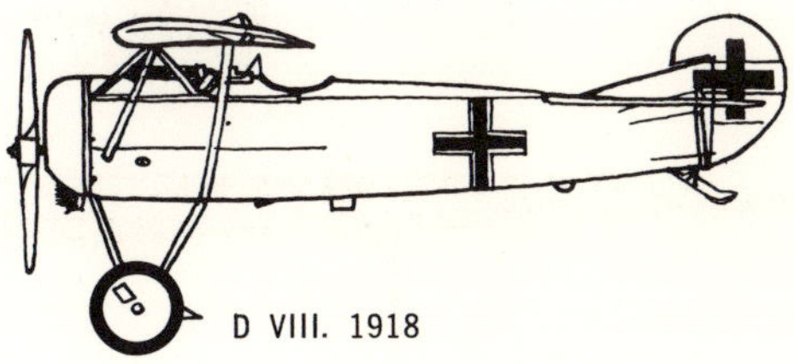
D VIII. 1918

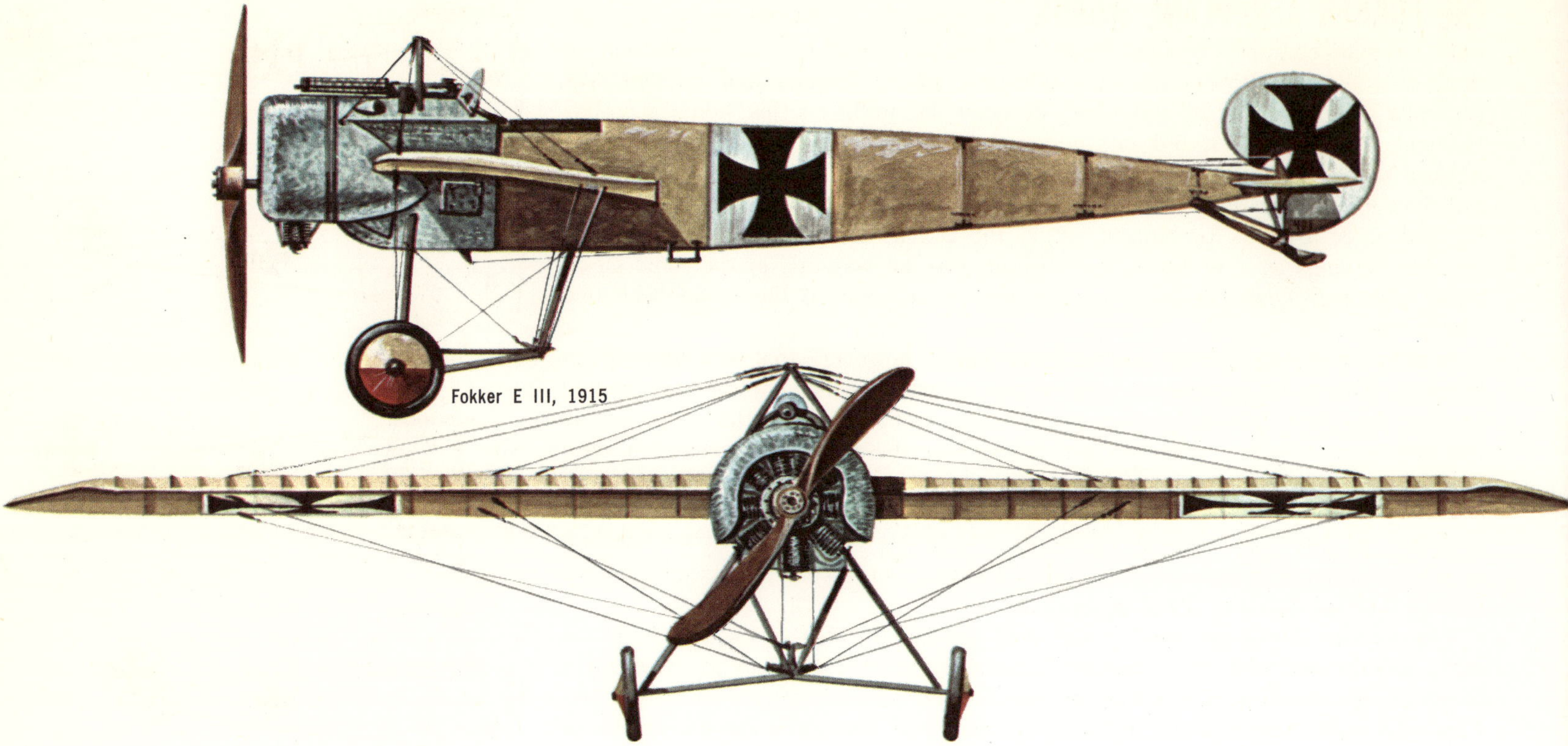

Fokker E III, 1915

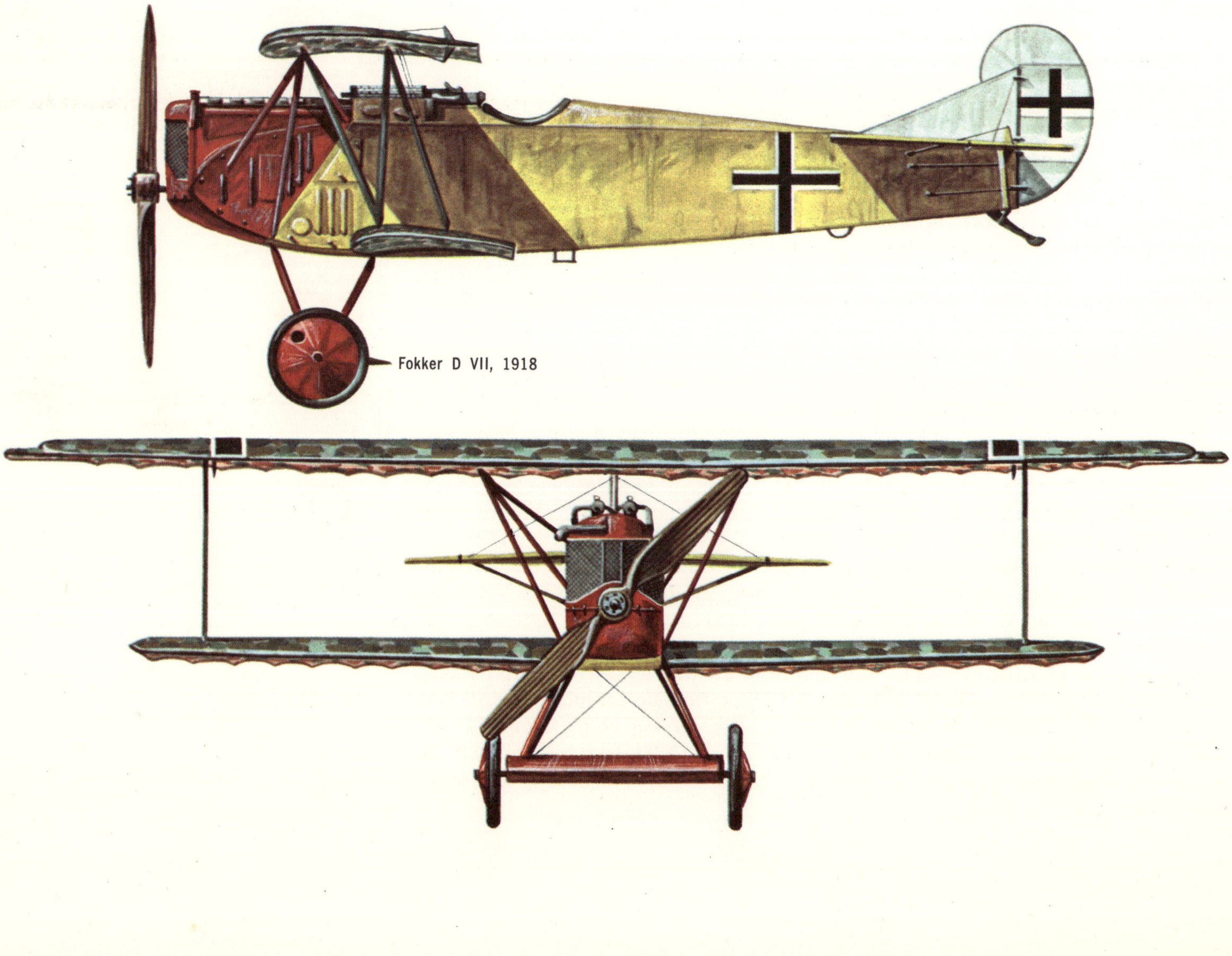

Fokker D VII, 1918

Nieuport 12, 1915

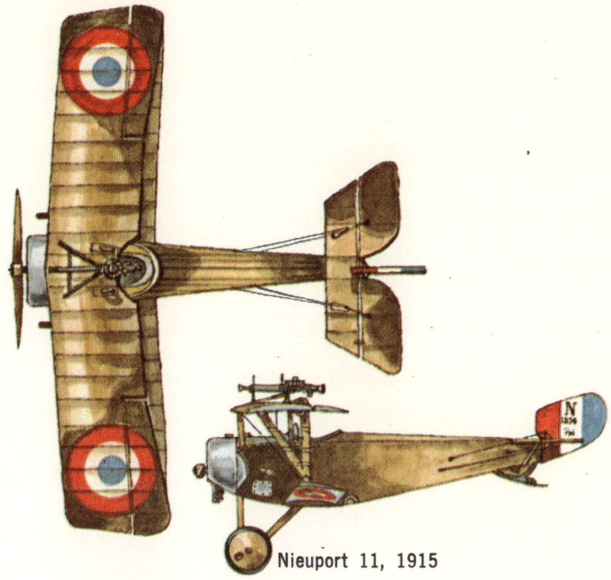

Nieuport 11, 1915

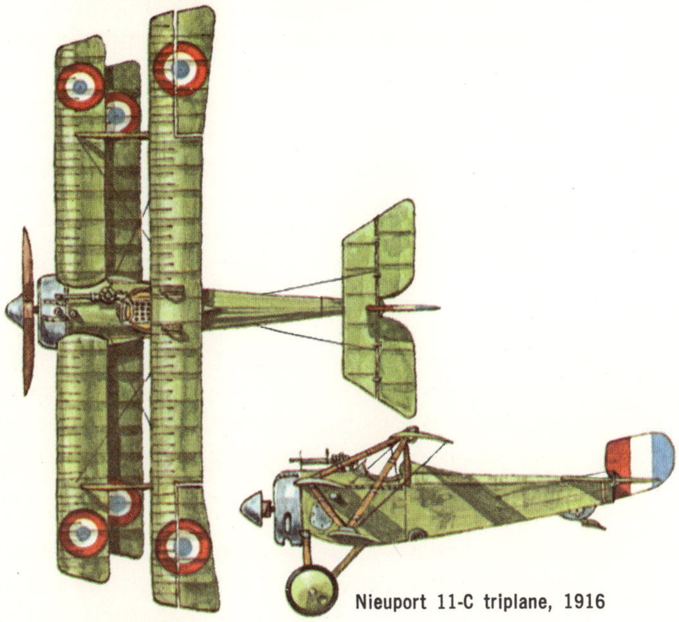

Nieuport 11-C triplane, 1916

Nieuport 17, 1916

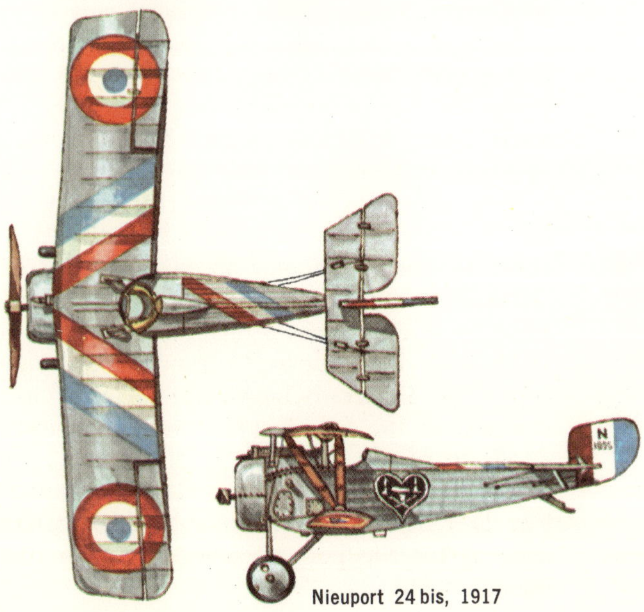

Nieuport 24 bis, 1917

Nieuport 28, 1918

Nieuport 24

NIEUPORT is a name that is synonymous with aviation pioneer. The Nieuport Company—*Société des Etablissements Nieuport*—was founded by Edouard de Niéport at Issy-les-Moulinaux in 1910, and before the war the company had won an international reputation as the producer of a fine series of fast monoplanes, a number of which were purchased as single-seater scouts for the French army. The founder de Niéport was killed in a crash in September 1911 at the age of thirty-six, but the company had been successfully launched and so grew and flourished. In January 1914 a naval engineer named Gustave Delage took over as chief of the design staff, and remained with the company all during the war years.

The first design by Delage, the Type 10, was also the first biplane to be produced by the company and went into production before the war as a two-seat general reconnaissance machine. It was powered with the Gnôme or Le Rhône 80 h.p. rotary engine and was the machine that introduced the famous Nieuport sesquiplane layout. The top wing was a conventional looking plane, but the bottom wing was hardly a plane at all, being little more than a streamlined support for the "V" interplane struts. The sesquiplane, or half-wing, layout was a Nieuport trademark until the appearance of the Nieuport 28 at the beginning of 1918. The Type 12 was almost identical to the Type 10, the difference being the installation of a more powerful engine, either the 110 or 130 h.p. Clerget rotary. The observer sat in the front seat in the early models of the Type 10, and when the machine was armed it was with a Hotchkiss machine gun mounted on the top wing. The observer stood up in his seat and stuck his head through a hole in the wing in order to reach the gun.

In the later models of the Type 10 and in the Type 12, the observer sat in the back seat and operated two Lewis guns, one behind his cockpit firing aft and one mounted at the trailing edge of the top wing firing forward.

The Types 10 and 12 were called "18 metre" Nieuports because their wing area was equivalent to 18 square metres. The "13 metre" Nieuport was the Type 11, also known as the *Bébé,* or Baby. Powered with the 80 h.p. Gnôme rotary engine and armed with a stripped Lewis gun on the top wing fixed to fire over the propeller, the *Bébé* was the best single-seater at the front in the latter half of 1915 and the first half of 1916, and was the aeroplane that ended the supremacy of the Fokker *Eindecker* at Verdun. A more powerful engine, the 110 h.p. Le Rhône rotary, was fitted to the type toward the end of 1915, whereupon it was redesignated the Type 16.

Various experimental triplane versions were tried out in 1916, but none of them was put into production. For the most part, they were based on the Types 17 and 24*bis*.

Early in 1916 the Type 17, or "15 metre" Nieuport made its debut. The 17 was a thoroughly redesigned single-seater with strengthened air-frame and wings, a much streamlined appearance, and either the 110 h.p. Le Rhône or the 130 h.p. Clerget rotaries. With the latter engine, the machine was known as the 17*bis*. In the summer of 1916 the 17 was equipped with a synchronized Vickers gun mounted in front of the cockpit; before then, it was armed with a Lewis gun on the top wing in the fashion of the *Bébé*. In many French *escadrilles* the two guns were used together, but British squadrons equipped with the type used only the top wing Lewis.

The Nieuport 24 had a fuselage that was rounded by means of light wooden stringers all the way aft, marking a mid-point in development from the slab-sided design of the *Bébé* to the circular cross section of the Type 28. It also had a rounded tailplane similar to what was to be used in the 28. It was powered with a 130 h.p. Le Rhône rotary engine. The 24*bis* was the same machine with a reversion to the earlier angular style of tail plane. The 27 came next and was the last of the sesquiplanes. It had a 120 h.p. Le Rhône rotary engine and the rounded tail and rudder of the 28.

The 28 was a most elegant and streamlined aeroplane, and was the last of the Nieuport family of single-seaters to see active service in the war. The engine was the 160 h.p. Gnôme-Rhône Monosoupape 9N rotary. The armament was two synchronized Vickers guns, both of which were mounted to port, one inside and one outside the cabane struts.

While the various models on the opposite page are all shown wearing French colors, the Nieuports served in the air services of all the Allied nations and on all fronts. From Russia to Italy, and from Belgium to Bulgaria, the Nieuports saw the whole war through, and have the unusual distinction of having been flown by both sides. In 1918, the Bulgarian air service regularly flew a number of captured 24*bis* machines when the Germans could spare no machines for their ally.

Even stranger than a Nieuport in German markings was a German-built Nieuport. In a desperate effort to find a machine to match the *Bébé,* the German Aviation Inspectorate delivered a captured *Bébé* to the Siemens-Schuckert company late in 1915 with instructions to produce an improved copy. The Siemens-Schuckert D I which ultimately emerged in the fall of 1916 was an almost exact duplicate of the *Bébé* save for a more powerful engine, the 110 h.p. Siemens-Halske geared rotary. The D I outclassed the *Bébé,* but was outclassed itself by the Nieuport 17, and fewer than 100 were manufactured.

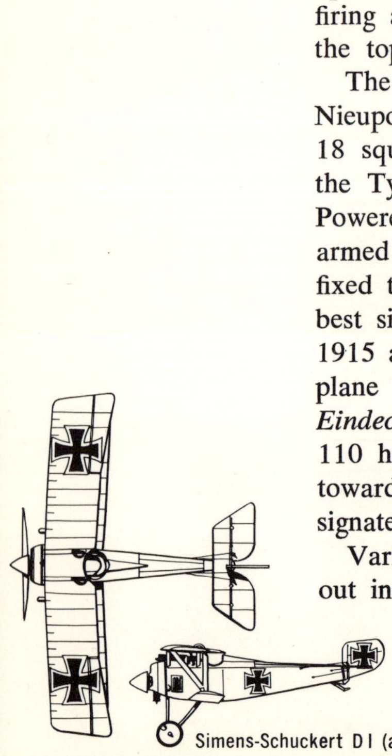
Siemens-Schuckert D I (adaptation of Nieuport 17)

24th

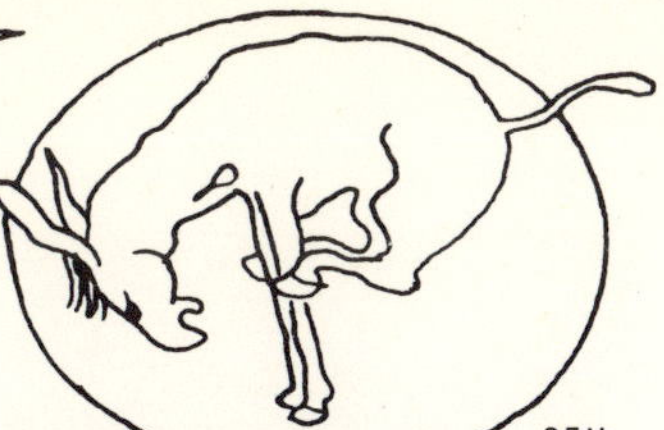
95th

27th

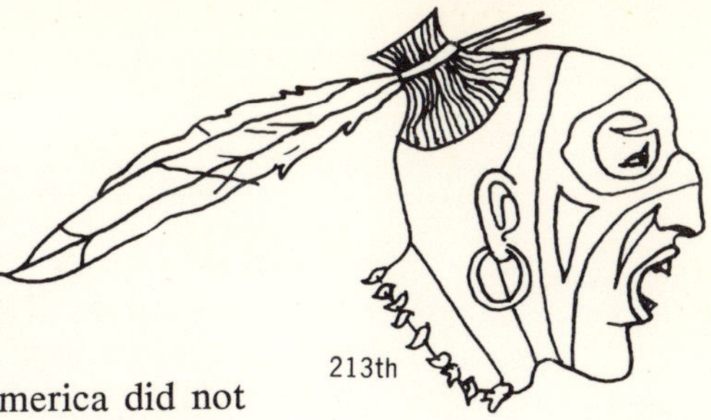
213th

9th

100th

99th

186th

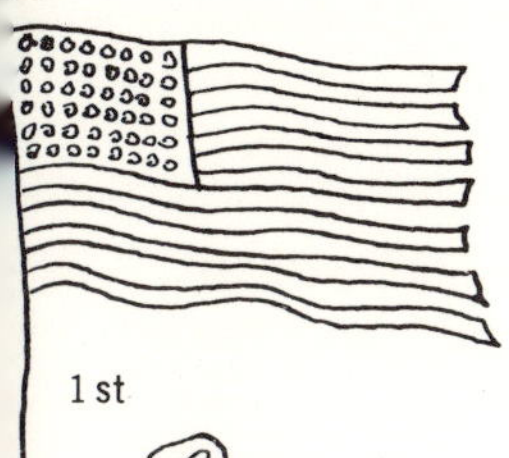
1st

25th

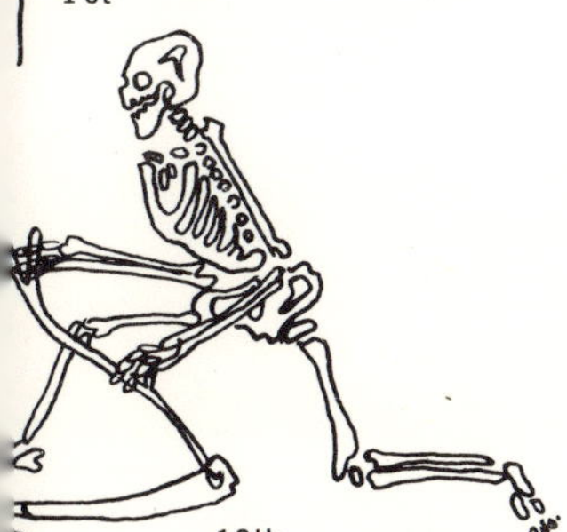
13th

135th

88th

50th

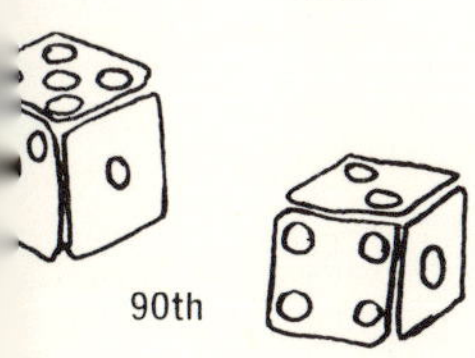
90th

AMERICAN ACES had but a short time to prove their worth; America did not really figure in the war until the last seven months. The buildup of American forces was astonishing to her allies once it had gotten started. It was to the Germans, too. In the last months of the war, the despondent question was asked over and over again by the exhausted Germans, "Where do they keep coming from?"

The Americans were like any other men, save that as a nation they had to learn everything from scratch. But the same rules applied to them as to their European contemporaries. In the air, the only men of any nation who stood a chance of surviving were those who were cool and businesslike, or better, cold and determined, who had keen eyesight and fast reflexes. And who had 100 good men behind them on the ground, because that is how many men it takes to put one man in the air.

The fighter pilots required one more attribute besides eyesight and reflexes, that rare mixture of depth perception, co-ordination, and timing that is commonly known as marksmanship. Those who are marksmen usually deprecate any suggestion that it is a rare gift, but those who are not are mystified by it. It is true that to some men it comes naturally, and one of these is George Augustus Vaughn, Jr., of New York, who served in both the R.A.F. and the U.S. Air Service and qualified as an ace in both. He simply shrugs his shoulders and says it came naturally to him. Edward Vernon Rickenbacker, the racing driver from Columbus, Ohio, who commanded the 94th Pursuit Squadron, says that shooting was sometimes as simple a matter as directing a stream of water with a garden hose. Reed McKinley Chambers, Rickenbacker's teammate from Tennessee, says that he never fired except at point blank range and then he did not need to aim.

So much for the qualities needed for survival. For outstanding success, one more was needed, an intuitive judgment of what the enemy pilots were going to do. Time after time in his wartime autobiography, *Fighting the Flying Circus,* Rickenbacker describes how he got his man by making his move a split-second before his opponent.

Rickenbacker logged more hours over the front than any other Air Service pilot, and his squadron more hours than any other American squadron. His own score of twenty-six was made in a few months, and is held by some to be the most intensive record of service of any fighter pilot in either world war.

The last American victory of the war was scored near Verdun, about noon on Sunday, 10 November 1918, by a Major Kirby, temporarily attached to Rickenbacker's 94th Pursuit Squadron. Kirby had taken off on a voluntary four-man patrol the evening before to have a look around the front. Lost in fog and separated from the rest of the flight, he had landed at the first field he had found and had spent the night there. When he took off the following morning to return to the 94th's field, he quickly ran into fog and cloudy weather again. While dodging around trying to stay in clear air, he suddenly found himself flying wing to wing with a Fokker D VII. Both pilots were taken so completely by surprise that for a few seconds neither one of them reacted and they continued to fly along in formation. The Fokker pilot broke first and dived toward the earth. Kirby dived after him. The diving chase went on all the way down to the deck where Kirby put a long burst into the Fokker from dead astern and at an altitude of no more than fifty or 100 feet. The Fokker smashed straight into the ground and Kirby made a daisy-cutting pull-out.

He returned to the 94th field to find that as he had neglected to phone in the night before everyone supposed that he was dead. To add to the surprise of his return was the news that he had scored a victory. It was confirmed by the French army four days after the armistice. It was Kirby's first and only victory.

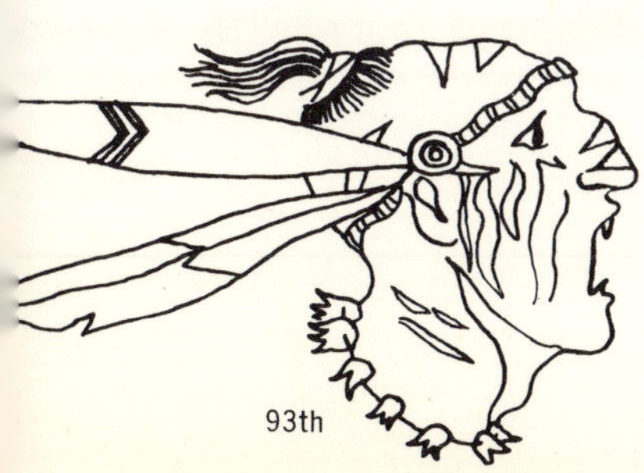
93th

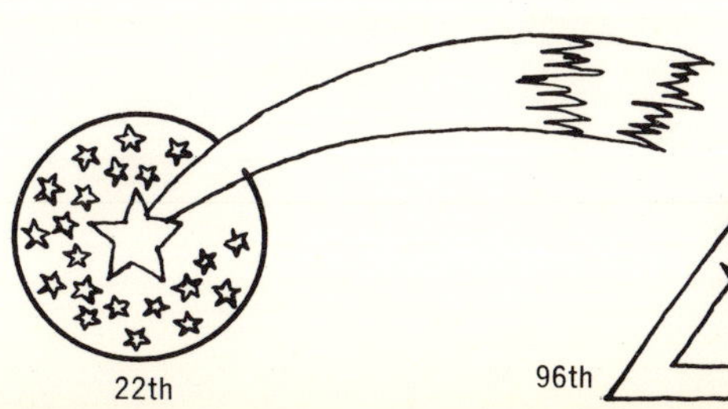
22th

96th

163th

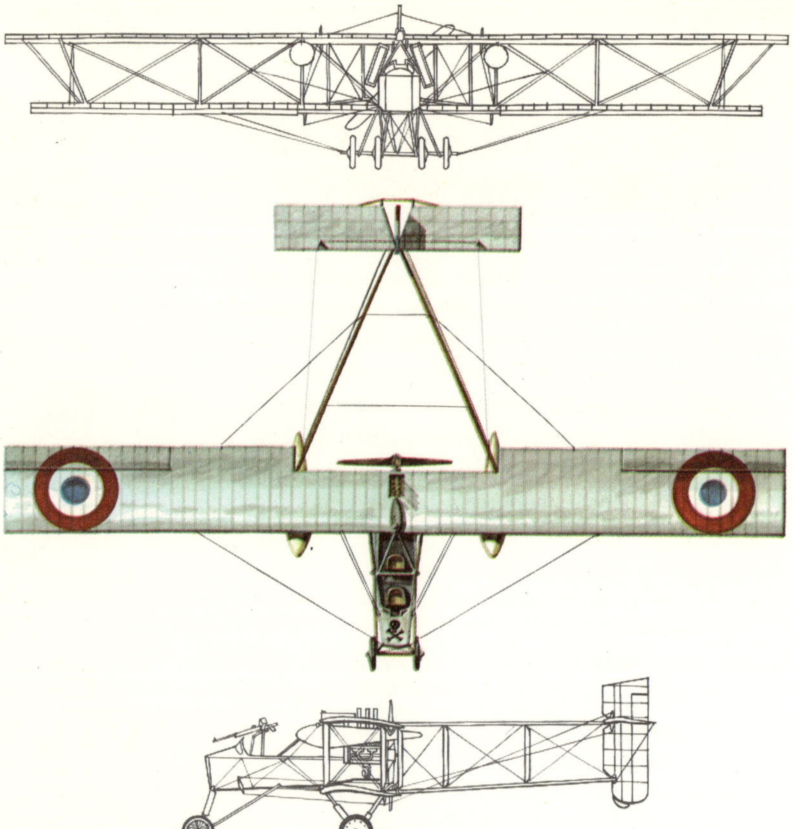

Voisin 8

LIEUTENANT CHARLES NUNGESSER was born in Paris on 15 March 1892. He learned to fly before the war but began his actual service with the 2nd Hussars, receiving his first citation when the war was still in its first month. He transfered to aviation at the end of 1914 and began operational flying at St-Pol, near Dunkirk, with V.B. 106. He scored his first victory while still flying Voisins and was shortly thereafter transferred to fighters, having completed over fifty bombing flights. His career as a fighter was remarkable for the number

of times he was wounded as well as for the number of victories—forty-five—he achieved. One victory that does not appear in his score is the one over a British pilot who attacked him in May 1917. Nungesser shot the British machine down in self-defense, supposing it was a captured machine flown by a German pilot. It was not, and it can only be guessed that the man was either stupid, horribly mistaken, or had lost his head. Nungesser had broad tricolor flashes painted on his Nieuport 24*bis* to prevent an occurrence of this tragedy. In September he was ordered on a convalescent leave. He had been injured so many times that he had to be carried to and from his aeroplane. He took off, and headed for Paris, was attacked en route by a Halberstadt scout. He and the pilot of the Halberstadt fought a long and inconclusive duel. Nungesser felt his strength ebbing and knew he must escape or die. He headed for the airfield at Le Touquet, expecting at each moment to be shot down by the man chasing him. When he touched down, the Halberstadt roared past and its pilot waved a salute.

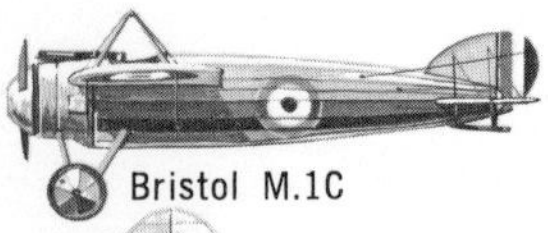

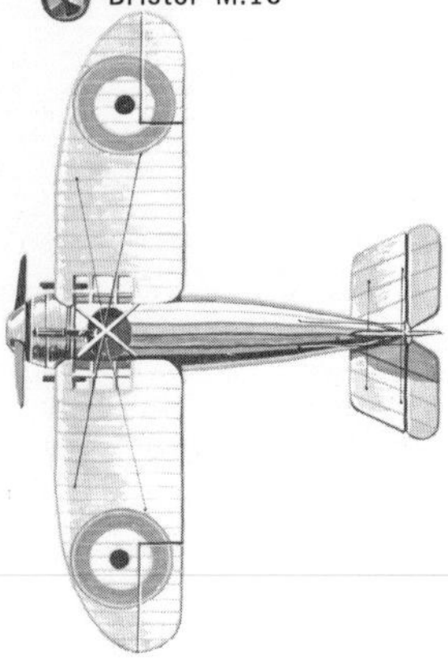

BRISTOL, or the British and Colonial Aeroplane Company, was established at Bristol, England, by Sir George White around 1909. The company first achieved prominence with the remarkable Bristol Baby Biplane early in 1914. The Baby, later known as the "B," "C," or "D" Scout, was designed by Captain F. Barnwell, as were the Bristol M.1 Monoplane and the immortal Bristol Fighter, or "Brisfit."

The Brisfit, also known as the "Biff," was the outstanding two-seat fighter of the war. It went into action in April 1917, and served to the end of the war, by which time over 3000 had been built. It remained in service with the R. A. F. until 1932, establishing one of the all-time longevity records for any aircraft.

Various engines were fitted to the Brisfit, including the 190, 220, and 274 h.p. Rolls Royce Falcons, the 150 h.p. Hispano Suiza, and the Siddeley Puma, and Sunbeam Arab engines. The only thing that remained the same was the "sting in the tail." The Bristol looked like a fighter, and many enemy pilots making a fast diving attack from astern found out too late that it was a two-seater with that sting in its tail—the rear gunner.

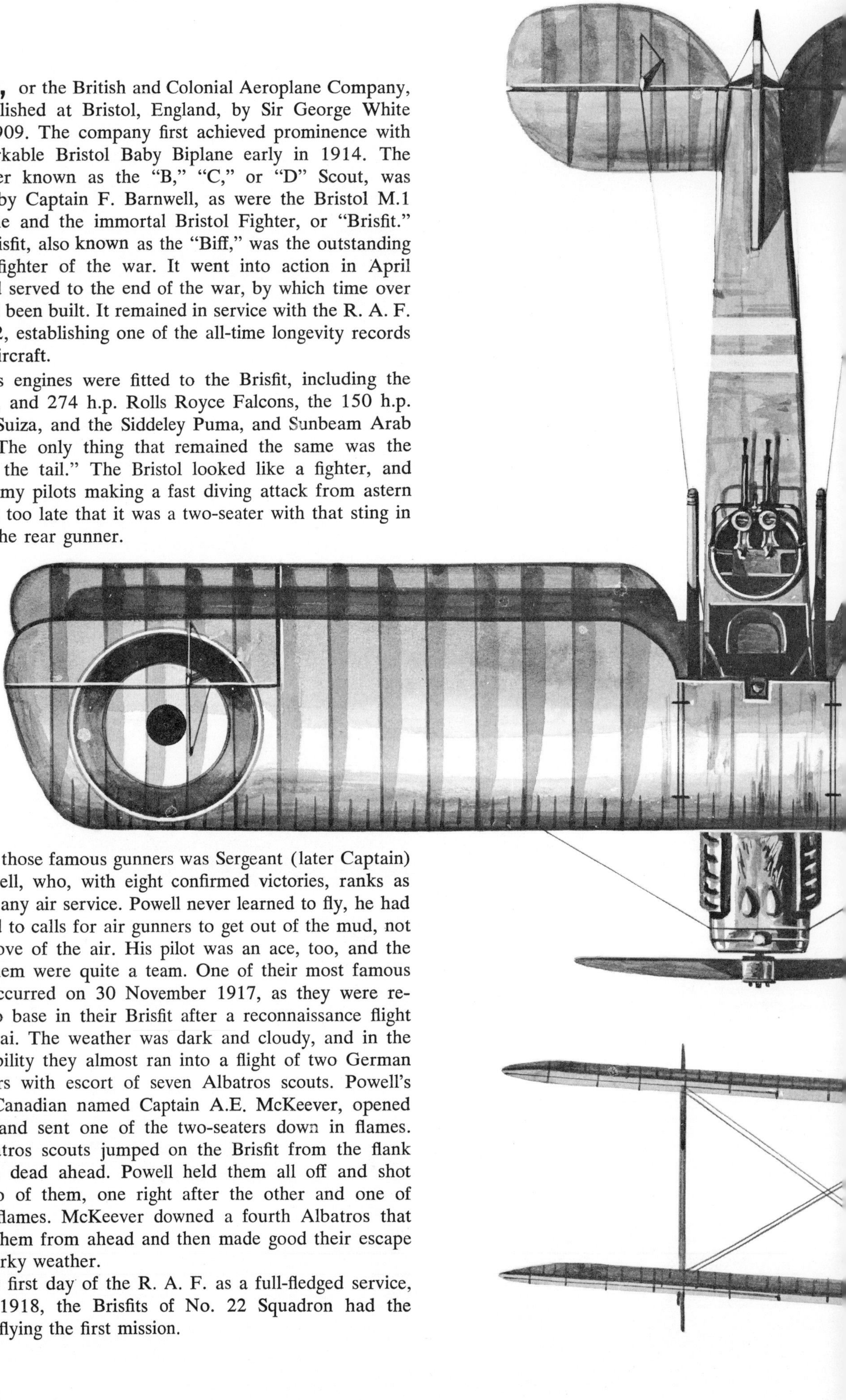

One of those famous gunners was Sergeant (later Captain) L.F. Powell, who, with eight confirmed victories, ranks as an ace in any air service. Powell never learned to fly, he had responded to calls for air gunners to get out of the mud, not for any love of the air. His pilot was an ace, too, and the pair of them were quite a team. One of their most famous explois occurred on 30 November 1917, as they were returning to base in their Brisfit after a reconnaissance flight to Cambrai. The weather was dark and cloudy, and in the poor visibility they almost ran into a flight of two German two-seaters with escort of seven Albatros scouts. Powell's pilot, a Canadian named Captain A.E. McKeever, opened fire first and sent one of the two-seaters down in flames. The Albatros scouts jumped on the Brisfit from the flank and from dead ahead. Powell held them all off and shot down two of them, one right after the other and one of them in flames. McKeever downed a fourth Albatros that came at them from ahead and then made good their escape in the murky weather.

On the first day of the R. A. F. as a full-fledged service, 1 April 1918, the Brisfits of No. 22 Squadron had the honor of flying the first mission.

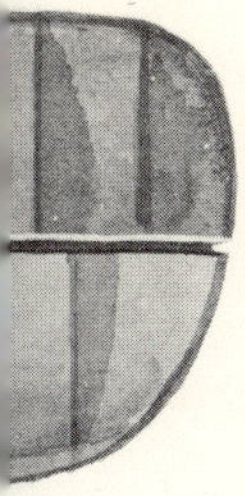

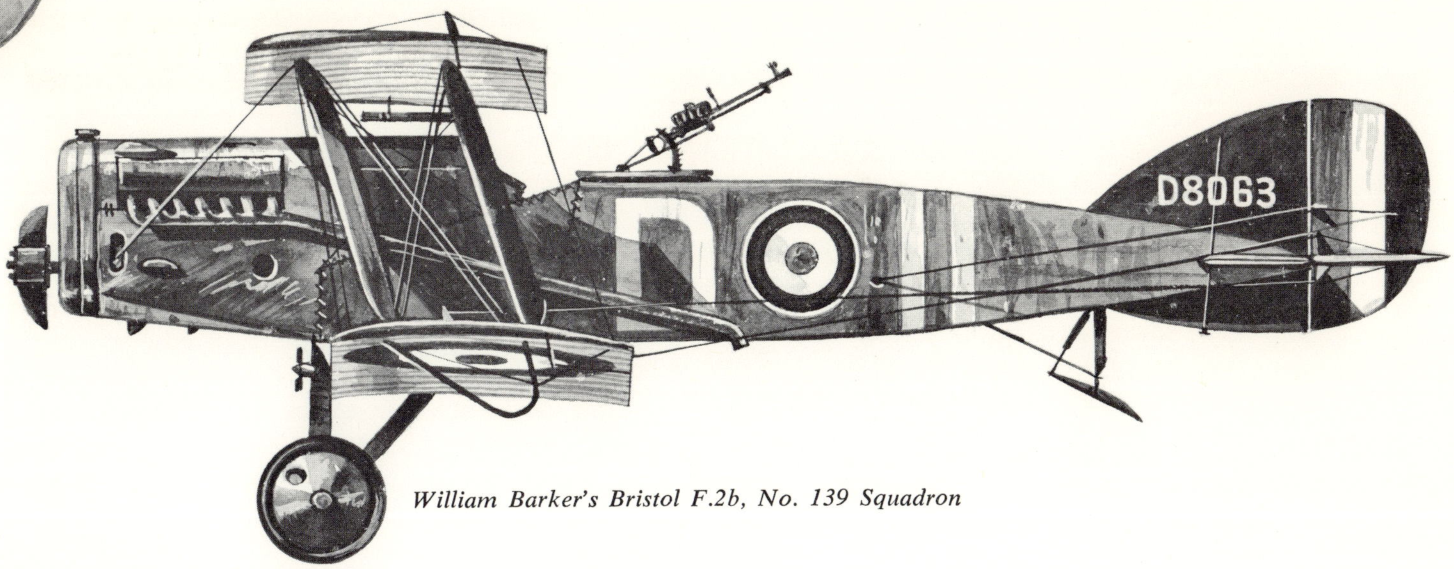

William Barker's Bristol F.2b, No. 139 Squadron

NAVAL AVIATION can be credited with having established some of the most significant policies of air power, possibly because of the wide outlook of navy men who traditionally consider the seven seas their domain. In the 1914–1918 war, long-range strategic bombing was essentially a naval innovation, and in the modern navy the aircraft carrier has virtually replaced the battleship.

The unlimited operational radius of ship-borne aeroplanes was given considerable thought by the Germans as early as the summer of 1916 when the British blockade was beginning to take effect. In an effort to give maximum effectiveness to the commerce raiders which were believed to be one of the answers to the blockade, the Germans assigned aeroplanes and crews to them. One of these auxiliary cruisers was the converted cargo steamer *Wolf,* which sailed from Kiel toward the end of November 1916. Abroad the *Wolf* was one Friedrichshafen FF 33e two-seater seaplane powered by a 150 h.p. Benz motor, equipped with a wireless receiver and sender, and armed with a small load of bombs. Throughout 1917 the *Wolf* cruised the Indian, South Pacific, and South Atlantic Oceans, and with the help of the aeroplane—dubbed the *Wölfchen,* or wolf cub—captured or sank twenty-eight Allied vessels.

In England one of the outstanding names in naval aviation, that of the Short brothers of Rochester, entered the aero industry in 1908 with a contract to build Wright Flyers on a royalty basis. Just before the outbreak of war, a Short seaplane had sucessfully performed the first torpedo-dropping experiments. Commodore Murray F. Sueter (later Rear Admiral Sir Murray Sueter), Director of the Air Department of the Admiralty, pressed for the development of

torpedo-carrying aeroplanes and the famous Short Type 184 (below) was the result. Powered with various engines of from 225 to 275 h.p., the first Short 184's entered active service in the early months of 1915. During the Dardanelles campaign they sank three enemy ships with torpedos, as well as flying many bombing, observation, and artillery-spotting missions. A Short 184 was the only seaplane to take part in the Battle of Jutland, being flown from the *Engadine* attached to the Battle Cruiser Fleet under Beatty. On the afternoon of 31 May 1916, the machine spotted three enemy cruisers and ten destroyers on a forty minute flight, in spite of bad weather and poor visibility. This reconnaissance was one of the milestones of naval aviation, for it was the first of its kind, and it demonstrated that henceforth the eyes of the navy, as those of the army, must be in the air.

Wölfchen

The Brandenburg C.C. was designed by Ernst Heinkel in 1916 for the Austrian navy. It was named after Camillo Castiglioni, the Austrian millionaire and financier, who had purchased the Brandenburg aircraft works in order to secure the design services of Heinkel. The C.C. was flown with great success by Linienschiffsleutnant" Gottfried Banfield, the Austrian ace who commanded the Trieste naval air station.

The Sopwith Baby began its naval career in 1915 as a wing warper; later models converted to ailerons. Fitted with wheels, it was the first seaplane to fly from a carrier, the H.M.S. Campania, in 1915. Sometimes required to haul two 65 lb. bombs, machine gun, ammunition, and sea-anchor, as well as fuel and pilot, the tiny aeroplane gave a rather modest performance. However, it served on reconnaissance flights continuously until the Armistice.

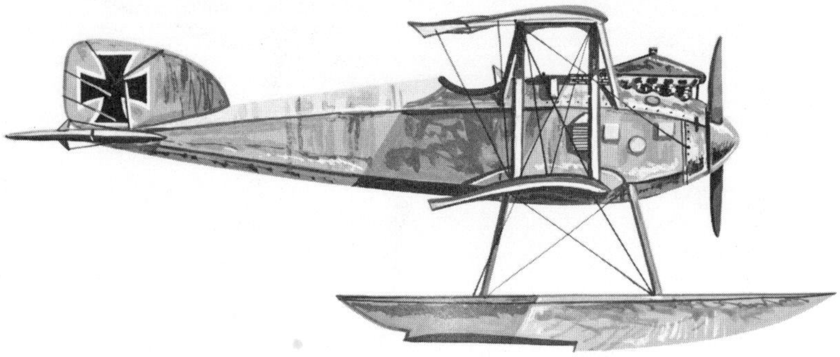

Over 100 Albatros W 4's were delivered to the German navy to fly defensive patrols over the North Sea. They were essentially enlarged D I's with floats, and for seaplanes, were capable of a fair turn of speed—100 m.p.h.—and were maneuverable and well-armed, having the two-gun arrangement of the D I's.

The Hansa-Brandenburg W 12 was designed by Heinkel on the back of a beer coaster. Although a two-seater, it could match single-seaters in speed and maneuverability, and was the machine that made the name of the German naval air station at Zeebrugge much respected by the Allies. Perhaps the most famous exponent of the W 12 was Oberleutnant Friedrich Christiansen, who commanded the air station. Among his twenty-one victories, Christiansen was acknowledged to have destroyed not only aeroplanes, balloons, and flying boats, but an airship and a submarine as well.

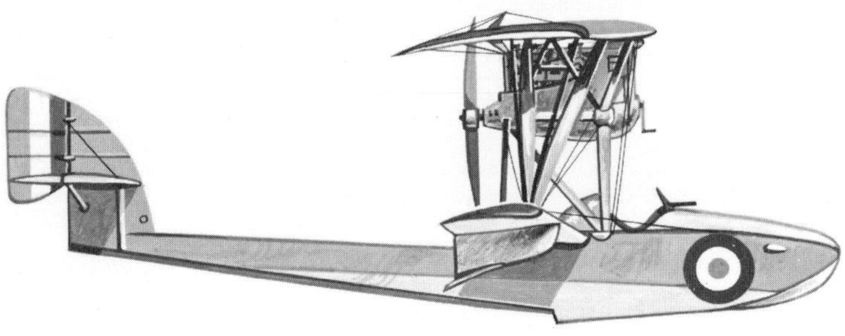

Considering that it was not only a flying boat but also a pusher, the Macchi M.5 had a phenomenal performance. It was extremely easy to handle, fully aerobatic, and had a top speed of 118 m.p.h. It was better than the Austro-Hungarian land-based fighters it faced across the Adriatic. The Macchi company of Varese began to manufacture Nieuport aeroplanes under license in 1912, and the M.5 was a descendant of a design inspired by a captured Austrian Lohner flying boat. Some 340 M.5's were delivered to the Italian navy during 1918.

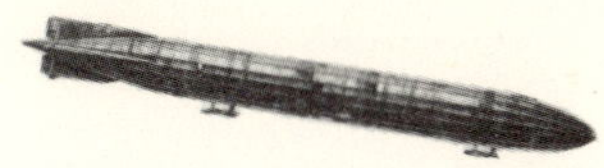

As a solution to the problem of getting first-class aeroplanes to sea in support of naval units, the towed lighter stands mid-way between the seaplane tender and the true aircraft carrier. Designed to be towed behind destroyers, the only class of ship that could work up a sufficient speed to assist an aeroplane in take off, the lighters went into service with the Royal Navy in the spring of 1918. Measuring fifty-eight feet in length with a sixteen foot beam, they supported a thirty foot take-off platform and could be towed at speeds up to thirty-two knots without throwing walls of water.

In the evening of 10 August 1918, Sir Reginald Tyrwhitt put to sea with the Harwich Force of cruisers and destroyers in the hope of luring out a Zeppelin. During the night the Force broadcast phoney wireless messages to give away its position, off Terschelling, one of the largest Frisian Islands. Just before 9:00 a.m. the following morning the L.53 commanded by *Kapitänleutnant* Eduard Prölss, a fifty-one year old Brandenburger, came snooping over at 19,000 feet.

Aboard the lighter towed behind the destroyer H.M.S. *Redoubt,* the pilot, who had made the first successful fighter take-off only a short time previously, Lieutenant Stuart D. Culley (a Group Captain in World War II), stood ready to attempt an intercept. His Sopwith 2F. 1 Camel was a naval version of the standard R.A.F. fighter, slightly shorter in the wings and with a detachable fuselage for easier shipboard stowage. The motor was started up, and as the destroyer raced into the wind, he took off.

The Zeppelin was in sight all the time, hovering over the Force at the same altitude at which it had first been sighted. Culley had little trouble maneuvering to stay with the airship as he climbed, but as he approached its altitude, he was also approaching the Camel's ceiling, and his machine began to feel sluggish at the controls. At one point the Zeppelin left him behind, but when it reversed course to cross over the Force once more, Culley came at it from dead ahead and only about 300 feet below. He pulled back on the stick, stood his machine on its nose and fired a long burst. The Camel stalled and fell away. He let it fall to pick up flying speed, straightened out, looked back at the L.53, and saw her start to burn. The flames quickly enveloped the entire ship and gutted her, leaving only a blackened and twisted skeleton that plunged into the sea and disappeared. The wreck burned out long before it finished its plunge and the plume of smoke that marked its fall was bent into a question mark by the wind.

Culley circled down to find that at various levels clouds had started to form and he could no longer spot the Force. He was not exactly certain of his position, but felt he might be able to find friendly fishing vessels near which to ditch. As he came down through a hole in the clouds he saw the Force spread out beneath him. He picked out the *Redoubt* and buzzed her, putting his Camel down in the water directly in her path. He and the aeroplane were hoisted aboard. The Camel was preserved at the Imperial War Museum and Culley was awarded the D.S.O.

3

AIRCRAFT CARRIERS have grown in two world wars from the tiny cross-Channel steamers converted by the British at the outbreak of World War I to the mighty nuclear-powered U.S.S. *Enterprise,* the largest ship in the world. The first aircraft carriers to be designed as such from the keel up, such as the British *Hermes* and the Japanese *Hosho,* were not completed until the 'twenties. The first British ship completed as an aircraft carrier, the *Ark Royal,* laid down as a collier and converted while building, was actually a seaplane tender and not an aircraft carrier in the modern sense. Her seaplanes took off from and landed on the water, and were hoisted on and off the ship with a crane. The *Ark Royal* served at Gallipoli and in the Eastern Mediterranean. After the war she was renamed *Pegasus* and was sold for merchant service in 1947.

Some of the converted cross-Channel steamers, such as the 3,000-ton *Nairana* (page 96), were also equipped with a short sloping flying-off deck foreward. Land planes were obliged to land in the water or fly to land bases after taking off.

Typical of the development of the aircraft carrier is the saga of the *Furious,* shown on these pages in the five stages of her career.

From about 1907 a new class of vessel called the light battle cruiser had been contemplated by the Royal Navy for fast raids against the Frisian Islands to secure bases for penetration of the Baltic. As it happened, no light battle cruiser was actually used for that purpose, and some of these ships

1

2

H.M.S. Furious, 1918

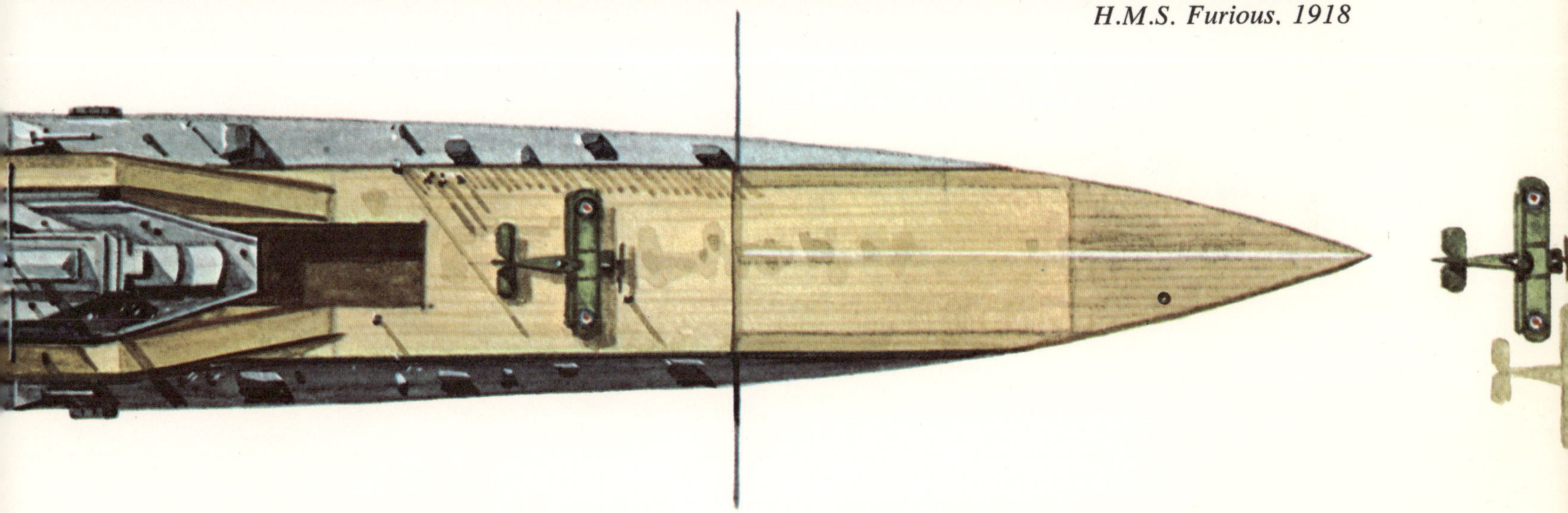

ended up in roles that the old-time navy men never imagined. The *Furious* was one of them. She was laid down as a proper light battle cruiser with a projected armament of 18-inch main batteries (1), but was converted while building to a carrier with a sloping flight deck foreward and only the after battery in place (2). In this form she was commissioned in 1917. In the spring of 1918, she emerged from alterations with the after battery removed and covered fore and aft with flight decks (3), after which she was dazzle-painted (4). Her 18-inch guns, the largest in the navy, were erroneously thought to have been installed in the shore defenses at Singapore—they were not. The 1918 conversion of the *Furious* was not altogether satisfactory since she still lacked the essential characteristic of the modern carrier—the uninterrupted flush deck. Her superstructure rose up amidships and effectively separated the two flight decks. Unsatisfactory or not, the *Furious* was the only carrier to launch a major strike during World War I. On 17 July 1918, escorted by the First Light Cruiser Squadron, she flew off seven 2F.1 Camels each armed with two 50-pound bombs, for a raid on the Zeppelin sheds at Tondern. Six of the Camels succeeded in reaching the target and blew up two new navy Zeppelins, the L.54 and L.60.

The *Furious* did not receive a proper flush deck until she was rebuilt in 1921–5 and her superstructure was moved well out to starboard (5). In this form she served throughout World War II. She was scrapped in 1949.

4

5

The only German seaplane Giant to achieve active service with the navy was the Rs. III, built in 1917 by the Zeppelin-Werke Lindau, on Lake Constance. The Giants and the contribution made by Graf von Zeppelin are briefly treated on page 106, but the Rs. III merits special attention as a most interesting and unusual aeroplane.

Professor Claudius Dornier, who was born in 1884 and at the time of writing is living in retirement in Switzerland, joined the design staff of the Zeppelin Airship Factory in 1910 with several years of experience in steel construction to his credit. He was, in those days, a daring experimenter who possessed the ability to bend ideas to practical applications. His genius soon came to the attention of Zeppelin himself and he was transferred to the design bureau of the major Zeppelin works on Lake Constance. Shortly after the outbreak of the war, Graf von Zeppelin commissioned Dornier to undertake the designing of an all-metal seaplane, and put him in charge of the design staff of a company formed expressly for this project, the Zeppelin-Werke Lindau, which was located in one of the old airship sheds at Lindau on Lake Constance.

The actual construction of the Rs. III was begun at the end of 1916, was completed in the autumn of 1917, and the machine's maiden flight was made on 4 November 1917. While highly individual in layout, there was nothing fanciful in the Rs. III, for the brilliant young Dornier was too practical in his creativity and knowledgeable in his ingenuity to waste time with any half-baked flashes of inspiration.

The Rs. III was composed of three parts: a boat-shaped hull, a fuselage and wing assembly, and, slung between these, the power pods. Four 245 h.p. Maybach engines were mounted in tandem on heavy streamlined struts, each pair of engines being composed of one tractor and one pusher, both enclosed in a streamlined nacelle. The four engines were much closer to the fore and aft axis of the ship than was possible in other multi-engined machines because of this tractor-pusher arrangement, and the asymmetrical thrust caused by the shutting down of one engine was correspondingly reduced. With this flight characteristic, it was possible, on long flights, to "rest" the engines in rotation and so conserve fuel.

The boat-shaped hull, stable in the water because of its ample beam, was fitted with two cockpits, one forward and one amidships, for the pilots and flight mechanics respectively. Forward of the pilot's cockpit was a gunner's position. The pilot's eye-level was about eight feet above the water when the machine was resting on the water and he enjoyed a far more comfortable "feel" of his true position in taking off and landing than did the pilots of some Giant aeroplanes who perched twenty or more feet off the ground. The flight mechanic's cockpit was set

R43

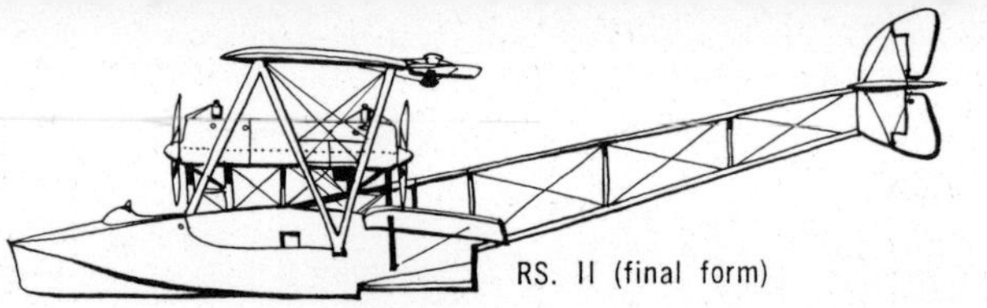

RS. II (final form)

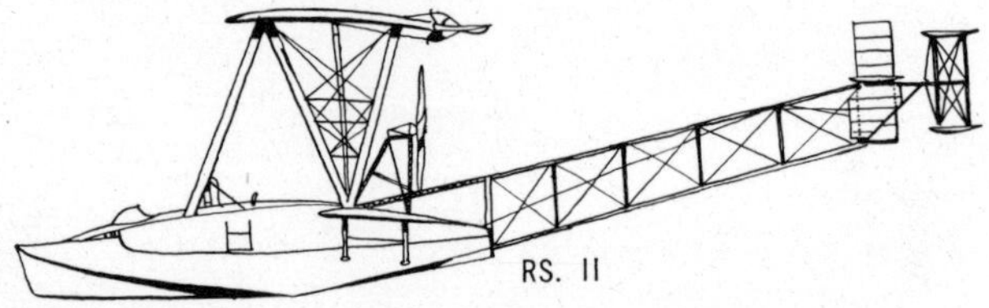

RS. II

between eight 380 litre (100 gallon) fuel tanks, and from this position the mechanics regulated the flow of fuel from the main tanks to the gravity tanks in the nacelles.

The nacelles enclosed all but the cylinder heads of the engines and the car-type radiators. Ladders led from the flight mechanic's cockpit to each nacelle, and a third ladder led to the underside of the wing center section where a trapdoor gave access to the fuselage. In the fore part of the fuselage was located a soundproofed wireless cabin, and just aft of mid-span a gunner's position was rigged atop the fuselage. At the rear of the fuselage was the tail, a biplane affair with two identical planes and elevators of roughly rectangular form with raked tips rather like the wings of an S.E.5. As a matter of fact, the biplane tail of the Rs. III was larger than the wings of an S.E.5.

For its great size, the Rs. III was a pleasant machine to fly; its well-designed hull relinquished its grip on the water smoothly on take-off, it responded to the controls without the pilot having to wrestle them, and when the load was properly distributed it could be flown on long patrols without fatigue.

In February 1918 it was delivered to the navy for operational use, the delivery flight from Lake Constance to the Frisian Islands being made non-stop in a few minutes over seven hours at an average speed of seventy-five m.p.h. The navy tested the Rs. III extensively after delivery, accepting her officially in June 1918. It is said that between then and the armistice, she flew many ten to twelve hour observation missions. After the war she was flown on numerous mine-spotting patrols during the clearance of the North Sea. She was finally broken up by order of the Allies in July 1921.

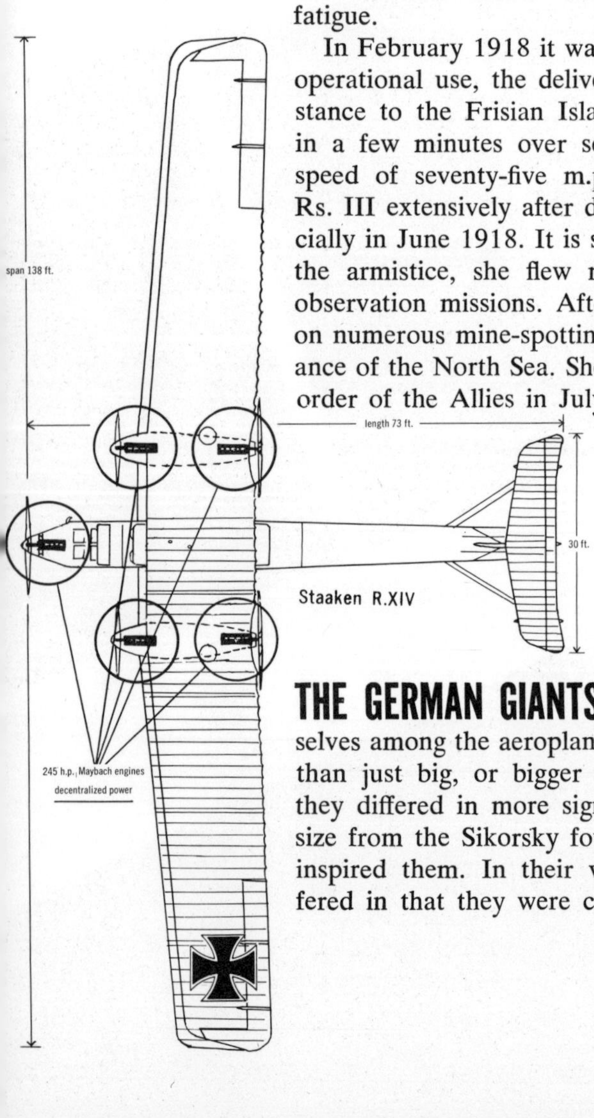

Staaken R.XIV

THE GERMAN GIANTS were a class by themselves among the aeroplanes of the Great War. More than just big, or bigger than any other machines, they differed in more significant aspects than mere size from the Sikorsky four-engined bombers which inspired them. In their very conception, they differed in that they were created to serve a strategic rather than a tactical purpose. Something has already been said about the nature of strategy and tactics, so it will suffice to say that the Giants were the only German aeroplanes built during the war for the purpose of long-range bombing raids against industry and political nerve centers.

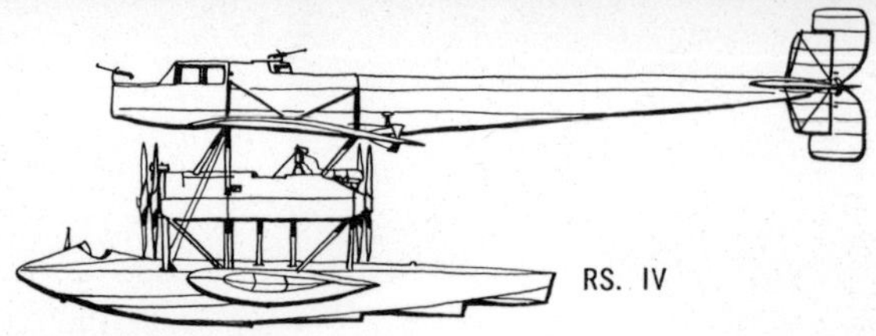

RS. IV

Several major German aircraft constructors built Giants, but the most successful of the class were those built by the Zeppelin-Werke Staaken, a company formed by the same Graf von Zeppelin who created the great airships that bear his name. The Graf was a visionary and imaginative man who had already lost interest in his Gothic monster, the Zeppelin, before the war began. Although the German army and navy placed considerable hope in the psychological profit of a Zeppelin campaign, the Graf was keenly aware of the severe limitations of the Zeppelins in a military context. They were dangerously inflammable, slow, cumbersome, expensive and time-consuming to produce, fragile for their bulk, and able to carry only a small fraction of their own weight.

When a proposed six-engine seaplane capable of crossing oceans came to his attention just before the war, the Graf saw in such a conception a long-range carrier to transport large bomb loads to vital targets far from the battle front. To develop such an aeroplane, a company was formed by Zeppelin and Robert Bosch, the founder of the Bosch company of Stuttgart. The company, located in the Berlin suburb of Staaken, was called Zeppelen-Werke Staaken. In September 1914, work commenced on the first Staaken Giant.

Construction and delivery specifications for German military aircraft were laid down by the aviation inspectorate in Berlin, which, late in 1915, expanded the air service establishment to accord permanent status to the Giants, or "R-planes." (*Riesenflugzeug*—Giant aeroplane.) By that time, the R-planes were definitely superseding Zeppelin in any consideration of long-range flight, since just about everybody was finally disillusioned with them.

The aviation inspectorate specified that R-planes were to be equipped with powerful engines, oxygen apparatus, navigational instruments, and communication devices; they were to be large enough for their crews to walk around in them to attend to defense, servicing; and navigation; and they were to have engines that were accessible for in-flight maintenance. This last was one of the most significant of the particularities of R-planes. Some were designed in such a way that the engines were buried in the fuselage, turning their propellers by various means of drive-linkage, and some had paired engines in nacelles which were large enough to accommodate bodily the mechanics who attended to in-flight servicing and repairs.

Staaken R. XIV is the type-name of a series of

three machines numbered R.43 to R.45. The R-planes were usually referred to by their individual serial numbers. The R.43, delivered in April 1918, was the only R-plane to be shot down by fighters. (See illustration, pages 104–105.) The R.43 was powered by five 245 h.p. Maybach engines, mounted one in the nose and two each in two nacelles between the wings. It had an all-up weight of 31,862 pounds, of which roughly one ton was bombs. It had a wing spread of 138 feet and a length of about seventy-four. Parachutes, regularly carried for all nine crew members, were operated by means of static lines running to fixed stations. The R.43 was defensively armed with six machine guns arranged in pairs in dorsal and ventral positions, and singly in the two upper wing positions.

The R.43 was on a night bombing mission on 10 August 1918, when it was caught by British searchlights in the neighborhood of Abbeville. It was held by a chain of lights until the unusual glare attracted several British night fighters who were prowling around in the vicinity. One of these pilots was Captain A.B. Yuille of No. 151 Squadron,

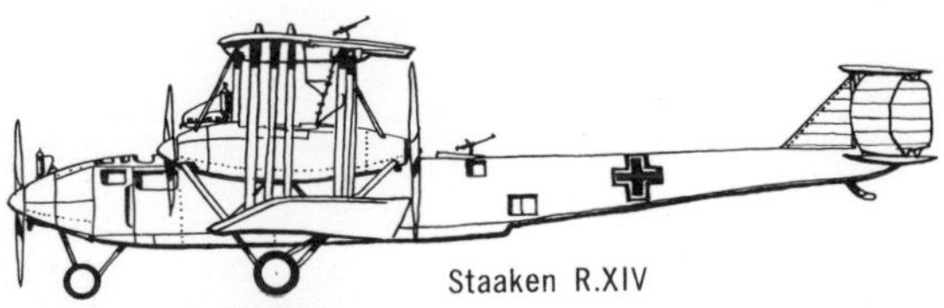
Staaken R.XIV

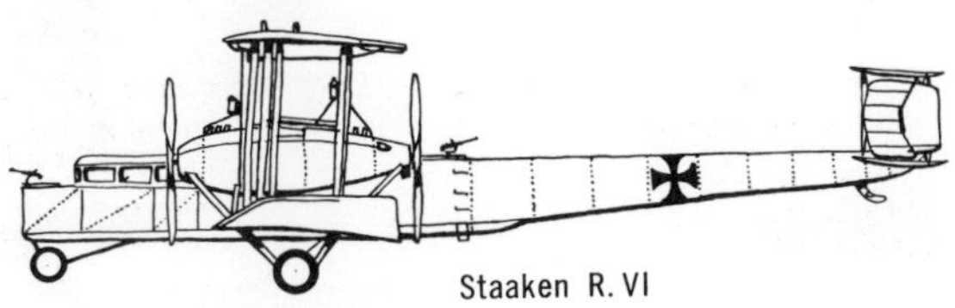
Staaken R. VI

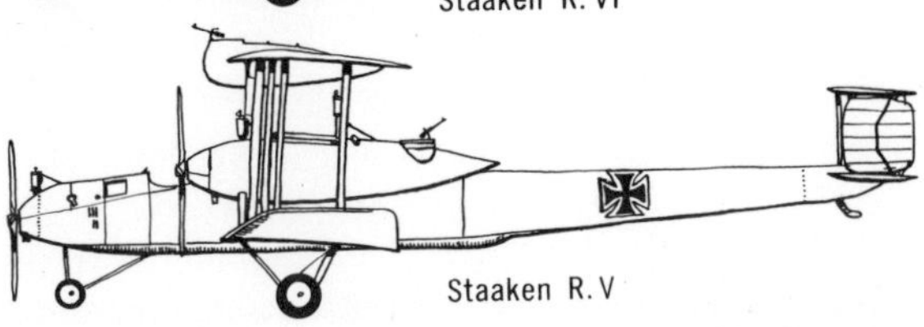
Staaken R. V

R.A.F. This squadron, at that time under the command of Major C.J.Q. Brand, was the first night fighter unit in the R.A.F., and scored a total of twenty-one confirmed victories in the four months of its active service. Captain Yuille himself achieved a score of six.

When Yuille got close enough to see the R.43, he worked himself into a good position behind and below the Giant's tail. He refrained from firing until he had closed to within twenty-five yards, and then with five short bursts stopped one engine and started a fire in the fuselage.

The R.43 went over on one wing and started down, diving more and more steeply, and then began to break up in the air. The entire crew perished in the flaming wreck.

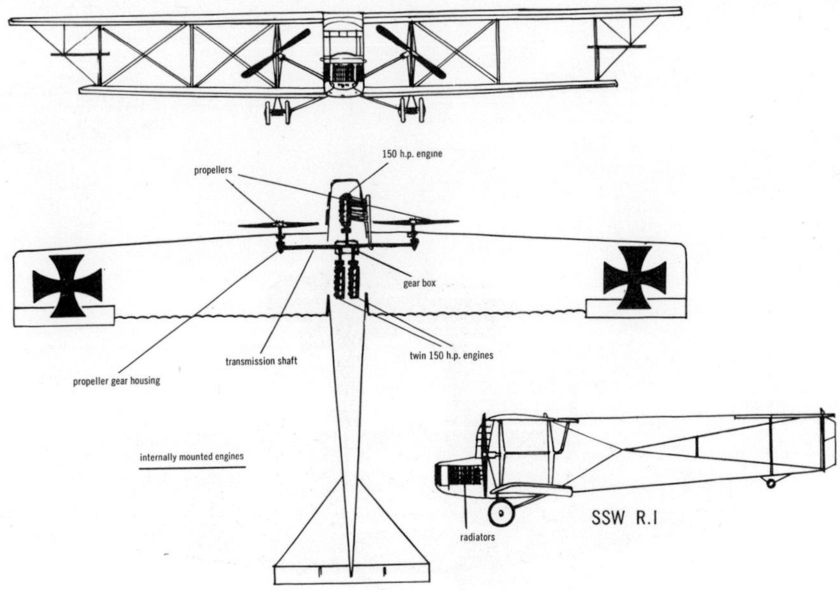

The Staaken R.V Giant is shown at the bottom of pages 108–109 in scale with two single-seaters and a number of bombers of both Allied and Central Power air services. Staaken R.V is a type name of a series of which only one aeroplane, the R.13, was built, although it is similar to a larger series designated R.VI. The R.V (or R.13) entered active service on the Western Front in the fall of 1917, being based in the vicinity of Ghent, and it was flown on a number of bombing raids against targets in England and France. It survived the war, and is supposed to have been turned over to an Allied commission after the armistice.

The R.V was one of the largest of the R-planes, with a span of 138 feet 5½ inches and a length of over seventy-five feet. (Compare, for example, the Avro Lancaster with a span of 102 feet, or the Flying Fortress with a span of 104 feet.) It was powered by five 245 h.p. Maybach engines, all of which were tractors driving fourteen foot propellers. The engines were arranged one in the nose of the fuselage and two each in nacelles between the wings. The nacelle engines were disposed in tandem, the drive shaft of the rearmost passing under the foremost into their common gear box.

In the leading edge of the upper wing was a large gravity tank whose plywood fairing also enclosed a gunner's position called the "swallow's nest." There were also dorsal and ventral machine gun positions, and the after portion of each engine nacelle was fitted with a cockpit and ring-mounted machine gun.

The R.V grossed an all-up weight of fourteen tons, of which nearly four tons was useful load. With a wing loading of 8.6 pounds per square foot, the aerodynamic qualities of the R.V's design compare favorably with any German fighter aeroplane with the exception of the Fokker Triplane (shown in scale to the left). The Triplane and the Sopwith Camel (right, shown as a night fighter) were the champions of the war for handiness and maneuverability. Both were light but strong, well-designed, compact, and possessed of markedly lighter wing loadings (both around 6.4 pounds per square foot) than their contemporaries.

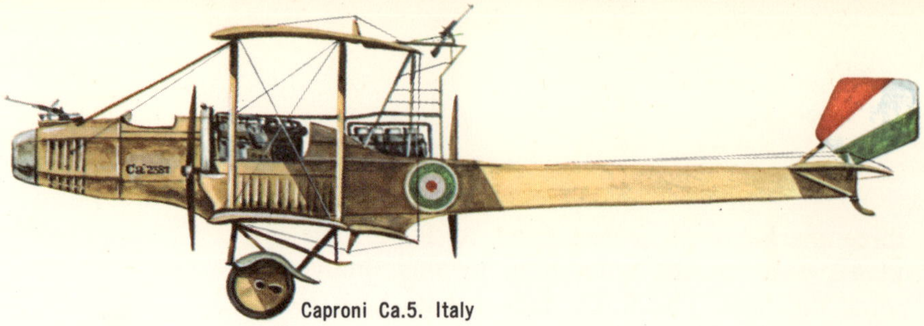

Caproni Ca.5. Italy

Handley Page 0/400, Great Britain

Gotha G V. Germany

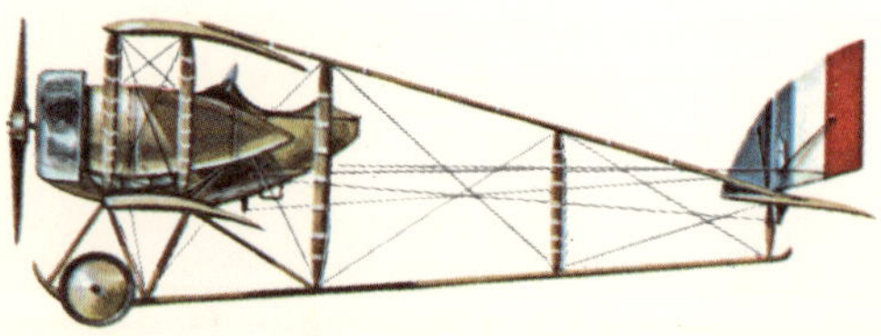

Caudron G.4. France

D.H.4. Great Britain (U.S. First Marine Aviation Force)

Bréguet 14B.2. France (U.S. 96th Aero Squadron)

Staaken R.V (Giant). Germany

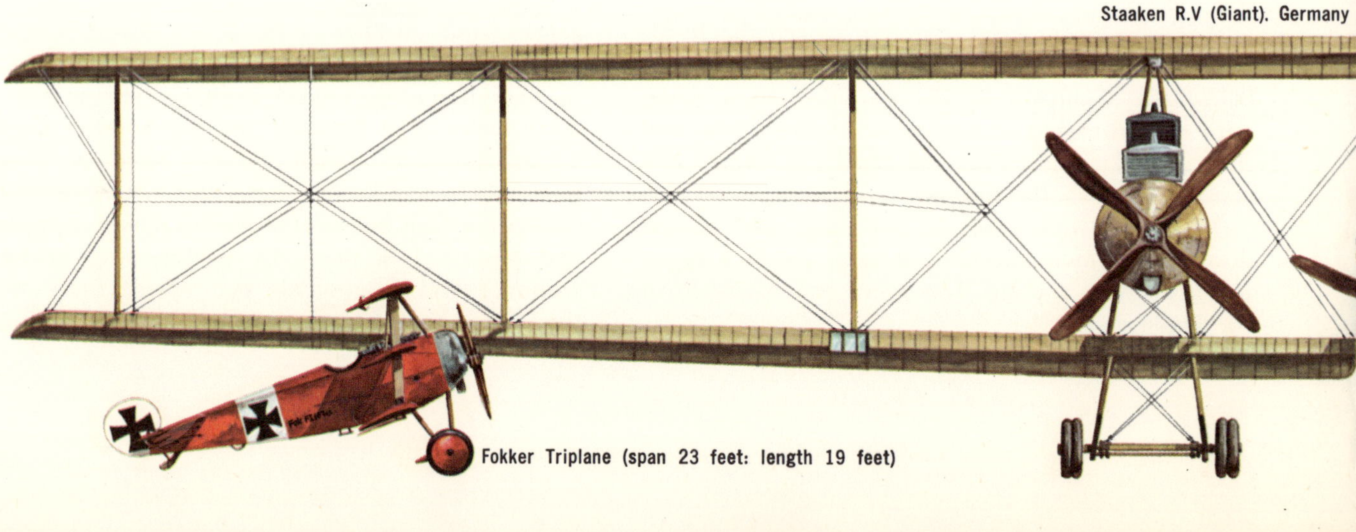

Fokker Triplane (span 23 feet: length 19 feet)

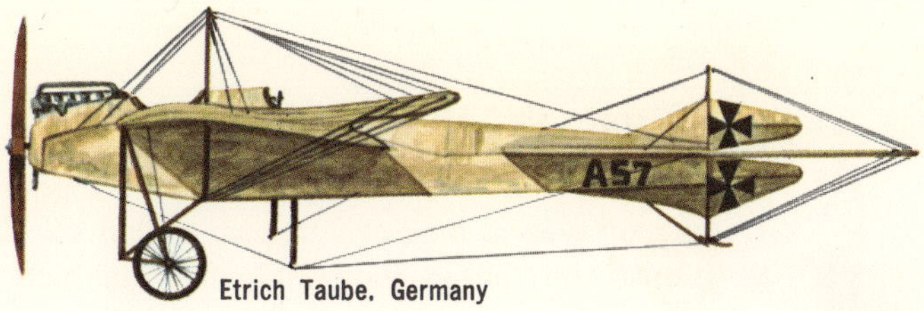

Etrich Taube. Germany

Hansa-Brandenburg C I. Austria

A.E.G. G IV. Germany

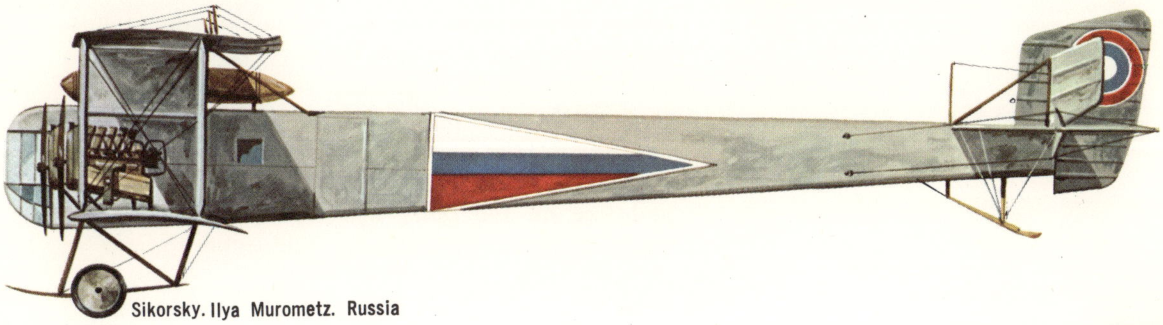

Sikorsky. Ilya Murometz. Russia

Bréguet 5. France

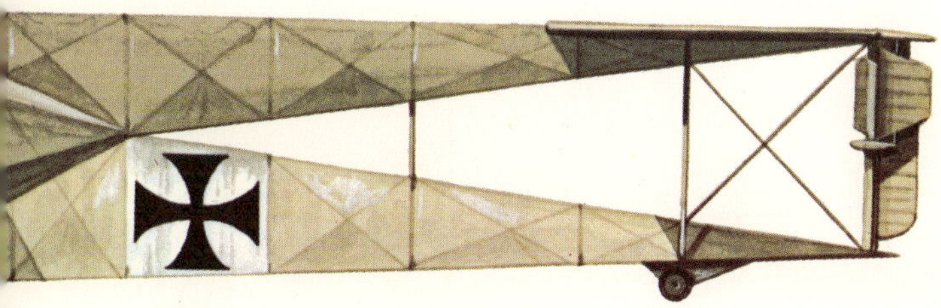

Siemens-Schuckert SSW R.I (Giant). Germany

Farman F.40. France (in Belgian colors)

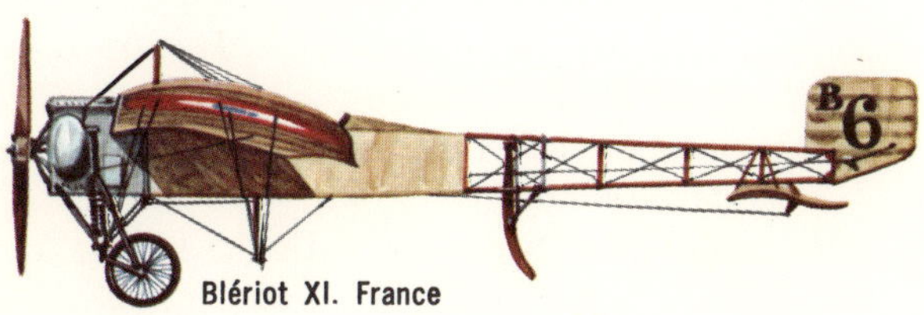

Blériot XI. France

(span 138 feet 5 inches: length 75 feet 7 inches)

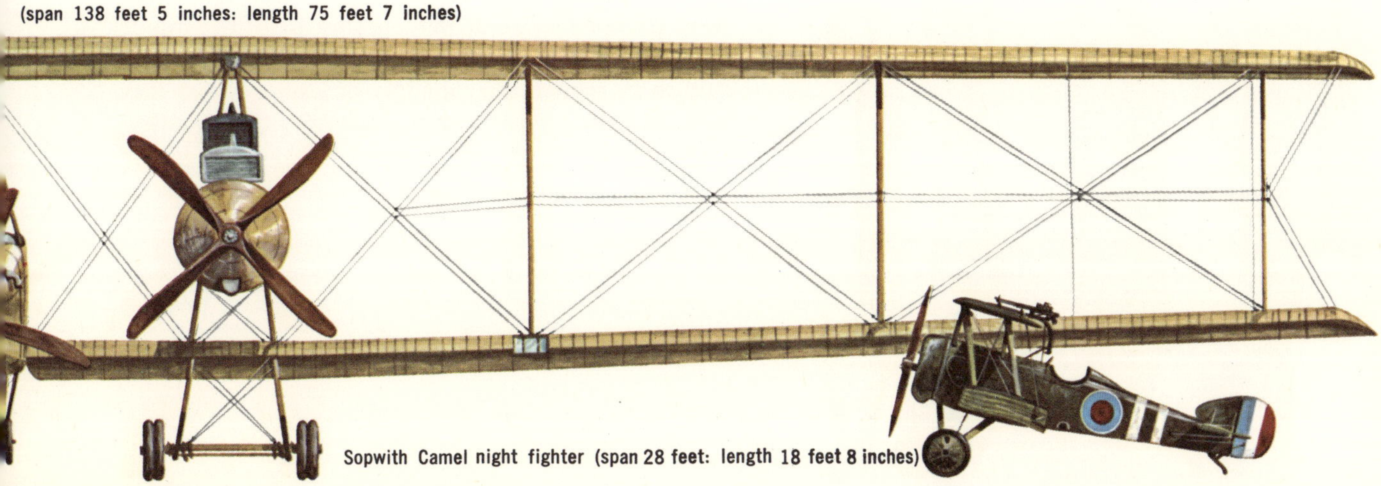

Sopwith Camel night fighter (span 28 feet: length 18 feet 8 inches)

AERIAL MISSILES dropped during the war ranged in size from a few ounces to 3,360 pounds. The former was a medieval device called a *"fléchette,"* a steel dart about three-eighths of an inch in diameter and about six inches long. Bundles of *fléchettes* were carried in boxes in the observer's cockpit of two-seaters and dumped over the side wherever appropriate targets could be found—troops, animal-drawn transport, or even observation balloons. The rare occasions when such haphazard missiles had any effect were confined to the early months of the war. The rapid development of antiaircraft artillery and the quick advance of such protective measures as camouflage and dispersion foiled the use of *fléchettes* and forced the development of real bombs whose effectiveness did not depend on direct hits. An intermediate step was taken by the French who for a time made a practice of dropping artillery shells as bombs, particularly the 3-inch, 3½-inch, and 6-inch sizes. The shell of the famous "75" was very effective. It was equivalent to a 3-inch shell and like all the other artillery shells so used, it could be fitted with tail fins and either instant or delayed fuses.

In England, it was the R.N.A.S. that pioneered bomb-dropping. They carried out the first British raids of the war against Zeppelin sheds with small twenty-pounders. The R.F.C. had developed no techniques other than reconnaissance and observation and so had no bombs or bombing experience when the war started. The Royal Laboratory at Woolwich and the Royal Aircraft Factory at Farnborough began working on bomb designs as soon as the war started, and by late 1915 had developed bombs weighing up to 585 pounds, while the R.F.C. had acquired experience enough to drop them.

The development of bombs was not always toward larger and larger sizes. In the spring of 1917 the R.F.C. began using an excellent small bomb called the Cooper bomb which was carried by fighters on a variety of low-level missions. The 112-pound medium bomb of the Royal Laboratory and the 230-pound bomb of the Royal Aircraft Factory were dropped in great numbers by British bombing machines in 1917–1918. The jumbo "S.N." series—said to be named after the city of Essen, where they were first dropped—were produced for the Handley-Page machines of the Independent Air Force in

661 lb. P.u W. bomb

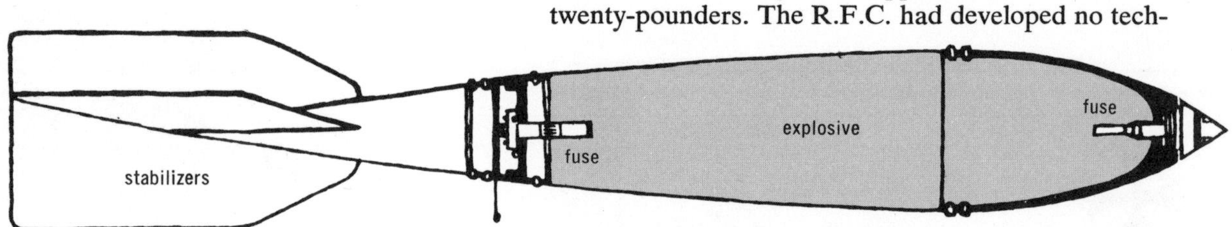

2205 lbs.
27 lbs.
661 lbs.
220 lbs.
110 lbs.

German P.u.W. high-explosive aerial bombs

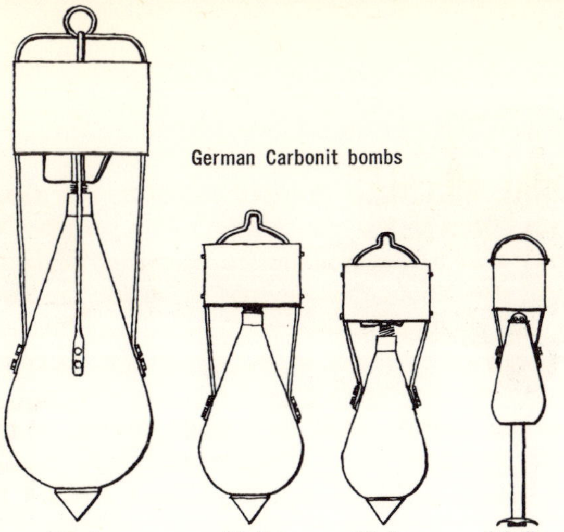

German Carbonit bombs

110 lbs.   44 lbs.   22 lbs.   9.9 lbs.

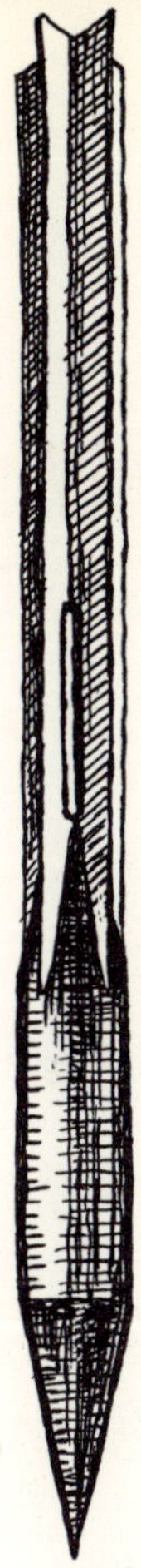

British fléchette (actual size)

1918. The S.N. bombs came in sizes of 1600, 1650, 1700, and 1800 pounds.

A German army department called Artillery Test Commission (A.P.K.—*Artillerie-Prüfungs-Kommission*) developed the first true aerial bomb for the German air service in 1913. Consisting of a cast iron shell and an impact fuse, and produced in eleven- and twenty-two-pound sizes (five and ten kilos), the A.P.K. bomb was too primitive even by 1914 standards to see service in the war.

The successor to the A.P.K. was the Karbonit series which had tear-drop-shaped bodies with cylindrical tail fins. For better penetration they were equipped with steel-tipped noses. They were armed by means of propeller-activated fuses, charged with T.N.T., and produced in 4.5-, 10-, 20-, and 50-kg. sizes. These bombs were generally carried vertically in bomb bays and were used from the end of 1914 until 1916. The Test Establishment and Works for Aviation Troops (P.u.W.—*Prüfanstalt und Werft der Fliegertruppe*) superseded the army A.P.K. with the growth of the German air service as an independent arm. The P.u.W. developed a modern bomb in 1916 which differed from the Karbonit in that its body was a streamlined steel torpedo instead of a cast iron lump. Its aerodynamic qualities were the result of serious study by its designers who thus produced a missile that would fall faster and truer than previous bombs. Its fins were so arranged that they imparted a high speed spinning motion to the bomb which stabilized it in flight, as the rifling of a bore imparts stability to an artillery shell. The spinning also armed the bombs by means of a centrifugal activator. The P.u.W. bombs were produced in various sizes from roughly thirty pounds to something over a ton, and were carried horizontally in bomb bays.

The biggest bomb designed during the war was a 3060–pound monster, so large that only one aeroplane—the Handley Page V/1500—could carry it, and then only one at a time.

British bombs

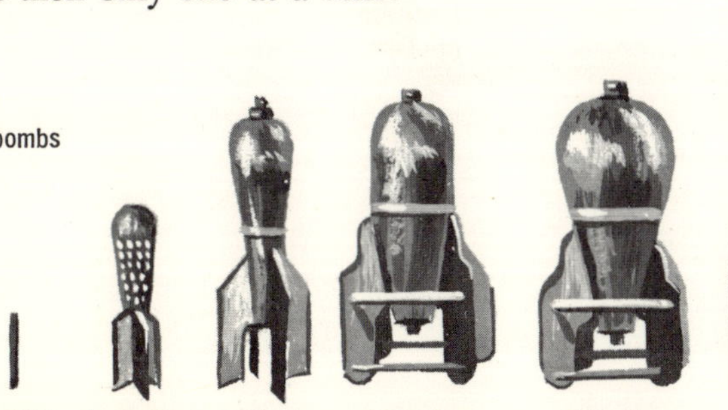

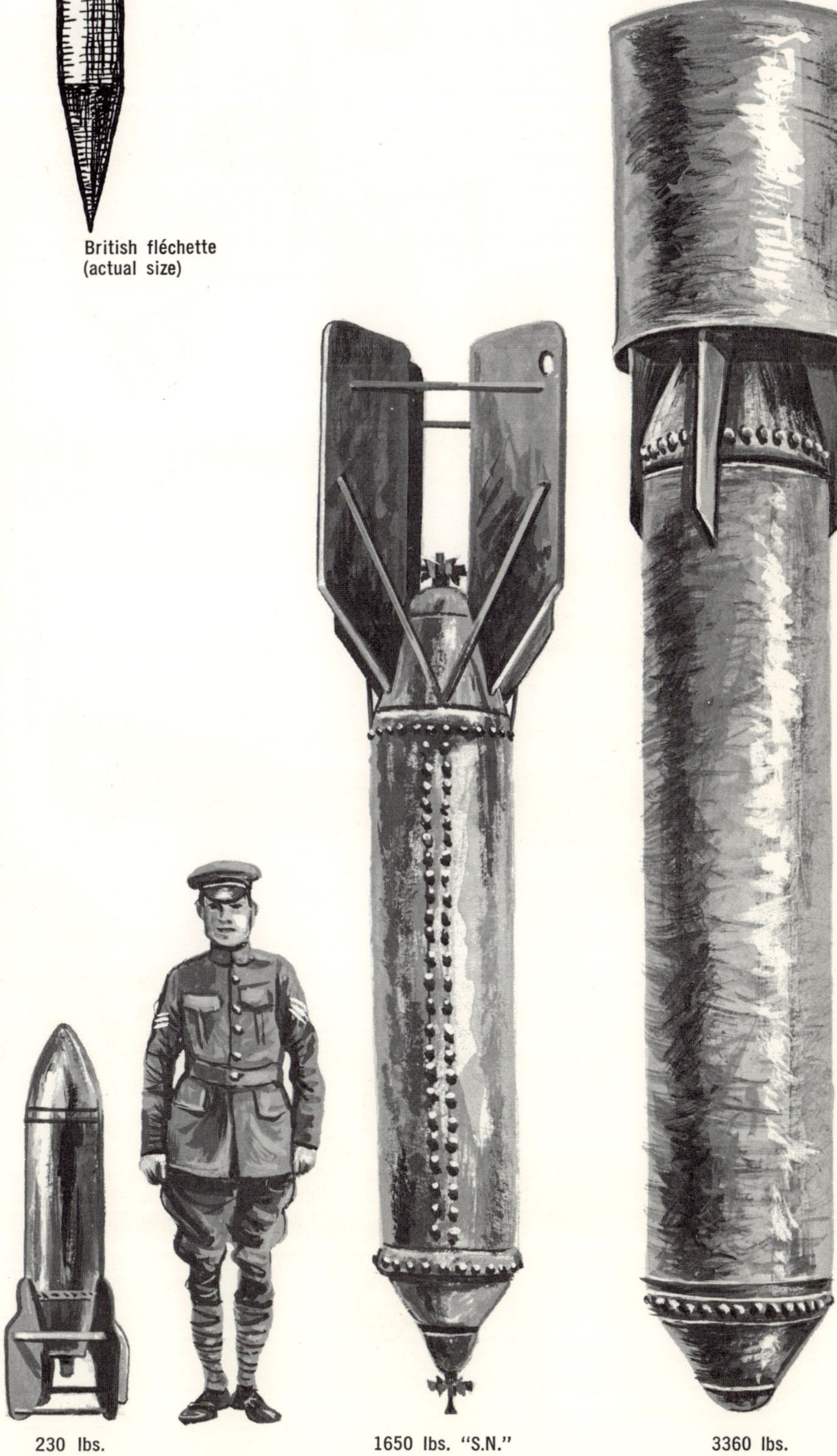

"B.I.B." incendiary   incendiary   65 lbs.   100 lbs.   112 lbs.   230 lbs.   1650 lbs. "S.N."   3360 lbs.

D.H. 10. Great Britain

Zeppelin Staaken R. VI. Germany

Handley Page V/1500. Great Britain

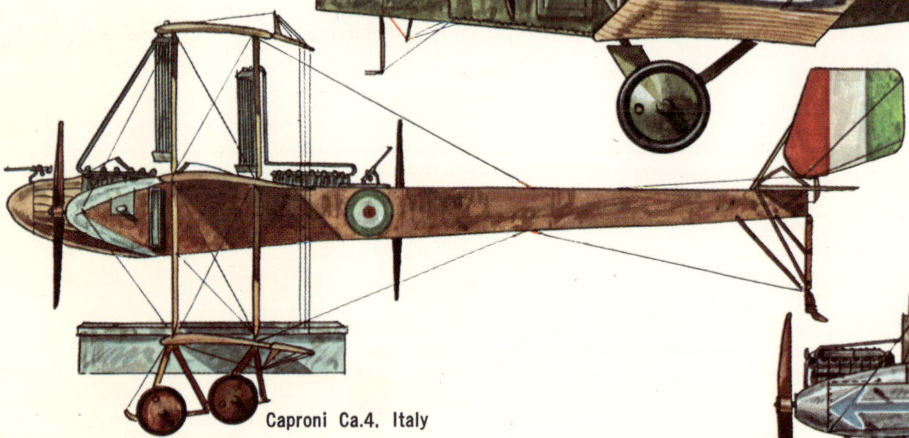

Caproni Ca.4. Italy

D.H. 9. Great Britain

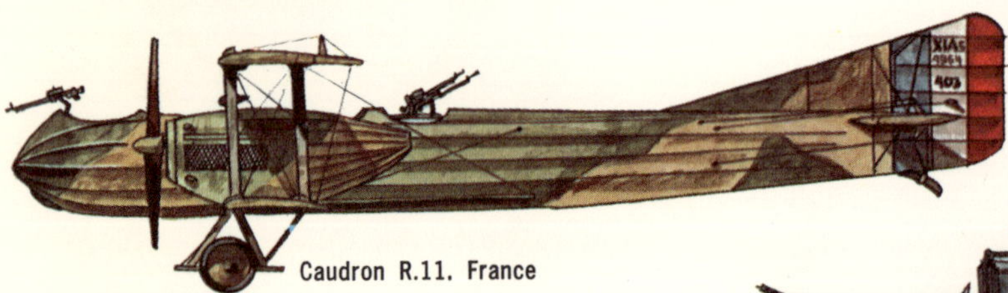

Caudron R.11. France

Friedrichshafen G III. Germany

Blackburn Kangaroo. Great Britain

D.H. 10—Great Britain. 1918. Two 400 h.p. Liberty engines. The D.H. 10 Amiens was too late to see operational service in the war. It was a good design that offered a ceiling of 20,000 feet, a top speed of 131 m.p.h. at sea level, and a bomb load of 900 pounds for 800 h.p.

Zeppelin Staaken R.VI—Germany. 1917-1918. Four 245 h.p. Maybach engines. The R.VI was one of the Giants to carry the 1,000 kg. (2200 pound) bomb, the largest bomb actually used during the war.

Handley Page V/1500—Great Britain. 1918. Four 375 h.p. Rolls Royce engines. The V/1500 arrived too late to see active service in the war, but had it been used, it would have been possible to raid targets in Germany from bases in England, as it had a range of 1300 miles and an endurance of seventeen hours.

Caproni Ca.4—Italy. 1918. Three 270 h.p. Isotta-Fraschini engines. Maximum bomb load for this unusual triplane bomber was a ton and a half.

D.H.9—Great Britain. 1918. 230 h.p. B.H.P. engine. The D.H.9 was not bad as a two-seater design. With its two cockpits moved together, it was an improvement over the D.H.4 whose cockpits were so far apart that communication between pilot and observer was impossible. It was the engine of the D.H.9 that gave all the trouble—the B.H.P. (Beardmore-Halford-Pullinger) was appallingly undependable and caused more losses than enemy action.

Caudron R.11—France. 1918. Two 220 h.p. Hispano Suiza engines. The R.11 served as a bomber, but did its best work as an escort for French day bombers, its guns manned by the sharpshooters of the French air service.

Friedrichshafen G III—Germany. 1917–1918. Two 260 h.p. Mercedes engines. The Friedrichshafen works on Lake Constance was another creation of the ubiquitous Graf von Zeppelin, and the company's G III, with the Gotha G IV, formed the backbone of the German bomber force.

Blackburn Kangaroo—Great Britain. 1918. Two 250 h.p. Rolls Royce engines. Only a few Kangaroos were delivered to the R.A.F., and these served mostly on anti-submarine patrols over the Channel and North Sea.

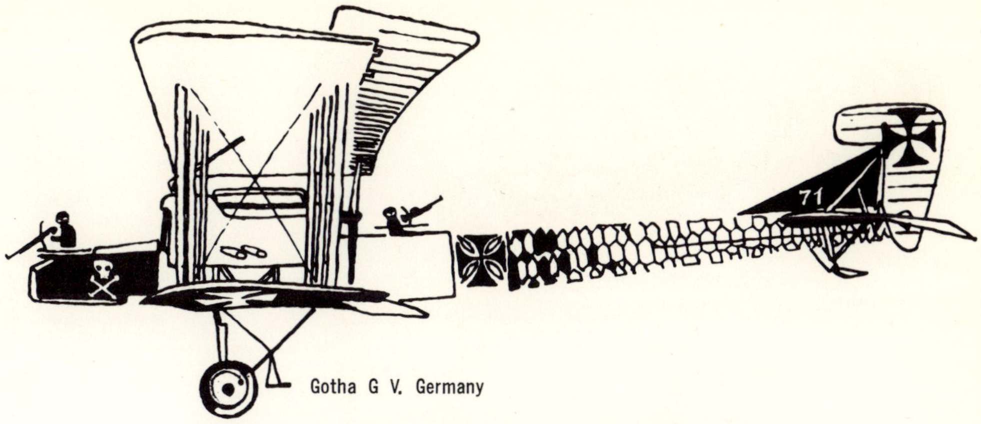

Gotha G V. Germany

The Gotha, along with the Friedrichshafen, was the standard German heavy bomber of the war. The Gothas carried out the major portion of the bombing raids against England and so were the best known—or most feared—and the name Gotha became a generic term for all bombers. At that, some of the British newspapers were referring to all German aeroplanes as *Taubes* as late as the summer of 1917.

The Gotha G IV and G V were developed from the G II of 1915 and reached a state of operational usefulness late in 1916 at about the time that the limited usefulness of the Zeppelins began to be apparent. With two 260 h.p. Mercedes six-cylinder engines and a crew of three, the G IV and G V types operated at altitudes of about 15,000 feet. Their ceiling was around 21,000 feet and it took them about an hour to get there.

In May 1917 when the first Gotha units based near Ghent flew their first raids against England, public indignation was so great that fighter squadrons were withdrawn from the front and brought back across the Channel to defend England against the "aerial invaders." Possibly this weakening of the Royal Flying Corps was one of the most significant results of the German air offensive, for the British were still struggling to recover from Bloody April.

The concrete results of the German bombing of England were not great. The offensive lasted one year—May 1917 to May 1918—and totaled twenty-seven raids, of which the last nineteen were perforce night raids owing to the rapid establishment of an effective antiaircraft and interceptor defense. On these twenty-seven raids, Gothas dropped a total of just under 100 tons of bombs, R-planes dropped about thirty, and damage of one and one half million pounds was caused. Fatalities in England amounted to 835, which makes an interesting comparison with the rule of thumb statistic for the Western Front that it required one ton of metal to kill one soldier. (The soldiers themselves used to say that it only took a man's own weight.)

German Gotha losses on these raids amounted to twenty-four destroyed by the defense and thirty-six destroyed through accidents, a two to three ratio that makes one wonder why the Germans persisted. It does tend to show one reason why the advocates of air power had an uphill struggle to get their ideas accepted.

OBSERVATION BALLOON, kite, *Drachen,* sausage—whatever its name, the floating blob of a balloon with its wicker basket dangling beneath was one of the characteristic sights on all fronts in World War I.

While balloon navigation had been to a large extent mastered by the end of the nineteenth century, it was purely as a "captive," that is to say tethered, aircraft that the balloon was used in the war, and its chief function was for artillery observation. In the American Civil War (1861–1865) captive balloons had been used for artillery observation, the signalling from balloon crew to battery commander being done by means of mirror flashes. The only improvement introduced since then had been to substitute wireless for mirrors.

The Germans developed the basic *Drachen* (dragon) kite balloon type, and gave considerable mobility to balloon companies by putting their hydrogen supply in high-pressure tanks on railroad cars. The *Drachen* originally had sails to keep its nose into the wind. Until the time when such improvements were made, the balloons were severely limited in the amount of flying they could do, for they were manageable only in the lightest of airs. The *Drachen* could operate in winds up to fifty m.p.h. A French officer, *Capitaine* Caquot, designed a more streamlined balloon with three large tail fins arranged at 120° intervals, and it is this type of *Drachen* (a German term, but used by both the Germans and the French) that was produced and used in the greatest numbers during the war.

Because they were so valuable for artillery observation, balloons were heavily protected from the ground by antiaircraft guns. As they were relatively stationary compared to aeroplanes, it was easy to range on them, and any fighter trying to attack a balloon had to run a gauntlet of zeroed-in fire. It was for this reason that balloons were counted equally with aeroplanes in fighter scores. Balloons could be quickly reeled in by motor winches, and unless an attack were delivered with speed and surprise (as by diving out of the sun with engine off), a pilot was likely to get nothing for his effort but a lot of holes in his own aeroplane.

Every air service produced its "balloon buster." There was the American, Frank Luke, who in seventeen days shot down sixteen balloons, five aeroplanes, and wrecked five of his own aeroplanes in the process. There was the French ace, *Lieutenant* Michel Coiffard of Spa 154, who served in the army from 1910 to 1914 in Tunisia and Morocco and was wounded three times in the course of those campaigns. He was sent to France in 1914 when the war began and was wounded again in August 1915. Considering that he had done his share by this time, the authorities discharged him, but Coiffard asked instead to be transferred to the air service. He began his flying training in January 1917 and reached an operational squadron, Spa 154, in June. Between then and October 1918 when he was wounded yet again, this time fatally, he shot down thirty-four enemy aircraft of which twenty-eight were balloons. There was the German ace, Heinrich Gontermann, of Westphalia, who commanded the famous *Jasta 15* in which Ernst Udet began his career as a fighter pilot. Gontermann himself began flying late in 1915 and flew a Roland C II *Wahlfisch* for a good part of 1916. He transferred to fighters at the end of 1916 and quickly showed himself to be a daring and resourceful pilot. He commanded a squadron and won the Blue Max when he was barely twenty-one. Gontermann's final score was eighteen balloons and twenty-one aeroplanes. He was killed in an accident on 30 October 1917, when the top wing of his Fokker Triplane collapsed as he was flying over his own field. Captain A.W. Beauchamp-Proctor, a South African ace, was awarded the Victoria Cross after the war for his generally outstanding work as a fighter and patrol leader rather than for any specific action. He served as a Flight Commander in No. 84 Squadron under Major Douglas (later Lord Douglas of Kirtleside, Marshal of the Royal Air Force), who said of him, ". . . that little man had the guts of a lion." Beauchamp-Proctor achieved a final score of fifty-four, of which sixteen were balloons.

These and many other fighter pilots specialized to a greater or lesser degree in attacking balloons and the work of a balloon observer was no cushy job even without the fighters. Enemy artillery could range on captive balloons almost as easily as the balloons' own antiaircraft defense, and there is nothing more inflammable than the hydrogen with which they were inflated. The balloon observers had one advantage—they were the only aircrews who always had parachutes.

French 75 mm. anti-aircraft gun mounted to pivot on concrete base. 1916

Nieuport 16 with eight LePrieur electrically fired rockets.

French observation kite used in 1915

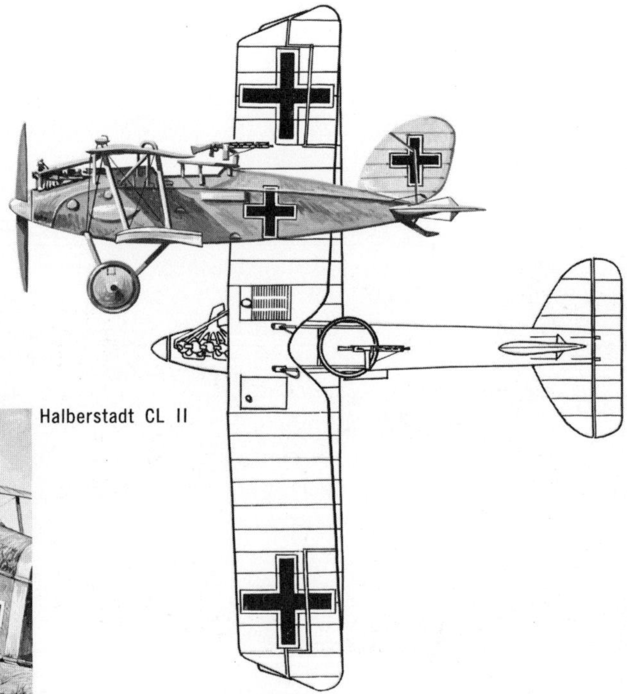

Halberstadt CL II

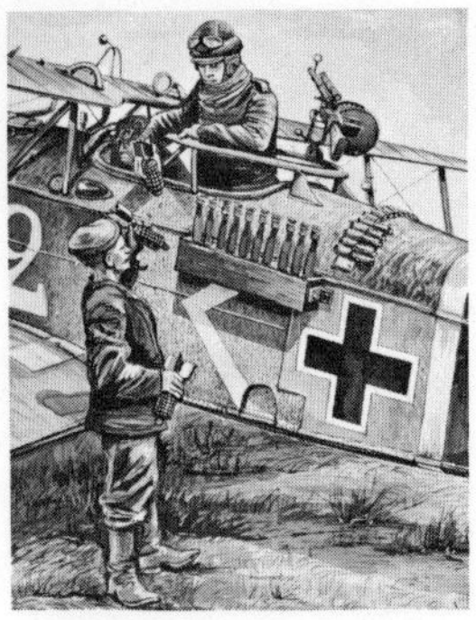

GROUND ATTACK in World War I was a combination of the roles of fighters and bombers. Significantly, it was originated by German two-seaters. Except for the tank, the Germans often came up with new ideas first, and the two-seaters of both sides were the most flexible class of aeroplanes.

In September 1917 six squadrons of Halberstadt CL II's threw an entire British division into disorder when they caught the infantry reserves on bridges over the Somme near Péronne and attacked repeatedly from tree-top height with machine guns and grenades.

Originally a variation of the "C" type of German observation two-seater, the "CL" came into being in the summer of 1917 as a two-seat fighter. Being two-seaters themselves, they could do any job the regular "C" types could, but with their performance and armament they could do it without escort because they could take care of themselves. The "CL" types were chosen to fly close-support missions coordinated with infantry attacks, for to the troops the morale value of their own machines going in right over their heads was considered very important. So

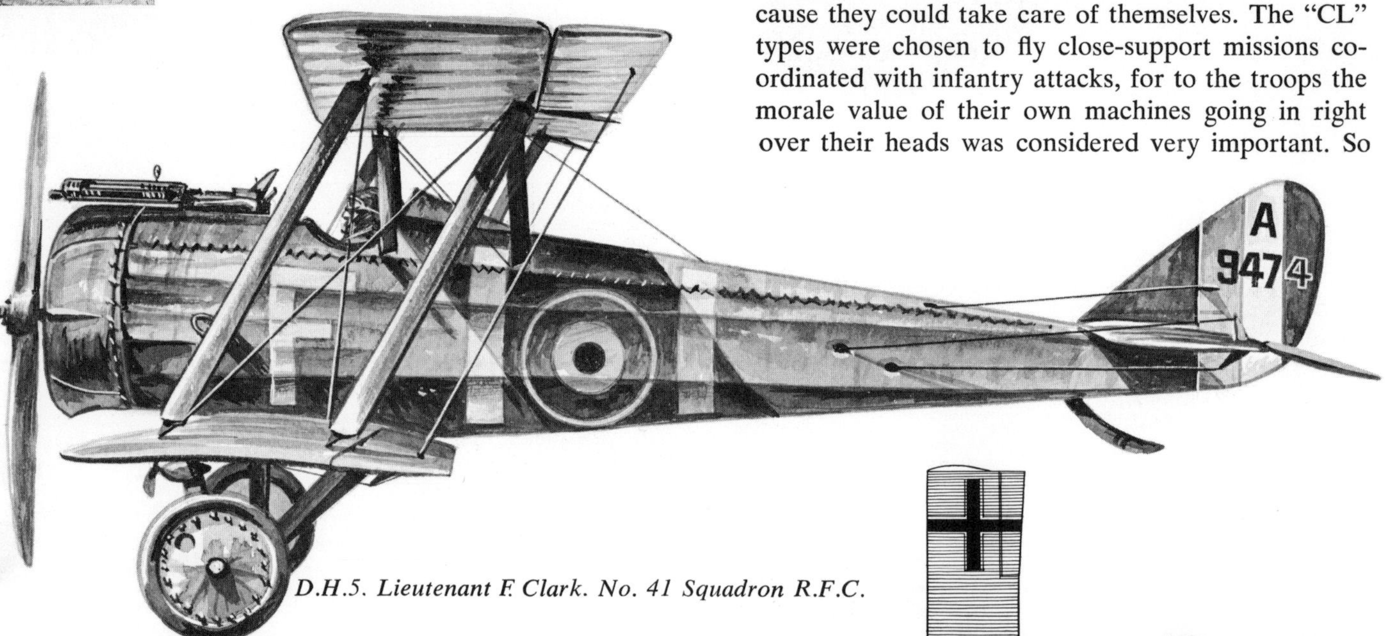

D.H.5. Lieutenant F. Clark. No. 41 Squadron R.F.C.

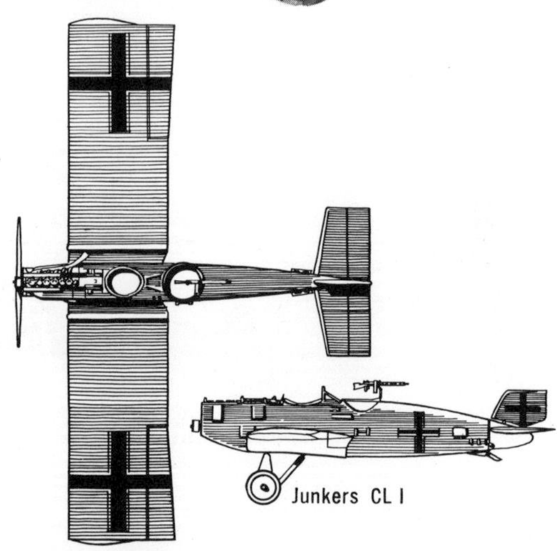

Junkers CL I

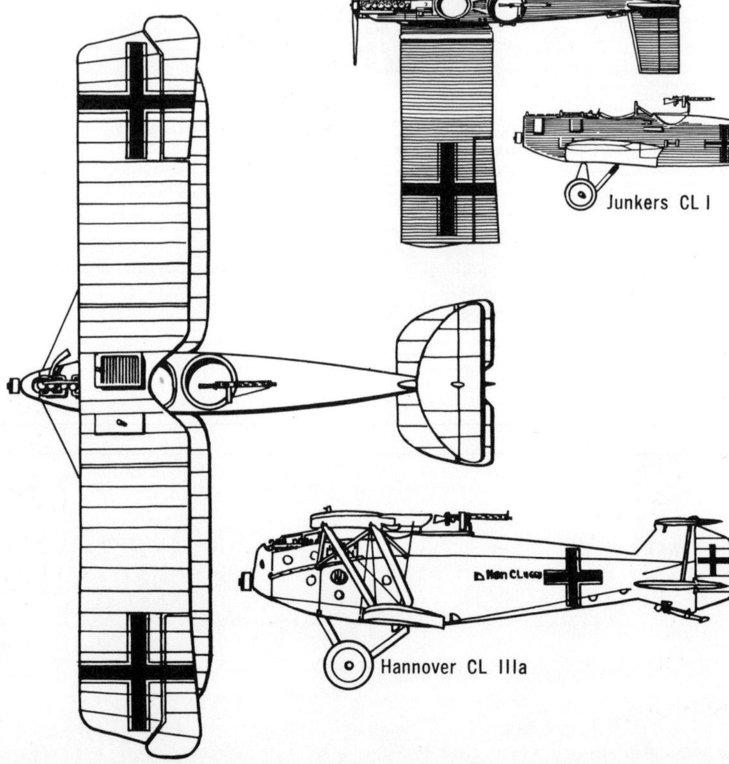

Hannover CL IIIa

important, in fact, that the general name for CL squadrons, *Schutzstaffeln* (Protection Squadrons), was changed to *Schlachtstaffeln* (Battle Squadrons). By the time of the great German offensive in March 1918, there were thirty *Schlastas* operating on the Western Front.

In the late autumn of 1917 several British squadrons took up ground attack work with varying success. The machine most used for the role was the unloved D.H.5. The D.H.5 was the victim of some ugly rumors which were quite unfounded, one of which was that it had a vicious stall at around eighty m.p.h. It didn't, of course, but aviators are a suspicious and superstitious lot and once a rumor gets started, they will hate the machine they are supposed to fly and then they are as good as dead. The D.H.5 did have a mediocre performance, but it was sturdy, and had a speed and rate of climb that did not put it at any disadvantage vis-à-vis the Albatros. It did have a poor performance at any height above 9,000 feet, so it was used chiefly for low-level attacks of the kind under discussion. The squadrons flying it carried four 25-pound Cooper bombs in external racks and a great many missions were flown before the last of the "stagger-wings" were retired from the front early in 1918.

The S.E.5a and the Camel replaced the D.H.5, and they also flew ground attacks sorties as well as regular offensive patrols. During the German offensive in March 1918, the experience gained in ground attack by the R.F.C. in 1917 was put to good use and various armored types were being developed.

The Junkers aeroplanes were the outstanding armored machines of the war. Developed from the J.1 of 1915, the world's first all-metal aeroplane, they were called "Tin Donkeys" because the J.1 was covered with thin sheet iron. The nick-name stuck although the later Junkers aeroplanes were covered with corrugated dural sheet. The major Junkers type to reach operational service was the J.1 of 1917. The J.1 was powered with the 200 h.p. Benz BZ IV six-cylinder engine which, like the cockpits and the fuel tank was armored with 5 mm. (3/16 inch) chrome-nickel sheet steel. Over 200 J.1's were built and from the end of 1917 they served the German army as the best of the machines assigned to contact patrol duties.

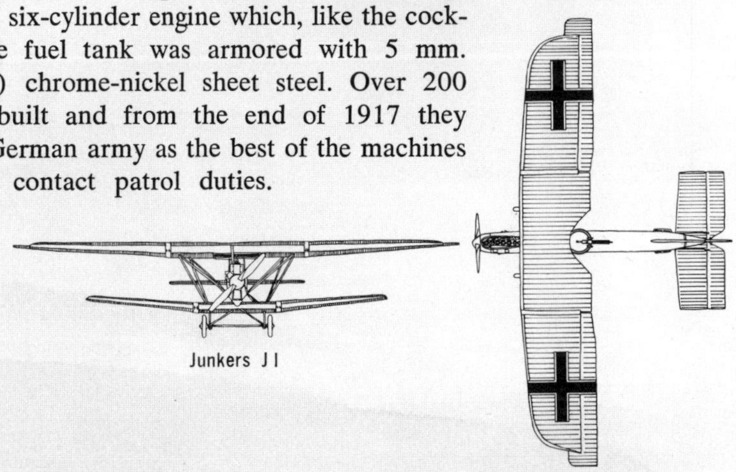

Junkers J I

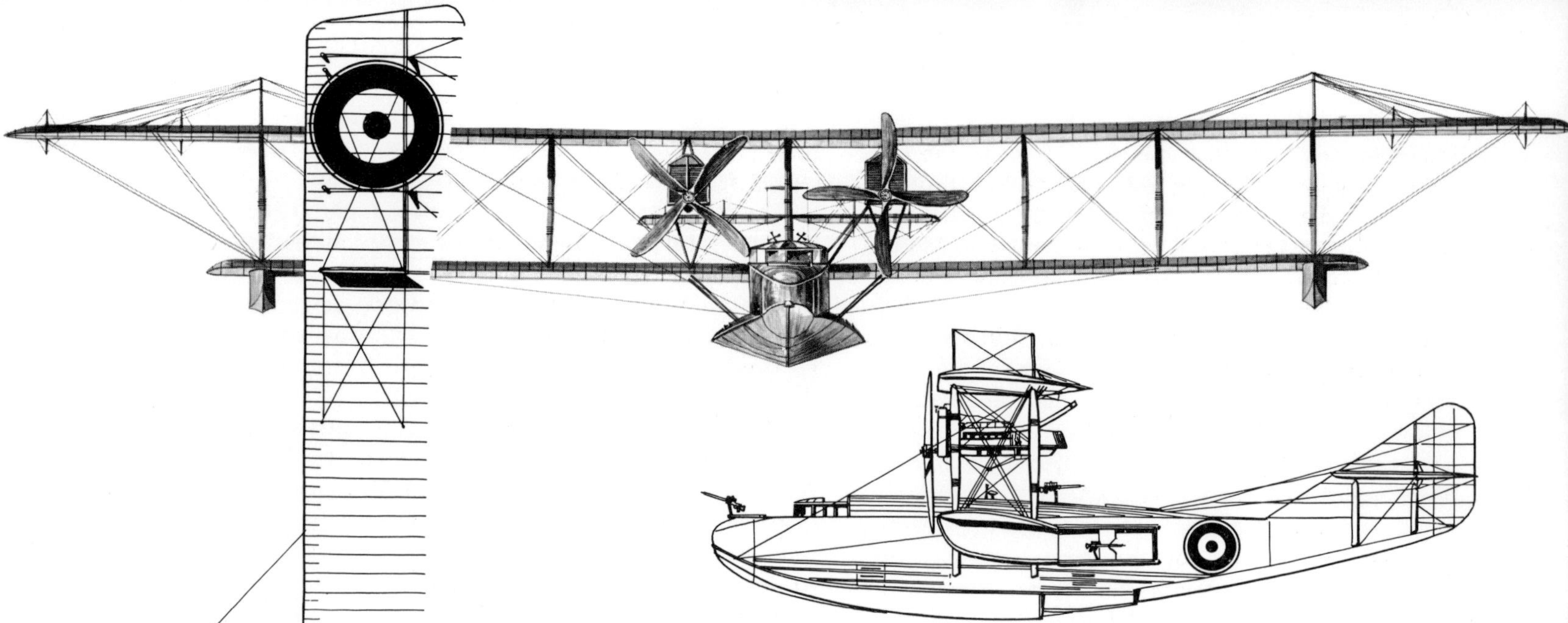

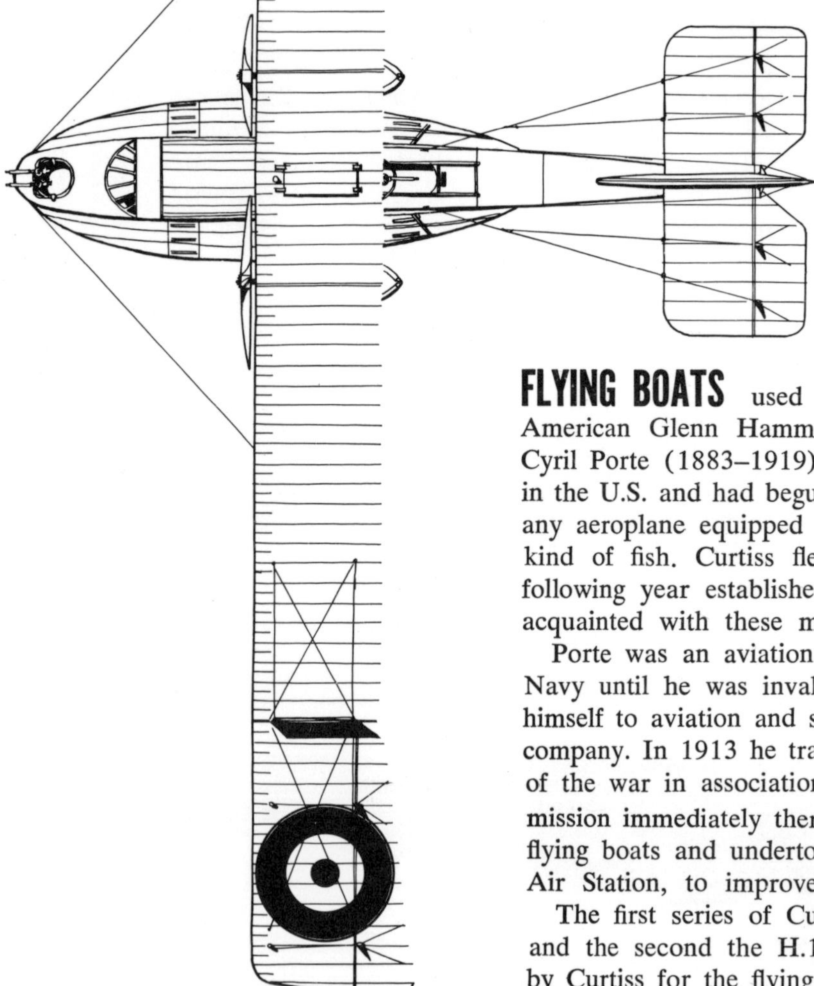

Felixstowe F.2A (span: 95 ft. length: 46 ft. 3 in.)

FLYING BOATS used during the war were the creation of two men, the American Glenn Hammond Curtiss (1878–1930) and the Englishman John Cyril Porte (1883–1919). In 1911 Curtiss had built the first successful seaplane in the U.S. and had begun work on a flying boat. A seaplane may be said to be any aeroplane equipped with floats, but a flying boat is an altogether different kind of fish. Curtiss flew his first flying boat in January 1912, and in the following year established an agency in England through which Porte became acquainted with these machines.

Porte was an aviation pioneer who had served as a lieutenant in the Royal Navy until he was invalided out because of poor health in 1911. He devoted himself to aviation and served for a time as director of the British Deperdussin company. In 1913 he traveled to America and spent the time until the outbreak of the war in association with Curtiss, returning to England and a naval commission immediately thereafter. He persuaded the Admiralty to purchase Curtiss flying boats and undertook himself, while he commanded the Felixstowe Naval Air Station, to improve their general design and seaworthiness.

The first series of Curtiss flying boats was called the H.4 "Small America" and the second the H.12 "Large America." "America" was the name chosen by Curtiss for the flying boat (shown on page 7) with which he hoped to win the £10,000 prize offered by the London *Daily Mail* for the first trans-Atlantic flight. The "small" and "large" were nick-names by which the two series were differentiated. The Curtiss H.12 "Large America" flying boats were flown operationally from the naval air stations at Felixstowe and Great Yarmouth on anti-submarine and anti-Zeppelin patrols. In the course of these patrols they destroyed two Zeppelins and sank three submarines. Powered by Rolls-Royce engines, the "Large Americas" had a crew of four, a maximum speed of eighty-five m.p.h. and an endurance of six hours.

The work of Porte at Felixstowe resulted in a new series of flying boats named after the air station. These Felixstowe flying boats had considerable influence on Curtiss in his own later series. The result was a Porte Felixstowe hull with Curtiss wings and tail.

The climax of the flying boat line was the Felixstowe *Fury* of 1918, a giant weighing fifteen tons and powered by five 360 h.p. engines.

Most important of the Felixstowe line, the F.2A appeared at the beginning of 1917, and between then and the armistice some 100 were built. With two Rolls-Royce engines producing about 700 h.p., the F.2A had a top speed of ninety-five m.p.h., and a ceiling of 10,000 feet. Its endurance was its chief virtue, for it could stay aloft for patrols of at least six hours' duration on normal tankage, but could extend this to ten hours by carrying extra fuel in tins. F.2A's from the Felixstowe and Great Yarmouth coastal air stations could sweep 2000 square miles of sea on anti-submarine patrols, and they carried two 230 pound bombs in external racks under the lower wings.

The Felixstowe was a well-armed flying boat, its crew had anywhere from four to seven Lewis guns at their disposal, and although it weighed over five tons loaded and was rather slow, the F.2A was no sitting duck. On 4 June 1918, in one of the few naval engagements of the war, three F.2A's and a Curtiss H.12, on a long reconnaissance from their bases at Felixstowe and Great Yarmouth, were attacked by fourteen seaplane fighters over the enemy coast. In the long running battle that ensued, the Curtiss was shot down, one boat was forced to drop out with a broken fuel pump (the crew landed safely on the water, repaired the pump, and made it home), and six of the enemy fighters were destroyed.

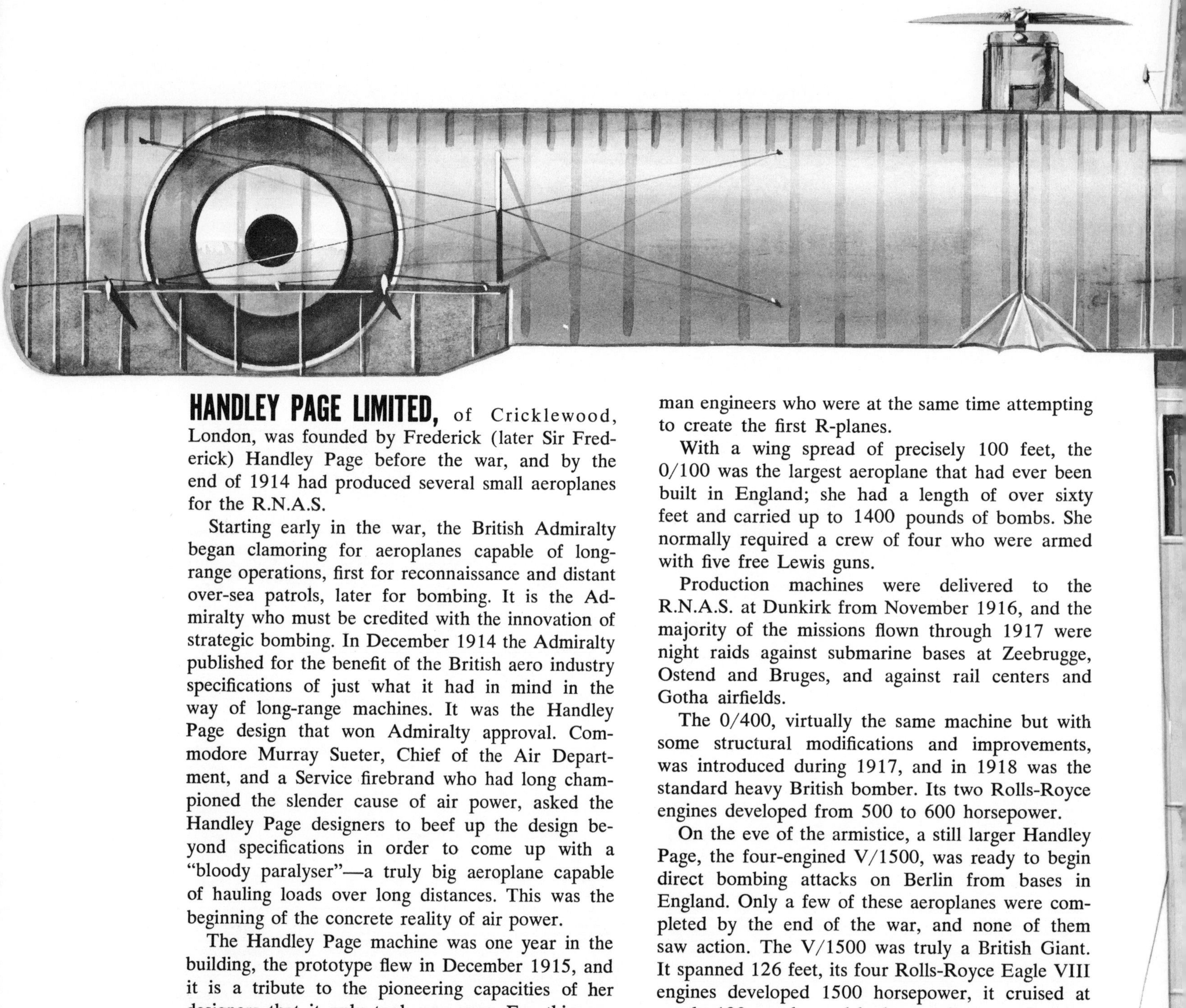

HANDLEY PAGE LIMITED, of Cricklewood, London, was founded by Frederick (later Sir Frederick) Handley Page before the war, and by the end of 1914 had produced several small aeroplanes for the R.N.A.S.

Starting early in the war, the British Admiralty began clamoring for aeroplanes capable of long-range operations, first for reconnaissance and distant over-sea patrols, later for bombing. It is the Admiralty who must be credited with the innovation of strategic bombing. In December 1914 the Admiralty published for the benefit of the British aero industry specifications of just what it had in mind in the way of long-range machines. It was the Handley Page design that won Admiralty approval. Commodore Murray Sueter, Chief of the Air Department, and a Service firebrand who had long championed the slender cause of air power, asked the Handley Page designers to beef up the design beyond specifications in order to come up with a "bloody paralyser"—a truly big aeroplane capable of hauling loads over long distances. This was the beginning of the concrete reality of air power.

The Handley Page machine was one year in the building, the prototype flew in December 1915, and it is a tribute to the pioneering capacities of her designers that it only took one year. For this was virgin territory. No experience existed for the solutions of the enormous new problems that developed. The British were as much in the dark as the German engineers who were at the same time attempting to create the first R-planes.

With a wing spread of precisely 100 feet, the 0/100 was the largest aeroplane that had ever been built in England; she had a length of over sixty feet and carried up to 1400 pounds of bombs. She normally required a crew of four who were armed with five free Lewis guns.

Production machines were delivered to the R.N.A.S. at Dunkirk from November 1916, and the majority of the missions flown through 1917 were night raids against submarine bases at Zeebrugge, Ostend and Bruges, and against rail centers and Gotha airfields.

The 0/400, virtually the same machine but with some structural modifications and improvements, was introduced during 1917, and in 1918 was the standard heavy British bomber. Its two Rolls-Royce engines developed from 500 to 600 horsepower.

On the eve of the armistice, a still larger Handley Page, the four-engined V/1500, was ready to begin direct bombing attacks on Berlin from bases in England. Only a few of these aeroplanes were completed by the end of the war, and none of them saw action. The V/1500 was truly a British Giant. It spanned 126 feet, its four Rolls-Royce Eagle VIII engines developed 1500 horsepower, it cruised at nearly 100 m.p.h., and had an endurance of seventeen hours.

In January 1918 an Air Ministry was set up with Lord Rothermere as Secretary of State for Air and

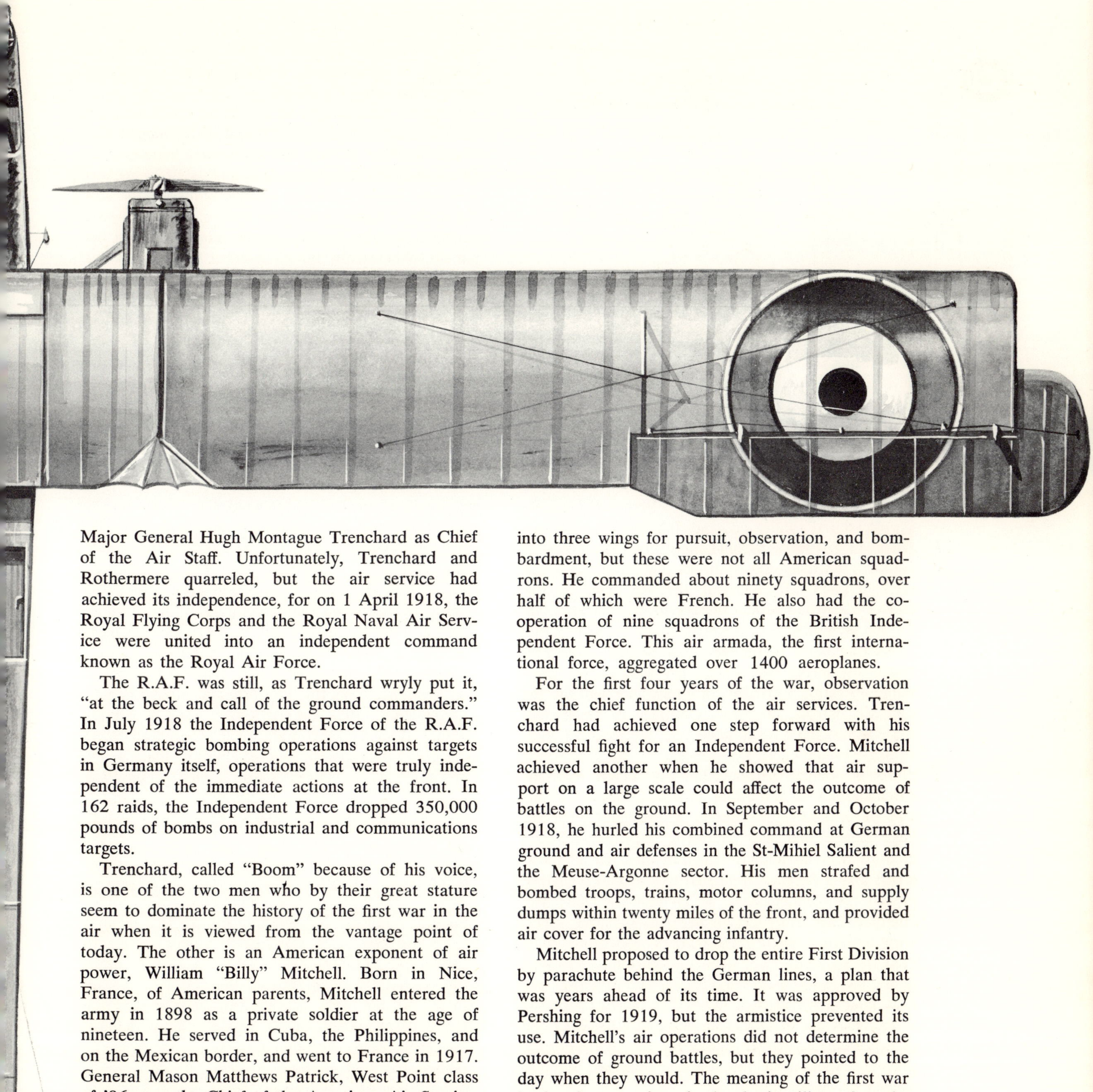

Handley Page 0/400

Major General Hugh Montague Trenchard as Chief of the Air Staff. Unfortunately, Trenchard and Rothermere quarreled, but the air service had achieved its independence, for on 1 April 1918, the Royal Flying Corps and the Royal Naval Air Service were united into an independent command known as the Royal Air Force.

The R.A.F. was still, as Trenchard wryly put it, "at the beck and call of the ground commanders." In July 1918 the Independent Force of the R.A.F. began strategic bombing operations against targets in Germany itself, operations that were truly independent of the immediate actions at the front. In 162 raids, the Independent Force dropped 350,000 pounds of bombs on industrial and communications targets.

Trenchard, called "Boom" because of his voice, is one of the two men who by their great stature seem to dominate the history of the first war in the air when it is viewed from the vantage point of today. The other is an American exponent of air power, William "Billy" Mitchell. Born in Nice, France, of American parents, Mitchell entered the army in 1898 as a private soldier at the age of nineteen. He served in Cuba, the Philippines, and on the Mexican border, and went to France in 1917. General Mason Matthews Patrick, West Point class of '86, was the Chief of the American Air Service, and his choice for the overall commander of U.S. air units at the front was Colonel Billy Mitchell. From August 1918 the Air Service was organized into three wings for pursuit, observation, and bombardment, but these were not all American squadrons. He commanded about ninety squadrons, over half of which were French. He also had the cooperation of nine squadrons of the British Independent Force. This air armada, the first international force, aggregated over 1400 aeroplanes.

For the first four years of the war, observation was the chief function of the air services. Trenchard had achieved one step forward with his successful fight for an Independent Force. Mitchell achieved another when he showed that air support on a large scale could affect the outcome of battles on the ground. In September and October 1918, he hurled his combined command at German ground and air defenses in the St-Mihiel Salient and the Meuse-Argonne sector. His men strafed and bombed troops, trains, motor columns, and supply dumps within twenty miles of the front, and provided air cover for the advancing infantry.

Mitchell proposed to drop the entire First Division by parachute behind the German lines, a plan that was years ahead of its time. It was approved by Pershing for 1919, but the armistice prevented its use. Mitchell's air operations did not determine the outcome of ground battles, but they pointed to the day when they would. The meaning of the first war in the air was written in the sky in pillars of smoke —if you do not hold the air, you cannot win on the ground.

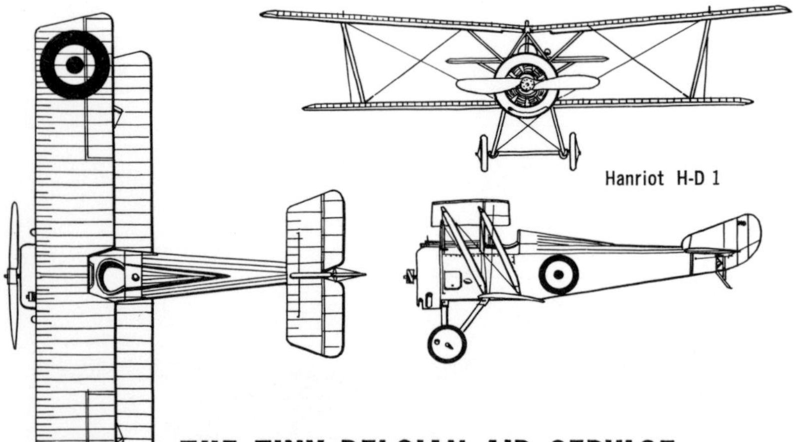

Hanriot H-D 1

THE TINY BELGIAN AIR SERVICE, which grew from four squadrons to eleven between the outbreak of the war and the armistice, was not considered very important by the Allies and was obliged to make do with their cast-off aeroplanes for the greater part of the war. For all that it was given such cavalier treatment, it was an air service whose morale and performance were second to none. Such pre-war aviators as Fernand Jacquet, a professional soldier and the first Belgian to shoot down an enemy aeroplane, and Jan Olieslagers, a famous motorcycle racer and exhibition pilot, served through the entire war and were an example and inspiration to the rest of the service.

The highest-scoring Belgian ace was Willy Coppens, a native of Watermael, near Brussels, where he was born on 6 July 1892. He was known as a balloon-buster, and when he was knighted for his gallantry he became Willy Coppens de Houthulst, after Houthulst Forest where he achieved his successes.

As a national service man, he served with the Grenadiers before the war and was recalled to his old outfit upon the general mobilization. He remained with the Grenadiers for one year, securing a transfer to aviation in the fall of 1915. He was given a two-month leave to go to England for flying lessons, which he took at Hendon on his own. He was given his certificate in December 1915, but had not even been taught that one must take off into the wind. Returning to Belgium, he was accepted for further training and was finally posted to a two-seater squadron in the summer of 1916. One year later, in July 1917, he was posted to a fighter squadron, the 1st *Escadrille,* having experienced his first air combat and received his first citations.

The 1st *Escadrille,* stationed at Les Moeres, was equipped at that time with Nieuport 17's and one Nieuport *Bébé*. Coppens, as low man on the totem pole, was given the old *Bébé*. This was bad enough, but the machine was something of a freak, having gone through its original 80 h.p. Le Rhône engine and having been re-engined with the standard engine for the later 17's, the 120 h.p. Le Rhône. It was as a result extremely nose-heavy. It had to be landed with power on because its glide angle was about that of a cannonball. Without power it simply dropped its nose and dived.

Coppens managed to fly his freak, but it was not a satisfactory aeroplane. A friend of his named Edmond Thieffry, of the 5th *Escadrille,* happened to fly an identical aeroplane. One day as Coppens was watching Thieffry make a landing approach, he saw the *Bébé* abruptly nose dive from a low level—the engine had quit. Thieffry barely managed to get the tail down before he hit the ground, but even so he was going in pretty steeply. The machine whammed into the runway, the landing gear was torn off, and the *Bébé* was flipped violently over on its back. As the spectators ran up to rescue Thieffry who was trapped upside down in the wreck, his own struggles to free himself triggered his machine gun. A burst of machine gun fire sent bullets whistling across the field and his rescuers scattered in all directions.

Thieffry was one of the few fighter pilots who was a college graduate. He had passed his final examinations in law at Louvain University on 28 July 1914, and was called up the same day. He scored ten victories before he was himself shot down in flames behind the German lines. Though seriously injured, he survived the crash and even settled the dispute between two German pilots, both of whom claimed him. He was killed in 1929 on a survey flight for a proposed airline in the Belgian Congo.

During the summer of 1917, a new single-seater was introduced on the Western and Italian Fronts. The machine, the Hanriot HD-1, was a French product designed and built at Carrières-sur-Seine by a firm known as Avions R. Hanriot. Only a few were used by the French air service which was committed to the Nieuport and Spad types, and it was delivered instead to France's allies, Belgium and Italy. The original Hanriot company was one of the pioneer aeroplane manufacturers in France. After the outbreak of the war the company began to produce various machines under contract to other companies and did not attempt any original designs before the HD-1. It was itself sub-contracted in considerable numbers in Italy by the Macchi company of Varese, and became the standard Italian fighter. At the time of the armistice, it was the equipment of sixteen out of eighteen active squadrons of the Regia Aeronautica.

When the first example arrived on the field of the 1st *Escadrille,* Willy Coppens was still low man on the totem pole. The senior pilots had first choice, but as it happened they all passed it up. It was offered first to André de Meulemeester who refused to have it because he hated any change and so preferred to keep his Nieuport 17. Jan Olieslagers didn't want anything de Meulemeester refused and so he passed it on to the next man. And so on down the line until it was at last offered to Coppens. He tried it once and loved it. It proved to be highly maneuverable and stronger than it looked, its one weak point being that it was armed with but one gun, a synchronized Vickers.

Actually, it had one other weak point . . .

On 14 October 1917, Coppens was flying a patrol with de Meulemeester when he spotted a formation of ten Friedrichshafen bombers escorted by about fifteen fighters. The two Belgians dived together, going down almost vertically, fired and pulled out. Coppens horsed his machine around hard to avoid a collision with his target and also to escape by a zoom climb. Under the strain of the sharp pull-out, the tubes supporting his seat gave way and he was slammed to the bottom of the fuselage. He lost control of the aeroplane and fell out of the fight. Possibly the Germans thought one of their number had shot him down, for there was no attack made on him during his fall, or if there was, he was not aware of it. He worked himself up to a position where he could see out, and with one arm locked over the cockpit side, he began heaving the wreckage overboard. The control cables had been blocked by his weight and the broken pieces of seat.

The other pilots of the squadron were eventually persuaded to try the machine. Both Coppens and de Meulemeester hated the factory camouflage applied to production aeroplanes. Coppens said it reminded him of a varnished toy snake. He had his painted blue. De Meulemeester had his painted yellow, and lest some trigger-happy British pilot suppose he had come up against a member of one of the German Circuses, he took the trouble to fly his canary around to all the British units in the vicinity to familiarize them with it.

Of his total score of thirty-seven, Coppens destroyed no fewer than twenty-six balloons, making him, next to Michel Coiffard of France, the champion balloon buster of the war. Balloon busting was not easy for anyone, but for Coppens it seemed to come especially hard, and he flew many months before he scored his first confirmed victory. The first time he tried it he drew a blank, but he gave his comrades something to talk about. He volunteered to take on one that was causing particular trouble near Bovekerke, and went in with a flight of Belgian fighters overhead to provide cover. He dived hard at his target and the German Archie opened up while the ground crew began frantically to reel in the balloon. Without incendiary ammunition it was hopeless, and Coppens blazed away without producing any visible result. He was forced to break off and admit that this was not his day, but he hated to slink off with his tail between his legs. On an impulse, he suddenly looped his Hanriot. It was better than thumbing his nose. It was pointless, but such a reckless gesture in the midst of the shell bursts showed a magnificent scorn of danger, and it is of such *beaux gestes* that legends are born.

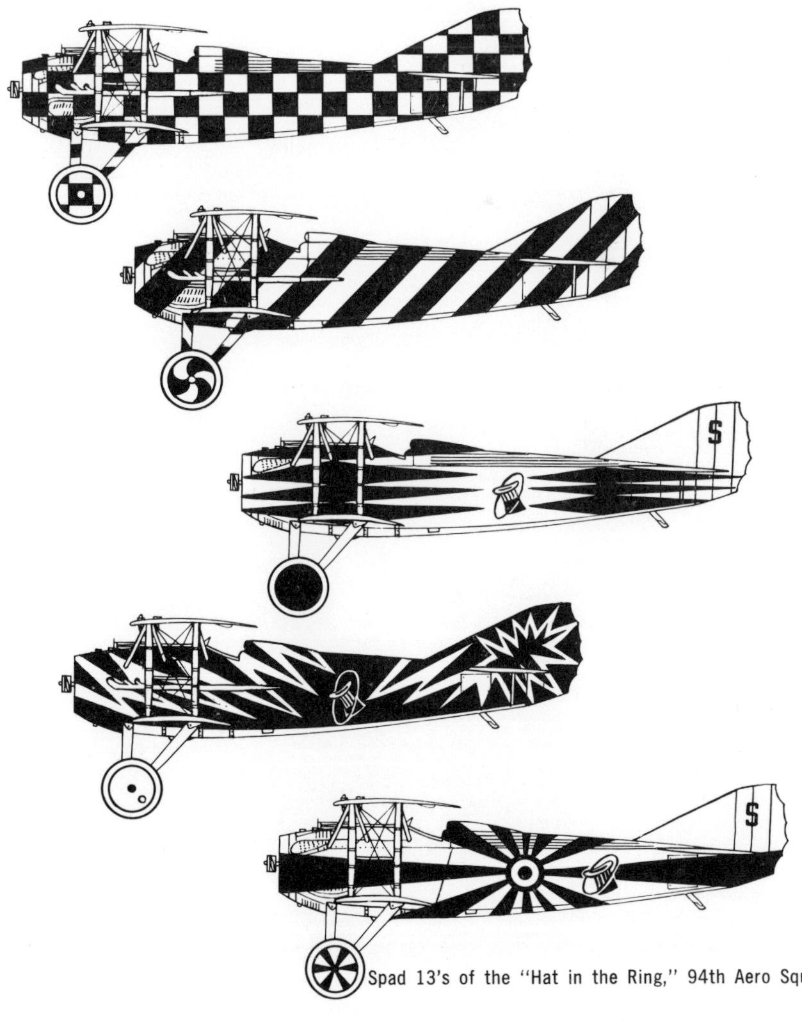

Spad 13's of the "Hat in the Ring," 94th Aero Squadron

On 20/21 May 1927, Charles Augustus Lindbergh, an airmail pilot born in Detroit in 1902, became the first man to fly solo across the Atlantic Ocean. Lindbergh's thirty-three hour flight in a Ryan monoplane from Long Island, New York, to Paris brought aviation back into the headlines after the nine-year period of public apathy which followed the war. His open and modest character, his dignity, and his dedication to aviation made "Slim" Lindbergh a popular hero and one of the noblest men to grace the history of aviation. His flight was a beacon of reason and sanity in a world already preparing itself for World War II — an epic of courage and skill that offered proof to those who were willing to see that the way of the air was at last open, and that the way of the air was the road to peace and international co-operation. As in the old folksong, those who have known freedom have, like the swallow, learned to fly. Equally, those who have learned to fly have known the real meaning of freedom.

N-X-211
RYAN
NYP
pirit
of
Louis

SCORES OF ACES OF THE GREAT WAR 1914-1918

GREAT BRITIAN

Score	
73	Major E. Mannock
72	Lieutenant-Colonel W.A. Bishop
60	Lieutenant-Colonel R. Collishaw
57	Major J.T.B. McCudden
54	Captain A.W. Beauchamp-Proctor
54	Major D.R. MacLaren
53	Major W.G. Barker
47	Captain R.A. Little
46	Captain P.F. Fullard
46	Captain G.E.H. McElroy
44	Captain A. Ball
44	Captain J. Gilmore
41	Major T.F. Hazell
40	Captain J.I.T. Jones
39	Captain W.G. Claxton
39	Major R.S. Dallas
37	Captain F.R. McCall
35	Captain H.W. Woollett
34	Captain F.G. Quigley
32	Major G.H. Bowman
31	Major A.D. Carter
31	Captain J.L.M. White
30	Captain M.B. Frew
30	Captain S.M. Kinkead
30	Captain A.E. McKeever
29	Captain A.H. Cobby
29	Captain W.L. Jordon
27	Captain J.E. Gurdon
27	Captain R.T.C. Hoidge
27	Captain H.G.E. Luchford
27	Major G.J.C. Maxwell
26	Captain W.C. Campbell
26	Captain W.E. Staton
25	Major K.L. Caldwell
25	Major R.J.O. Compston
25	Major J. Leacroft
25	Captain R.A. Mayberry
24	Major J.O. Andrews
24	Captain W.E. Shields
23	Captain J.S.T. Fall
23	Captain A. Hepburn
23	Captain D. Latimer
23	Captain E.J.K. McLoughry
23	Lieutenant A.P.F. Rhys Davids
23	Captain S.W. Rosevear
23	Captain H.A. Whistler
22	Major C.D. Booker
2	Major W.J.C.K. Cochrane-Patrick
	Captain R. King
	Lieutenant McK. Thomson
	aptain C.J. Venter
	ptain P.J. Clayson
	ain R.P. Minifie
	n G.E. Thompson
	D.J. Bell
	T.S. Harrison
	W.L. Harrison
	.C. Johnston
	F. King
	Lieutenant J.J. Malone
	R. McDonald
	M. MacEwen
	Murlis-Green
	rk
	tewart
	ver
	l-Irving
	anachan
	aunders
	nson
	arlow
	llett
	ber
	on
	e
	i
18	Lieutenant E.V. Reid
18	Captain F.A. Thayre
18	Captain J.L. Trollope
18	Lieutenant W.B. Wood
17	Captain J.H. Burden
17	Captain G.H. Cock
17	Captain L.F. Jenkins
17	Captain M.A. Nounhouse
17	Captain Edwin Swale
16	Captain O.M. Baldwin
16	Captain W. Gillette
16	Captain C.R.R. Hickey
16	Captain H.T. Mellings
16	Captain T.P. Middleton
16	Lieutenant S.A. Oades
16	Major K. Oxspring
16	Major S.F. Pender
16	Captain B. Roxburgh-Smith
15	Captain P.C. Carpenter
15	Captain M.H. Findley
15	Captain R.A. Grosvenor
15	Lieutenant H.B. Richardson
15	Captain J.H. Tudhope
15	Captain W.A. Tyrrel
15	Lieutenant C.T. Warman
14	Captain M. Galbraith
14	Captain G.E. Gibbs
14	Captain S.W. Highwood
14	Captain F. Libby
14	Major N.F.K. McEwan
14	Captain R.T. Mark
13	Captain C.P. Brown
13	Captain R.A. Delhaye
13	Captain J.H. Hedley
13	Captain A.G. Jones-Williams
13	Lieutenant C.H.R. Lagesse
13	Lieutenant N.W.R. Mawle
13	Captain G.P. Olley
13	Captain H.G. Reeves
13	Captain C.G. Ross
13	Lieutenant-Colonel A.J.L. Scott
13	Captain F.R. Smith
13	Captain O.H.D. Vickers
12	Lieutenant L.B. Bennit
12	Captain A.R. Brown
12	Captain R.W. Chappell
12	Captain E.S. Coler
12	Captain C.M. Crowe
12	Major C. Draper
12	Captain H.F.S. Drewitt
12	Lieutenant Alan Gerrard
12	Lieutenant F.D. Gillete
12	Major P. Huskinson
12	Captain H.P. Lale
12	Lieutenant M.E. Mealing
12	Lieutenant K.B. Montgomery
12	Lieutenant-Colonel R.H. Mulock
12	Major R.C. Phillips,
12	Captain L.H. Rochford
12	Captain W.A. Southey
12	Lieutenant L.T.E. Taplin
12	Lieutenant F.D. Travers
12	Captain N.W.W. Webb
12	Major J.T. Whittaker
12	Captain P. Wilson
11	Captain S. Carlin
11	Captain R.E. Dodds
11	Captain G.B. Gates
11	Captain H.A. Hamersley
11	Lieutenant P.T. Iaccaci
11	Captain S.C. Joseph
11	Captain A.C. Kiddie
11	Captain K.M.St.C.G. Leaske
11	Captain C.N. Lowe
11	Lieutenant A. McCudden
11	Lieutenant R.W. McKenzie
11	Captain N. McMillan
11	Lieutenant A.J. Morgan
11	Captain W.R.G. Pearson
11	Lieutenant A.E. Reed
11	Captain W.W. Rogers
11	Captain M.D.C. Scott
11	Lieutenant J.E. Sharman
11	Captain S.F.H. Thompson
10	Major B.E. Baker
10	Captain G.B.A. Baker
10	Captain C.C. Banks
10	Captain A.J. Boswell
10	Lieutenant G.L. Graham
10	Captain E.T. Hayne
10	Lieutenant T.S. Horry
10	Captain W.H. Hubbard
10	Captain V. Kearley
10	Captain D.V. MacGregor
10	Lieutenant R.M. Makepeace
10	Lieutenant R.F.S. Maudit
10	Captain J.W. Pinder
10	Lieutenant H.B. Redler
10	Lieutenant L.L. Richardson
10	Lieutenant T. Rose
10	Captain J. Scott
10	Captain S.P. Smith
10	Captain A.T.B. Tonks
10	Lieutenant K.R. Unger
10	Major G.M. Vaucour
10	Lieutenant H.G. Watson
10	Lieutenant W.L. Wells
10	Major W.E. Young

UNITED STATES

Score	
26	Captain E.V. Rickenbacker
21	Second Lieutenant Frank Luke, Jr.
17	Maj. Raoul Lufbery
13	1/Lt. George A. Vaughn, Jr.
12	Captain Field E. Kindley
12	First Lieutenant David E. Putnam
12	Captain Elliot W. Springs
10	Major Reed G. Landis
10	Captain Jacques Michael Swaab

BELGIUM

Score	
37	Second Lieutenant W. Coppens
11	Adjudant A. de Meulemeester
10	Second Lieutenant E. Thieffry

ITALY

Score	
34	*Maggiore* Francesco Baracca
26	*Tenente* Silvio Scaroni
24	*Tenente-Colonnello* Ruggiero Piccio
21	*Tenente* Flavia Torello Baracchini
20	*Capitano* Fulco Ruffo di Calabria
17	*Sergente* Marziale Cerutti
17	*Tenente* Ferruccio Ranza
12	*Tenente* Luigi Olivari
11	*Tenente* Giovanni Ancillotto
11	*Sergente* Antonio Reali

RUSSIA

Score	
17	Staff-Captain A.A. Kazakov
15	Captain P.V. d'Argueeff
13	Lieutenant-Commander A.P. Seversky
12	Lieutenant I.W. Smirnoff
11	Lieutenant M. Safonov
11	Captain B. Sergievsky
11	Ensign E.M. Tomson

FRANCE

Score	
75	*Capitaine* René Paul Fonck
54	*Capitaine* Georges M.L.J. Guynemer
45	*Lieutenant* Charles E.J.M. Nungesser

41 *Capitaine* Georges F. Madon
35 *Lieutenant* Maurice Boyau
34 *Lieutenant* Michel Coiffard
28 *Lieutenant* Jean P.L. Bourjade
27 *Capitaine* Armand Pinsard
23 *Sous-Lieutenant* René Dorme
23 *Lieutenant* Gabriel Guérin
23 *Sous-Lieutenant* Claude M. Haegelen
22 *Sous-Lieutenant* Pierre Marinovitch
21 *Capitaine* Alfred Heurtaux
20 *Capitaine* Albert Deullin
19 *Capitaine* Henri J.H. de Slade
19 *Lieutenant* Jacques L. Ehrlich
18 *Lieutenant* Bernard de Romanet
16 *Lieutenant* Jean Chaput
15 *Capitaine* Armand O. de Turenne
15 *Capitaine* Paul V. d'Argueeff
15 *Lieutenant* Gilbert Sardier
14 *Lieutenant* Marc Ambrogi
13 *Sous-Lieutenant* Omer Demeuldre
13 *Lieutenant* Hector Garaud
13 *Lieutenant* Marcel Noguès
12 *Sous-Lieutenant* Bernard Artigau
12 *Lieutenant* Jean H. Casale
12 *Sous-Lieutenant* Gustave Daladier
12 *Capitaine* Xavier de Sévin
12 *Sous-Lieutenant* Fernand Guyou
12 *Lieutenant* Marcel Hugues
12 *Sous-Lieutenant* Lucien Jailler
12 *Capitaine* Jacques Leps
12 *Sous-Lieutenant* Jean M.D. Navarre
12 *Lieutenant* Paul A.P. Tarascon
11 *Adjutant* Armand Berthelot
11 *Sous-Lieutenant* Jean Bouyer
11 *Lieutenant* Benjamen Bozon-Verduraz
11 *Sous-Lieutenant* William Hérisson
11 *Adjutant* Maxime Lenoir
11 *Sous-Lieutenant* Ernest Maunoury
11 *Adjudant* René Montrion
11 *Sous-Lieutenant* Léon Nuville
11 *Lieutenant* Jacques Georges Ortoli
10 *Adjudant* Maurice Bizot
10 *Adjudant* André Chainat
10 *Adjudant* Marcel Gasser
10 *Sous-Lieutenant* André R. Herbelin
10 *Capitaine* Auguste Lahoulle
10 *Adjudant* Charles Macé
10 *Adjudant* Jean Pezon
10 *Sous-Lieutenant* Charles Quette
10 *Sous-Lieutenant* Robert Waddington

GERMANY

Score

80 *Rittm.* Manfred *Frhr.* v. Richtofen
62 *Oberleutnant* Ernst Udet
53 *Oberleutnant* Erich Loewenhardt
48 *Leutnant* Werner Voss
45 *Leutnant* Fritz Rumey
44 *Hauptmann* Rudolph Berthold
43 *Leutnant* Paul Bäumer
41 *Leutnant* Josef Jacobs
41 *Hauptmann* Bruno Loerzer
40 *Hauptmann* Oswald Boelcke
40 *Leutnant* Franz Büchner
40 *Oblt.* Lothar *Frhr.* v. Richthofen
39 *Leutnant* Karl Menckhoff
39 *Leutnant* Heinrich Gontermann
36 *Leutnant* Max Müller
35 *Leutnant* Julius Buckler
35 *Leutnant* Gustav Dörr
35 *Hpt.* Eduard *Ritter* von Schleich
34 *Leutnant* Josef Veltjens
33 *Leutnant* Otto Koennecke
33 *Oberleutnant* Kurt Wolff
33 *Leutnant* Heinrich Bongartz
32 *Leutnant* Theo Osterkamp
32 *Leutnant* Emil Thuy
31 *Leutnant* Paul Billik
31 *Rittmeister* Karl Bolle
31 *Oblt.* Gotthard Sachsenberg
30 *Leutnant* Karl Allmenröder
30 *Leutnant* Karl Degelow
30 *Leutnant* Heinrich Kroll
30 *Leutnant* Josef Mai
30 *Leutnant* Ulrich Neckel
30 *Leutnant* Karl Schaefer
29 *Leutnant* Hermann Frommerz
28 *Leutnant* Walter von Bülow
28 *Leutnant* Walter Blume
28 *Oblt.* Fritz *Ritter* von Röth
27 *Oberleutnant* Fritz Bernert
27 *Vizefeldwebel* Otto Fruhner
27 *Leutnant* Hans Kirschstein
27 *Leutnant* Karl Thom
27 *Hpt.* Adolf *Ritter* von Tutschek
27 *Leutnant* Kurt Wüsthoff
26 *Oberleutnant* Harald Auffahrt
26 *Oblt.* Oscar *Frhr.* von Boenigk
26 *Oberleutnant* Eduard Dostler
26 *Leutnant* Arthur Laumann
25 *Lt.* O. *Frhr.* von B.-Marconnay
25 *Oblt.* Robert *Ritter* von Greim
25 *Leutnant* Georg von Hantelmann
25 *Leutnant* Max Näther
25 *Leutnant* Fritz Pütter
24 *Leutnant* Erwin Böhme
23 *Leutnant* Hermann Becker
23 *Leutnant* Georg Meyer
22 *Oberleutnant* Hermann Göring
22 *Leutnant* Hans Klein
22 *Leutnant* Hans Pippart
22 *Leutnant* Werner Preuss
22 *Vizefeldwebel* Karl Schlegel
22 *Leutnant* Rudolph Windisch
21 *Leutnant* Hans Adam
21 *Oblt.* Friedrich Christiansen
21 *Leutnant* Fritz Friedrichs
21 *Leutnant* Fritz Höhn
20 *Vizefeldwebel* Friedrich Altemeir
20 *Oberleutnant* Hans Bethge
20 *Leutnant* Rudolph von Eschwege
20 *Leutnant* Walter Goettsch
20 *Leutnant* Friedrich Noltenius
20 *Hauptmann* Wilhelm Reinhard
19 *Vizefeldwebel* Gerhard Fieseler
19 *Leutnant* Wilhelm Frankl
19 *Leutnant* Otto Kissenberth
19 *Oberleutnant* Otto Schmidt
18 *Leutnant* Hartmuth Baldamus
18 *Leutnant* Franz Hemer
18 *Vizefeldwebel* Oskar Hennrich
18 *Leutnant* Kurt Wintgens
17 *Leutnant* Walter Böning
17 *Leutnant* Ernst Hess
17 *Leutnant* Franz Ray
17 *Leutnant* Hans Rolfes
17 *Vfw.* Josef Schwendemann
16 *Leutnant* Hans Boehning
16 *Leutnant* Hans von Freden
16 *Leutnant* Ludwig Hanstein
16 *Leutnant* Rudolf Klimke
16 *Leutnant* Karl Odebrett
16 *Leutnant* Hans Weiss
15 *Leutnant* Albert Dossenbach
15 *Vfw.* Christian Donhauser
15 *Vizefeldwebel* Albert Haussmann
15 *Leutnant* Aloys Heldmann
15 *Oberleutnant* Max Immelmann
15 *Leutnant* Johannes Klein
15 *Leutnant* Otto Löffler
15 *Leutnant* Victor von Pressentin
15 *Leutnant* Theodor Quandt
15 *Leutnant* Julius Schmidt
15 *Leutnant* Kurt Schneider
14 *Leutnant* Ernst Bormann
14 *Vizefeldwebel* Rudolf Francke
14 *Offz. Stellv.* Edmund Nathanael
14 *Leutnant* Franz Piechurek
14 *Leutnant* Karl Plauth
14 *Vizefeldwebel* Wilhelm Seitz
14 *Vizefeldwebel* Emil Schäpe
14 *Leutnant* George Schlenker
14 *Leutnant* Paul Straehle
14 *Leutnant* Rudolf Wendelmuth
13 *Vizefeldwebel* Karl Bohnenkamp
13 *Hpt.* Hans Joachim Buddecke
13 *Leutnant* Siegfried Büttner
13 *Leutnant* Heinrich Geigl
13 *Vizefeldwebel* Robert Heibert
13 *Vizefeldwebel* Reinhold Jörke
13 *Leutnant* Johann Janzen
13 *Vizefeldwebel* Christel Mesch
13 *Vizefeldwebel* Otto Rosenfeld
13 *Oberleutnant* Kurt Schoenfelder
13 *Oblt.* Erich Rüdiger von Wedel
12 *Vizefeldwebel* Erich Buder
12 *Leutnant* Diether Collin
12 *Oberleutnant* Theodor Cammann
12 *Vizefeldwebel* Gottfried Ehmann
12 *Offz. Stellv.* Otto Esswein
12 *Vizefeldwebel* Sebastian Festner
12 *Leutnant* Walter Höhndorf
12 *Vizefeldwebel* Max Kuhn
12 *Leutnant* Hans Mueller
12 *Vfw.* Friedrich Manschott
12 *Oberleutnant* Franz Schleiff
12 *Leutnant* Richard Wenzl
11 *Leutnant* Heinrich Arntzen
11 *Leutnant* Joachim von Busse
11 *Lt.* Raven *Frhr.* von Barnekow
11 *Oberleutnant* Kurt von Doering
11 *Leutnant* Xaver Dannhuber
11 *Leutnant* Heinz Dreckmann
11 *Vizefeldwebel* Willi Gabriel
11 *Oberleutnant* Stephan Kirmaier
11 *Leutnant* Hans von Keudell
11 *Leutnant* Alfred Lindenberger
11 *Leutnant* Fritz Loerzer
11 *Leutnant* Hermann Pfeiffer
11 *Leutnant* Hugo Schaefer
11 *Leutnant* Renatus Theiller
10 *Offizier Stellvertreter* Paul Aue
10 *Vizefeldwebel* Dietrich Averes
10 *Oberleutnant* Hans Berr
10 *Leutnant* Franz Brandt
10 *Vizefeldwebel* Fritz Classen
10 *Leutnant* Martin Dehmisch
10 *Leutnant* Wilhelm Frickart
10 *Leutnant* Justus Grassman
10 *Leutnant* Max Mulzer
10 *Leutnant* Rudolf Matthaei
10 *Vizefeldwebel* Alfons Nagler
10 *Leutnant* Wilhelm Neuenhofen
10 *Oberleutnant* Hans Schuez
10 *Leutnant* Werner Steinhaüser
10 *Leutnant* Paul Turck
10 *Leutnant* Erich Thomas
10 *Offz. Stellv.* Bernhard Ultsch
10 *Leutnant* Paul Wenzel
10 *Leutnant* Joachim Wolff

AUSTRIA-HUNGARY

Score

40 *Hauptmann* Godwin Brumowski
32 *Offizierstellvertreter* Julius Arigi
30 *Oberleutnant* Frank Linke-Crawford
29 *Oblt.* Benno Fiala *Ritter* von Fernbrugg
19 *Leutnant* Josef Kiss
16 *Leutnant* Franz Gräser
15 *Stabsfeldwebel* Stefan Fejes
15 *Feldwebel* Eugen Bönsch
14 *Offizierstellvertreter* Kurt Gruber
14 *Oberleutnant* Ernst Strohschneider
12 *Hauptmann* Raoul Stojsavljevic
10 *Leutnant* Franz Rudorfer
10 *Hauptmann* Adolf Heyrowsky
10 *Oberleutnant* Friedrich Navratil
10 *Hauptmann* Josef von Meier

This list of aces includes only
those who scored ten or more victories.

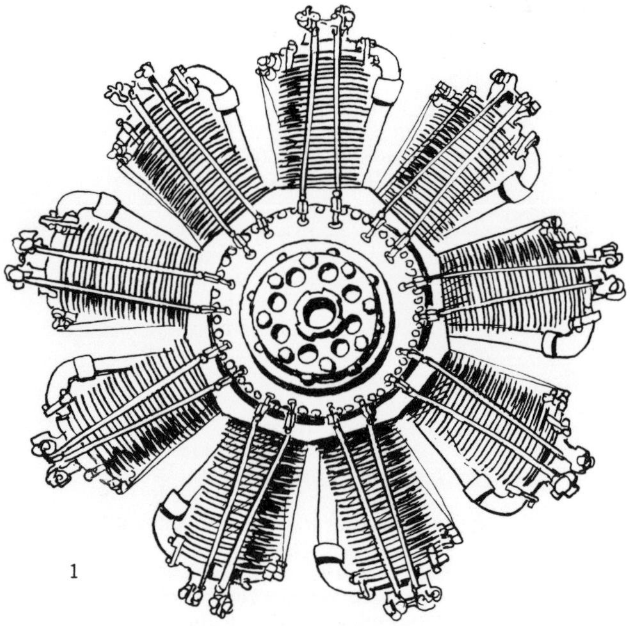

1

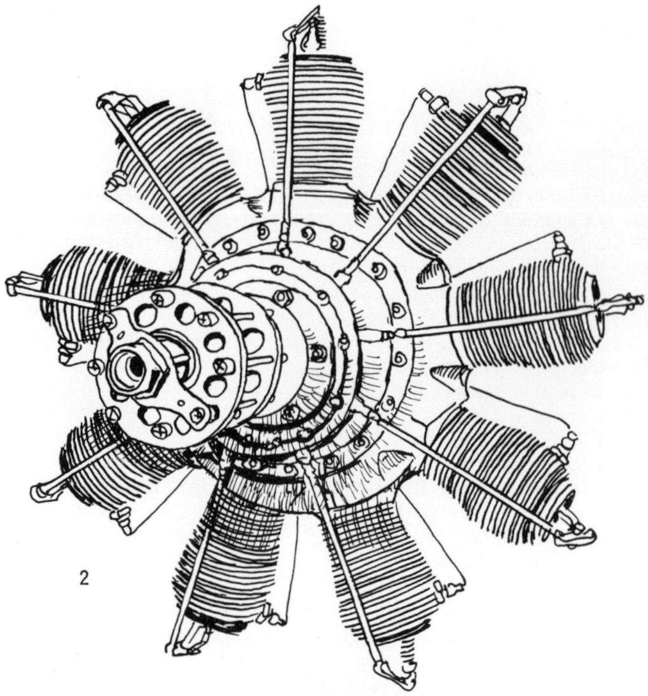

2

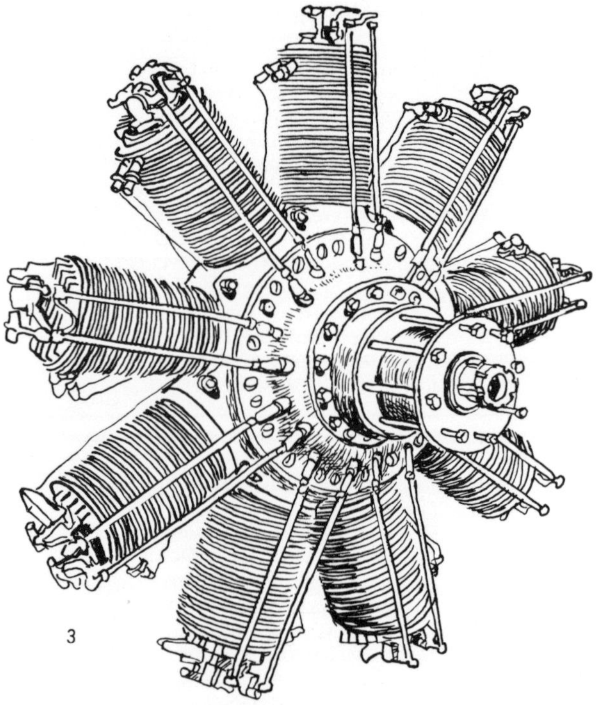

3

4

5

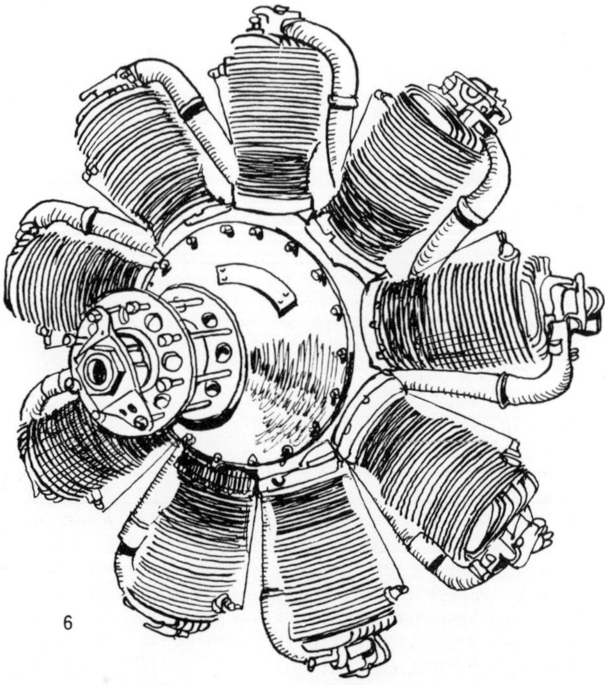

6

ROTARY ENGINES

1/ Bentley B.R.1 9-cylinder 150 h.p. Great Britain 2/ Gnôme-Monosoupape 9-cylinder 100 h.p. France 3/ Clerget 9-cylinder 130 h.p. France 4/ Oberürsel 9-cylinder 110 h.p. Germany 5/ Oberürsel 14-cylinder 160 h.p. (rear view). Germany 6/ Le Rhône 9-cylinder 110 h.p. France

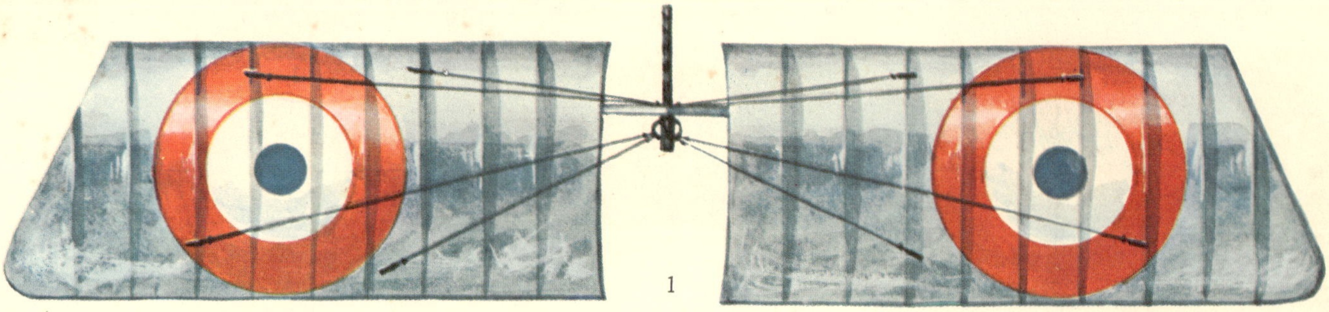

1

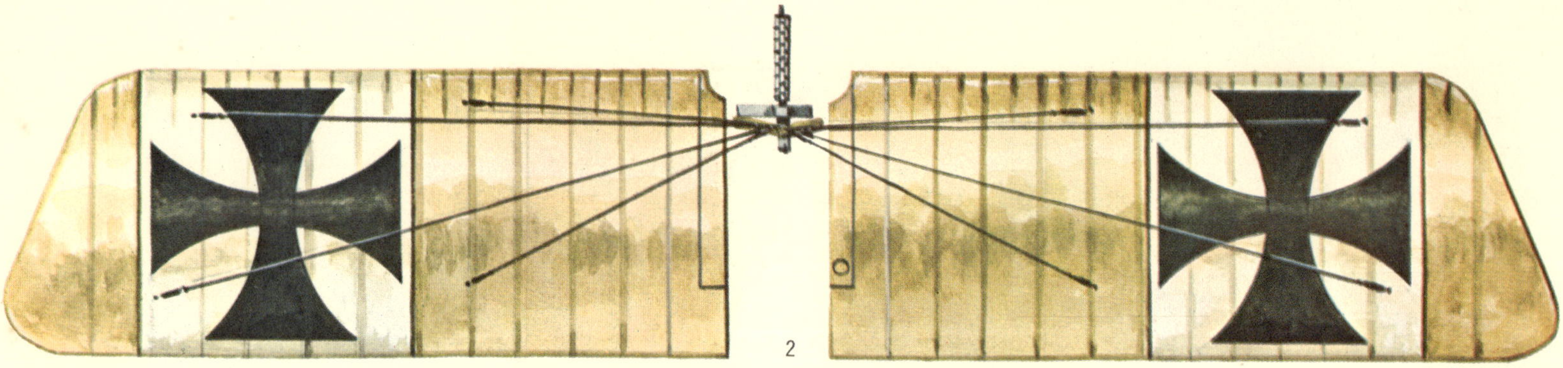

2

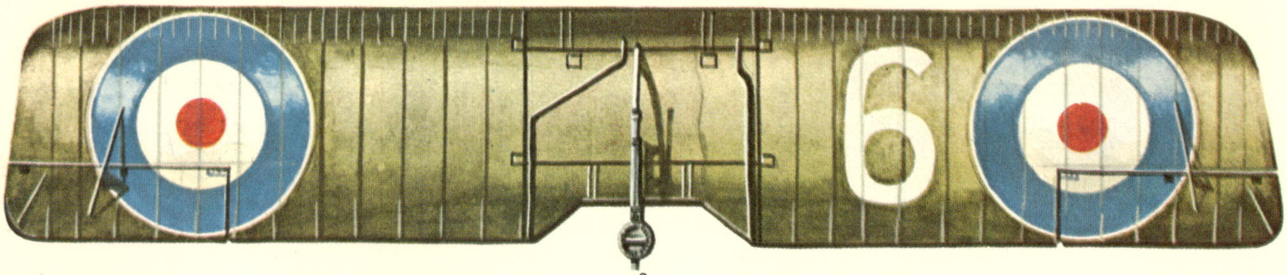

3

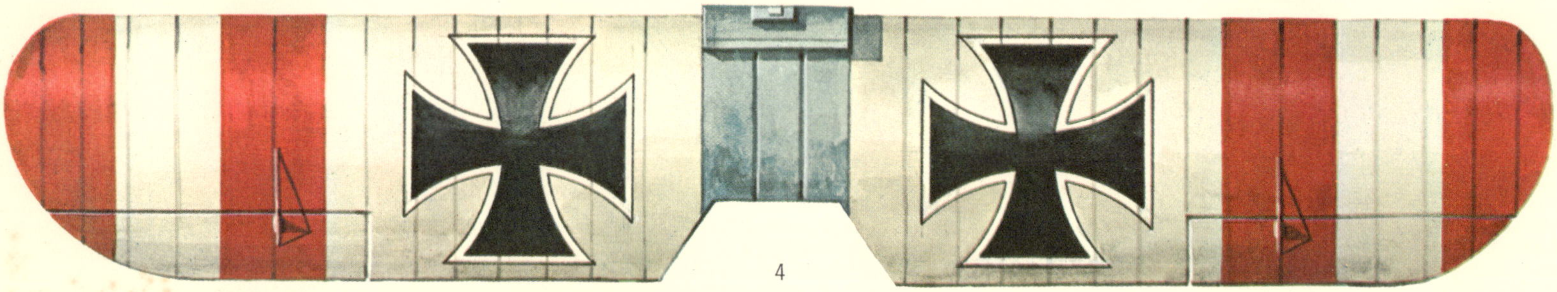

4

5

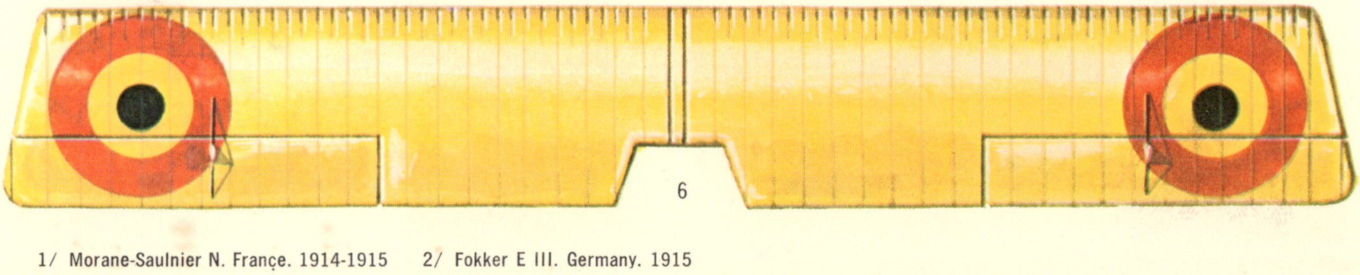

6

1/ Morane-Saulnier N. Françe. 1914-1915 2/ Fokker E III. Germany. 1915
3/ S.E.5a. Great Britain 1917-1918 (Captain J. T. B. McCudden, V.C., No. 56 Squadron, R.F.C.) 4/ Phonix D III. Austria-Hungary. 1917 (Naval Squadron)
5/ Spad 13. France. 1917-1918 (Capt. E. V. Rickenbacker, 94th Aero Squadron, U.S.A.S.) 6/ Hanriot H-D 1. France. 1916-1918 (in Belgian colors)